9/11: The New Evidence

The original bestseller, fully updated and revised with startling new facts

9/11: The New Evidence

The original bestseller, fully updated and revised with startling new facts

Ian Henshall

CARROLL & GRAF PUBLISHERS
NEW YORK

Every effort has been made to locate the person(s) having rights in the pictures
and figures appearing in this book and to secure permission for usage from
such persons. We apologize in advance for any unintentional omission and we
would be pleased to insert appropriate acknowledgement in any subsequent
edition.

Carroll & Graf Publishers
An imprint of Avalon Publishing Group, Inc.
245 W. 17th Street, 11th Floor
New York, NY 10011-5300
www.carrollandgraf.com

AVALON
publishing group incorporated

US ISBN-13: 978-0-78672-041-5
US ISBN-10: 0-7867-2041-7

Printed and bound in the US

Contents

Acknowledgements

I could not have produced this book without the massive endeavours of a band of brave, mostly web-based investigators who were the first to raise the questions I explore. Their websites and books are cited in the bibliography. Others have given me direct help too; in particular, I should like to mention Rowland Morgan, my co-author on *9/11 Revealed*, many of whose ideas and insights have found their way into this book; Calum Douglas, who helped with the physical issues; Michael Wright, who dug up valuable leads on the CIA connection; my family for their forbearance; and the people who work at my coffee shop, for keeping things running smoothly during my absence.

Introduction

As debate rages over the justness and tactics of the war in Iraq, another issue is all too frequently ignored: the justness and tactics of the "war on terror". Some opponents of the Iraq war even seem to believe the best way to put the case for getting out of Iraq is to swear allegiance to this greater war.

The attack on Iraq was based on the false allegation that it was developing weapons of mass destruction (WMD), but this allegation would not have been enough. The real danger, explained the pro-war lobby, was that Saddam Hussein might give his weapons to "terrorists", that 9/11 had – in a phrase uttered many thousands of times – "changed everything".

Any war must have its driving philosophy of "them and us", "with us or against us". Despite protestations by those on the liberal wing of the war on terror, the official philosophy underlying this war is the "clash of civilizations". If the old empires justified themselves through the ideal of imposing civilization on heathens, the extension of the US and NATO into vast swathes of other peoples' territory is proclaimed as supporting human rights and the reform of Islam. The war on terror lobby is a coalition of "liberals" who snarl about *Shari'a* law but turn a blind eye to torture, and "conservatives" who say all means necessary must be used in self-defence against terrorism. The cement binding this unholy enterprise is the belief that we face a threat from people in the Islamic world so massive that we must go there and change them. The 9/11 attacks are the crown jewels of this war on terror.

It is therefore astonishing, and suspicious, that the official story of 9/11 has never been validated by anything more than the discredited report of Washington's 9/11 Commission. For all we know, the official story of 9/11 may be, like the WMD story, a baseless, officially sanctioned conspiracy theory. If Al-Qaeda was involved, we need to be sure it was not acting in its historical role as an ally (if not a tool) of the CIA. And if Al-Qaeda was acting autonomously, we need to be sure it was not helped by plotters in Washington fully aware of the impending attacks, who decided to clear a path for the terrorists because they wanted a war. The issue is not whether, in a world with billions of inhabitants, some people hate "us". Of course, some do, and a few always will. The issue is whether they have the capability to do great harm.

But five years of official investigations have drawn out little more than morsels of information from a contemptuous executive that believes it is above the law. As *Los Angeles Times* columnist Robert Sheer put it a few months before he was sacked in 2005:

> Let's be clear: The failure to fully disclose what is known about the 9/11 tragedy is not some minor bureaucratic transgression. Not since the Soviets first detonated an atomic bomb more than half a century ago has a single event so affected decision-making in this country, yet the main questions as to how and why it happened remain mostly unanswered.

We live in a corporate world ruled by an arrogant and increasingly integrated political class. Perhaps there is not so much a clash of civilizations as a clash between civilization as a whole and this global plutocracy manipulating the "war on terror" as a distraction from its own unpopular activities – accumulating ever more power and wealth, hollowing out democracy, nobbling the media and stealing centuries-old democratic rights. Scrutinizing the official story of 9/11 is a test of these rival theories.

This book does not try to offer a detailed account of what exactly happened, though an ominous outline takes shape. Its intention is to assess evidence that has become public and evaluate the feasibility of various scenarios. This is an investigation, not an indictment. Some reports will turn out to be false; much has yet to come to light. Readers may determine that the full complicity of plotters in Washington is inescapable; others will feel that not very much has been proven. But some conclusions can be drawn, most importantly that the truth *can* be discovered, despite the possibility of a wide-ranging cover-up. It is for a well-resourced legal enquiry to take the matter further and decide whether individuals participated in the 9/11 attacks through wilful negligence, obstructing investigations after the event or worse.

Just about any enquiry that can protect witnesses would likely produce bombshells, providing the momentum for what is really needed: a well-funded, extensive criminal investigation run by a team of prosecutors with no connections to Washington or London, closely supervised by the relatives of the 9/11 victims, with unfettered access to all public or privately held files. Were such files accessed, we might discover quite a lot more about the ways of the plutocracy; in the end, perhaps we could even get democracy back.

Certain officials are named here because they appear to be in a position to answer the many questions such an enquiry would pose, not because there is any assumption of guilt. It would be unwise to jump to conclusions at this stage. If there is a tone of hostility towards people like Dick Cheney, Condoleezza Rice and George Tenet, it is because of what the record shows clearly already: that the 9/11 attacks could have been stopped had officials been more vigilant; that the same officials used 9/11 as part of a fraudulent case for launching a war in the Middle East, sheltering behind language like "pre-emptive attack" and "harsh interrogation".

A book like this is only as good as its sources; most of the sources seem to believe in the official 9/11 story, which if anything gives more weight to the evidence they have produced. In addition to openly sourced reports, I have made use of a few books by Washington journalists based on briefings by senior officials. This is dangerous, however; it is precisely how the media is fed false information. Nevertheless, in these cases it is clear who the sources are, or at least where in the apparatus they are. They reveal information that contradicts the line they try to promote.

Information presented here known for years by Internet sleuths will be brand-new for those unfortunates relying on the BBC or CNN. To make it accessible to all, I have told the whole story from scratch, giving less emphasis than in *9/11 Revealed* to the continuing vast gaps in the official story and more to the new information.

The two big omissions are the details of the Flight 93 story and the insider trades. Flight 93 is covered very well in Rowland Morgan's book *Flight 93 Revealed*. The insider trades look highly suspicious, but official stonewalling has rendered the issue impenetrable.

Part 1
The Background

1
The First Draft
of History

It is a commonplace that journalism is the first draft of history but, more precisely, the first draft is the flow of news reports coming in. What media people call "the story" is already the second draft. However, in the case of 9/11 the story was proclaimed before most of the reports: CNN reported that "a White House source" told it Al-Qaeda was responsible for the attacks even before the South Tower of the World Trade Center had collapsed and the Pentagon had been struck.

This chapter outlines the key events from the morning of the attacks, presenting a parallel point of view of how the official story and skeptic views developed. (All unreferenced details are from the 9/11 Commission or referenced later.)

THE ATTACKS: 7.30 A.M.-10.30 A.M. HIJACK TIMELINE

Flight	Takes off	Last contact	Crashed
Flight AA11	7.59	8.14	8.46.40
Flight UAL175	8.14	8.42	9.03.11
Flight AA77	8.09	8.51	9.37.46
Flight UAL93	8.42	9.28	10.03.11

Source: 9/11 Commission. Last contact times were established from air traffic control tapes but what happened on the planes, when the Federal Aviation Authority (FAA) knew and when the military knew have never been clarified.

7.30 a.m.
Presumed hijackers Mohamed Atta and Abdulaziz al-Omari arrive in Boston on connecting flight; their bags are not put on Flight 11. Other presumed hijackers ready for embarkation.

8.14-8.17
Flight 11 apparently hijacked.

8.30
Brigadier-General Montague Winfield transfers command of Pentagon's National Military Control Center (NMCC) Operations Room to Captain Charles Leidig; North American Aerospace Defense Command (NORAD) exercises proceed, including hijacking exercise.

8.55 (approximately)
President George W. Bush informed of first crash (later claims he had seen it, which according to official story cannot be true), concludes pilot error; by 8.55 media helicopters filming events, but NORAD aircraft have yet to arrive in New York.

9.03
In the most spectacular live political event in history, South Tower hit; Bush informed but remains seated in schoolroom; press secretary Ari Fleischer holds up sign: "Don't say anything yet".

9.06-9.35 (times still disputed)
Vice President Dick Cheney rushed to White House basement; National Security Council (NSC) counterterrorism boss Richard Clarke chairs key White House videoconference; Defense Secretary Donald Rumsfeld hears news, returns to non-urgent briefing; White House evacuated.

9.37 (some say earlier, citing clocks stopped at 9.34)
Pentagon hit, first reports say car bomb, truck bomb, explosion.

9.40-10.00
Pentagon press briefing says Rumsfeld walked to crash site to help.[1]

9.58
Media reports say South Tower collapses after explosions.

10.00 (approximately)
General Winfield returns to NMCC.

10.03 (some say 10.06)
Plane presumed to be Flight 93 crashes in Pennsylvania.

10.28
North Tower collapses.

OTHER EVENTS THAT DAY

9.20 a.m.
Most experts, including firefighters, believe total building collapses are impossible, but New York firefighters get message from Mayor Rudolph Giuliani's office that collapse is expected.

9.25
Bush makes short speech denouncing terrorist attack; multiple reports say warning received that Air Force One will be attacked. Bush flies to Barksdale Airbase, Louisiana; FAA orders all aircraft over mainland US grounded immediately; order carried out successfully. (9/11 Commission will later judge FAA too incompetent to inform Pentagon that hijackings had taken place.)

9.30 (approximately)
Evacuation of a third building, World Trade Center 7, ordered.

9.50
CNN reports that at around 9.30 it was told by an official: "The initial assumption . . . was that this had something to do, or . . . possible connection with Osama Bin Laden."

1.30 p.m.
Bush sets off for US Strategic Command Headquarters, Offutt Airbase, Nebraska – military nerve centre. Bush leaves at 4.30 for Washington.

All Day
Orgy of repetition as iconic photos of collapsing towers plays repeatedly on TV, often next to footage from Palestine allegedly

CREDIT: Eric Draper, White House

Bush returning to Washington on Air Force One. The 9/11 Commission later said phone communications with Air Force One were poor. Multiple reports from Bush officials said the extent of the attacks was unclear, and Air Force One received anonymous threats that included secret codes. Skeptics see this as evidence that 9/11 was a "palace coup"; anti-Bush journalists dismissed the reports as a lie to cover up indecision.

depicting Palestinians celebrating the events. Phrase "The world has changed" uttered ceaselessly on TV worldwide.

3.00
Tenet already communicating with key nations, "lining up the forces for the counterstrike" against Al-Qaeda;[2] Bush returns to Washington in the evening.

Afternoon
CNN reports correspondent and Flight 77 passenger Barbara Olson called her husband twice, reaching him at the Justice Department; also, CNN witness Tim Timmerman, described as a pilot, declares certainty in seeing a 757 hit the Pentagon; his corroborative details later prove wrong. Other witnesses who ID a 737 are ignored.

5.20
World Trade Center Building 7 reported expected to collapse, as though routine event; indeed it does, falling neatly into its own footprint late in the afternoon.

Evening
In the White House, Richard Clarke walks into "a series of discussions about Iraq": "I realized with almost a sharp physical pain that Rumsfeld and [Deputy Secretary of Defense Paul] Wolfowitz were going to try to take advantage of this national tragedy to promote their agenda . . . my friends in the Pentagon had been telling me . . . we would be invading Iraq sometime in 2002."[3]

THE NEXT FORTY-EIGHT HOURS

Wednesday 12 September

Bush to Clarke: "See if Saddam did this. See if he's linked in any way. I want to know any shred."[4] Official story takes form; experts and officials make the following assertions, later deemed wrong or in doubt:

- attacks came as a complete surprise;

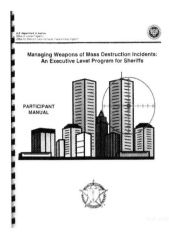

PARTICIPANT MANUAL

Managing Weapons of Mass Destruction Incidents: An Executive Level Program for Sheriffs

Officials were quick to claim that nobody could have foreseen the 9/11 attacks, but this image appeared on many official publications in the months before 9/11. This version is taken from a US Department of Justice publication.[5]

CREDIT: United States Department of Justice

- what happened was previously unthinkable;
- collapse of the Towers was due to fiery heat melting steel frames;
- it would not have been difficult for barely competent pilots to fly planes into the buildings;
- Al-Qaeda has many sleeper cells in America and billions of dollars at its disposal;
- more attacks were likely.

Evidence produced to support official theory; passport from one of the hijackers found at Ground Zero (many assume it is Atta's; in fact, it was Satam al-Suqami's). Photo of Atta boarding plane in Portland flashed around the world (many think they have seen a hijacker getting on a hijacked plane). Documents described as will and confession found in Atta's bags, which for some reason did not get onto Flight 11.

Asked about 9/11's effect on US-Israel relations, former Israeli prime minister Benjamin Netanyahu says: "It's very good . . . well, not very good, but it will generate immediate sympathy."[6] Pro-Israel lobby will become particularly hostile to 9/11 skeptics.

Wednesday 13 September

At a meeting, CIA counterterrorism chief Cofer Black makes presentation to NSC principals and Bush outlining CIA plan to invade

Afghanistan. Bush gives approval in principle to "take off the shackles" from CIA and its "Worldwide Attack Matrix".[7]

THE FIRST FEW WEEKS

Wave of grief and sympathy engulfs mainstream media in most parts of the world. No one doubts Washington's version of events. Bush regime announces war on terror, but precise meaning unclear. Main issue is extradition of bin Laden from Afghanistan; dossier promised by Secretary of State Colin Powell proving culpability. Later, responsibility for the dossier is shifted to British Prime Minister Tony Blair. Dossier finally evolves into oral presentation delivered in secret to NATO.

Friday 14 September

According to insiders, well before the attacks, White House lawyers – "seeded" by Cheney – have been secretly "incubating theories about how to expand Presidential power". Draft Congressional resolution allowing President to exercise "all necessary and appropriate force in the United States", arguably making him *de facto* dictator, is narrowly headed off – but applies to rest of the world. Bush will use this resolution as legal basis for arbitrary imprisonment and torture by CIA abroad. He will assume he has right to override Constitution as a "war president" from now on at home, too.[8]

Sunday 16 September

Cheney on *Meet the Press*: the government needs to "work through sort of the dark side . . . it's vital for us to use any means at our disposal." The road to Abu Ghraib is now open. Skeptics wonder if Cheney has already embarked on "dark side" prior to 9/11.

Pittsburgh Post-Gazette breaks "Let's roll" story of passenger Todd Beamer and resistance on Flight 93, told to reporter by wife Lisa Beamer, who has been briefed by phone supervisor Lisa Jefferson. Jefferson took call from Todd but somehow failed to record it. "We know he's in Heaven. He was saved," says Lisa. Slogan "Let's roll" later used to sell invasion of Iraq.

Monday 17 September

Bush secretly authorizes Worldwide Attack Matrix (probably a subject of Tenet's calls to foreign governments on 11 September).[9] Programme will grow into "largest CIA covert action program since the height of the Cold War".[10]

During interview in Pakistan, bin Laden denies responsibility and repeats his 1998 *fatwa* making killing innocent women and children unacceptable. Bin Laden's position will shift slowly until, in 2004 election video, a fuzzy figure takes full responsibility.

Thursday 20 September

Bush, Lisa Beamer beside him, addresses Congress with "war on terror" speech. "War" appears twelve times. Bush:

> Our grief has turned to anger, and anger to resolution . . . We will direct . . . every necessary weapon of war to the disruption and to the defeat of the global terror network . . . Every nation, in every region, now has a decision to make. Either you are with us, or you are with the terrorists.[11]

Bush also says: "We'll remember the moment the news came –

Ten days after the attacks, Bush melded grief with aggression as he addressed Congress.

CREDIT: Eric Draper, White House

where we were and what we were doing."[12] But his own officials produce major conflicts of evidence in their accounts of 9/11 events. Bush also claims: "The terrorists' directive commands them to kill Christians and Jews, to kill all Americans, and make no distinction among military and civilians, including women and children."[13] In reference to bin Laden's 1998 *fatwa*, it is false in several respects. (*Fatwa* to be discussed later.)

"War on terror" seems to involve little more than intense pressure on foreign countries to stop harbouring terrorists; on Taliban in Afghanistan to close down Al-Qaeda camps and deliver its leaders to the US; and reversion to CIA activities abandoned during Cold War. The phrase "every necessary weapon of war" tucked in after list of diplomatic and other solutions.

Meanwhile, in Middle East, many take bin Laden's statement at face value. Taliban refuse to extradite him in the absence of evidence. Bin Laden will still not be cited for 9/11 on FBI's "most wanted" list years later; FBI spokesman Rex Tomb says in 2006: "The FBI has no hard evidence connecting Usama Bin Laden to 9/11."[14]

Media news reports, mostly foreign, raise doubts about the official story, particularly that the attacks were unthinkable and no warnings had been received. Sources in Israel, Germany, Russia and Egypt all claim to have warned of an attack within the US.

Threats against Afghanistan mount. The Taliban offers to extradite bin Laden but not to the US. Offer rejected, forfeiting best chance of bringing him to justice; after the invasion he will escape capture.

Al Gore, having lost election to Bush only months earlier after vote-rigging allegations, nonetheless supports Bush on TV as commander-in-chief. At the UN, Bush declares: "Let us never tolerate outrageous conspiracy theories concerning the attacks of September the 11th, malicious lies that attempt to shift the blame away from the terrorists themselves, away from the guilty."[15] (However, conspiracy theories are fostered by FBI's refusal to release basic evidence even following terror suspect Zacarias Moussaoui's 2006 trial.)

French newspaper *Le Figaro* reports bin Laden had clandestine meetings with CIA in Dubai a few weeks before 9/11. Diplomats also recall US threatening invasion of Afghanistan before attacks.

Both the strain and the highly weaponized quality of the anthrax supposedly sent by Islamic extremists later led the FBI to assume the source was in US military or industry. Some letters were posted before the 9/11 attacks.[16]

15 October

Anthrax letter arrives at Senate leader Tom Daschle's offices on Capitol Hill, claiming to be from Islamic radicals. Letters target key senators in position to demand proper investigation into 9/11 attacks or obstruct planned US Patriot Act. Senate Judiciary Committee chair, Democrat Patrick Leahy, receives one on 16 November. New media panic starts. Americans far from New York and Washington now feel vulnerable to Al-Qaeda. Neocons blame Iraq.[17]

23 October

US Patriot Act introduced and passed by Congress in about forty-eight hours; some Congressmen say afterwards they did not read it. Skeptics suspect long, detailed bill drafted before 9/11. Only about four members vote against or abstain.

Shock at the enormity of Constitution-busting Patriot Act breeds suspicion, reminds libertarians of Hitler's Enabling Act, passed in panic following Reichstag Fire. Skeptical questions spread on Internet: Why did the Pentagon fail to scramble jets to intercept hijacked aircraft? Why was Bush not removed immediately by Secret Service from Florida schoolroom? Why were alleged hijackers having drinking sessions and visiting strip clubs? How could pilots trained only on small planes pull off the attacks?

Cheney strenuously opposes any investigation by Congress. Eventually, compromise is reached: Congress intelligence committees will investigate jointly but secretly and with limited access to documents. No one in the US is to be blamed, limiting this and all future investigations. How can there be certainty there were no other Al-Qaeda moles like Ali Mohamed (discussed later) in the CIA or FBI?

FBI names "person of interest" in anthrax case as Dr Stephen Hatfill, one-time arms inspector and worker in US government bio-warfare laboratory. Hatfill is innocent; skeptics say officials have ignored the real culprit, named on popular website. Discovery that elements in the US were behind anthrax attacks does not prompt media to take another look at official 9/11 story.[19]

Afghanistan is invaded.

Subsequent Years: 2002-03

Skeptical attitudes spread to doubts over physical issues like what hit the Pentagon and how the Towers collapsed. Over five million "Deception Dollars" – initially among few publicity tools available to skeptics – circulated. Videos appear highlighting spectacular collapse of Towers based on TV footage that media has long stopped showing.

News of blocked FBI investigations pre-9/11 breaks into mainstream media. *New York Post* proclaims "Bush knew" about attacks. Attention focuses on Bush's then-secret 6 August briefing from CIA. Things go

"Deception Dollar".   CREDIT: Blaine Machan

GOVERNMENT
EXHIBIT
P200037
01-455-A

M-CSP-00000588

Few TV viewers saw pictures of the Pentagon before collapse of wall. When they circulated on the Internet, many thought there was suspiciously little debris and began to doubt the official story.

CREDIT: US Department of Defense/Jason Ingersol

briefly into freefall; the storm combines with pressure from victims' relatives and leads to formation of 9/11 Commission.

French authors Jean-Charles Brisard and Guillaume Dasquie write – based on interview with FBI counterterrorism expert John O'Neill, who died in collapse of the South Tower – that O'Neill resigned from FBI because White House had stopped investigations of Al-Qaeda to avoid embarrassment to Bush's Saudi friends. Skeptics see more evidence here of deliberate inaction prior to attacks.

Another French citizen, Thierry Meyssan, grabs Internet attention by challenging world to find any visual evidence that Pentagon was hit by a plane. Countered by rare release of information: five frames from a Pentagon CCTV camera (see later chapter on Pentagon); but plane-like object is obscured, almost invisible and, say some skeptics, seems too small. Some skeptics say it appears to have a contrail indicating a missile.

Invasion of Iraq dominates 2003; 9/11 skeptics active in anti-war movement. Failure to find Iraq's alleged WMD undermines trust in media and government, provides long-term boost to 9/11 truth movement – though mainstream media yet again fails to re-examine official 9/11 story.

2004–Present

Skeptics find plenty of interest in 9/11 Commission testimony, but whistleblowers like FBI translator Sibel Edmonds, WTC building manager William Rodriguez and FBI special agent Coleen Rowley are ignored. Richard Clarke releases controversial book criticizing Bush for negligence, but otherwise underpins official story.

9/11 Commission's report released in summer 2004 amidst atmosphere of bonhomie; media announces the matter closed. Why the Towers collapsed is barely discussed, though other buildings logically now at risk. WTC 7 unmentioned. Skeptics point out that Commission's story of hijackers based almost entirely on evidence from the torture of people the Commission is barred from meeting.

Bush 2004 re-election campaign damaged by Michael Moore's film *Fahrenheit 9/11*; though many skeptics disappointed on details, film conveys the big skeptical picture well, with Bush portrayed hobnobbing with rich Saudis and exploiting 9/11 attacks for Iraq war.

Bush pushed ahead in polls by November video from "Osama bin Laden", helpfully released three days before election. Bin Laden cites Moore by name, has somewhat different nose and looks hardly older than three years earlier. CIA analysts decide video is aimed to secure Bush election victory.[20]

In 2005, "Able Danger" affair becomes biggest mainstream media disaster for official story since 2002 "Bush Knew" crisis. Republican congressman Curt Weldon and Pentagon's Colonel Anthony Shaffer reveal that Pentagon intelligence team identified presumed hijackers Atta and Marwan al-Shehhi in 2000. The 9/11 Commission, informed of this, nevertheless falsely concluded Atta not identified by US authorities before attacks.

Actor Charlie Sheen dominates CNN entertainment programme for three days in March 2006, expressing doubts about official 9/11 story; senior executives order further coverage stopped. Release of *Loose Change*, radical film criticized by many skeptics as too speculative; described as "first Internet Blockbuster".

Trial in Spring 2006 of Moussaoui, said to be twentieth hijacker. Unlike alleged ringleader Khalid Sheikh Mohammed, Moussaoui was not held by CIA and tortured; nevertheless he appears highly deranged. Reports of behaviour leading to his arrest suggest he was no professional terrorist. FBI agents testify and repeat original Rowley allegations that FBI blocked investigations that might have foiled attacks.

Bombshell confirmation (long suspected by skeptics) arrives in August that hijacking exercise proceeded at time of 9/11 attacks; leaked by trusted *Vanity Fair* journalist given exclusive access to Pentagon tapes discovered by Commission. Pentagon officials, it emerges, were considered for criminal charges for knowingly giving false information.

Fifth anniversary of 9/11 sees mainstream media breakthrough: long, sympathetic articles in *New York Times*, *Time* and *Washington Post*. However, backlash comes from the left. In hysterical spring 2007 *Guardian* article, George Monbiot describes 9/11 skepticism as "virus" and skeptics as "morons". Letters page sees massive outpouring of protest.

October *New York Times* poll finds only 16 per cent of Americans believe government is telling truth about 9/11; 53 per cent believe it is mostly telling truth but hiding something; 28 per cent believe it is mostly lying.[21]

Newly Democratic Congress cautiously begins to re-establish accountability in January 2007, but strong pro-Israel lobby still very reluctant to question 9/11 attacks. Outside US/UK, debate surges forward. Venezuelan President Hugo Chávez says notion that Twin

Towers were brought down by explosives not absurd. In countries from Malaysia to Holland permitting free debate, 9/11 skepticism booms.

Khalid Sheikh Mohammed appears in Guantánamo Bay in March; long confession released incriminating him for extraordinary litany of events real and planned. Unlikely mastermind to skeptics; others say he has been destroyed by prolonged CIA torture (now known as "harsh interrogation methods").

2
The Skeptical View Develops

In December 2006, BBC *Newsnight* editor Peter Barron wrote in his blog:

> Last night an amateur film-maker spoke to me about his belief that there's been a huge cover-up in the official reporting of both 9/11 and 7/7. Why, he asked, doesn't the BBC report the many discrepancies and oddities surrounding the accounts of these hugely significant events? In fact, on *Newsnight* we have briefly examined some of these questions . . . The reason we haven't gone deeper is that there's surely no rational explanation for the attacks other than that they were carried out by two groups of Islamist terrorists, however puzzling some of [the] apparent inconsistencies.[22]

Nevertheless, even for many believers of the official story, the possible motive is pretty clear.

9/11 solved strategic problems worrying policymakers in Washington and other Western capitals; it enabled little-noticed plans by the Bush White House for a massive expansion of the US military and the invasion of Iraq; and it neutralized several major domestic problems threatening an already unpopular president.

THE OLD AMERICAN CENTURY

The 1999 manifesto for the Project for a New American Century (PNAC) was barely noticed. "Rebuilding America's Defenses" hardly seemed the stuff of high political drama. However, this was not a project defending anything, but a plan for a global military empire. The PNAC was the latest and most virulent manifestation of an evolving faction of Washington hawks whose resurgence would come with the Bush presidency.

After the invasion of Iraq, conservatives and liberals alike started looking more closely at the teachings of the University of Chicago's Leo Strauss, a German émigré under whom many PNAC advocates – the neoconservatives – studied. Neocons argue that it is a travesty to describe Strauss as a closet Nazi, despite his close relationship to top Nazi lawyer Carl Schmitt, who wrote the emergency clauses into the Weimar Republic constitution, enabling the Nazis to seize power.[23]

Stanley Hilton, longtime Republican stalwart and former senior aide to presidential contender Robert Dole, was already suspicious when the 9/11 attacks occurred:

> At the University of Chicago in the late sixties with Wolfowitz and [Undersecretary of Defense Douglas] Feith and several of the others . . . we used to talk about this stuff all of the time . . . how to turn the US into a presidential dictatorship by manufacturing a bogus Pearl Harbor event.

Eminent law professor Francis Boyle, who helped draw up treaties on bioweapons and alert the FBI to the domestic origins of the anthrax attacks, told radio listeners in 2006:

> Well, you have to understand the Neo-conservative mentality. I went to the University of Chicago with these people . . . the Department of Political Science run by the Neocon founder Leo Strauss. His mentor in Germany before he came to the United States was Carl Schmitt, who went on to become the most notorious Nazi law professor . . . They are extremely dangerous, very bright, cunning and ruthless.[24]

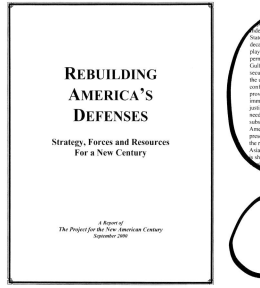

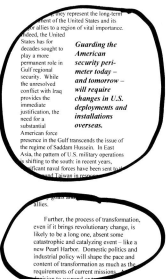

REBUILDING AMERICA'S DEFENSES

Strategy, Forces and Resources For a New Century

A Report of
The Project for the New American Century
September 2000

... they represent the long-term ...ment of the United States and its ...r allies to a region of vital importance. ...deed, the United States has for decades sought to play a more permanent role in Gulf regional security. While the unresolved conflict with Iraq provides the immediate justification, the need for a substantial American force presence in the Gulf transcends the issue of the regime of Saddam Hussein. In East Asia, the pattern of U.S. military operations is shifting to the south: in recent years, ...ificant naval forces have been sent to... ...und Taiwan in respon...

Guarding the American security perimeter today – and tomorrow – will require changes in U.S. deployments and installations overseas.

...y goals and... ...llies.

Further, the process of transformation, even if it brings revolutionary change, is likely to be a long one, absent some catastrophic and catalyzing event – like a new Pearl Harbor. Domestic politics and industrial policy will shape the pace and content of transformation as much as the requirements of current missions. ...cision to suspend or...

9/11 was the Pearl Harbor-type event Bush's people had dreamed of before coming to power. Their plans for global military supremacy could now proceed.

Washington hawks in power have always used the CIA, not as intended under the 1947 National Security Act but through the Directorate of Operations, as a proactive instrument of foreign policy, recruiting local militias and destabilizing governments refusing to embed themselves in the US military network or yield up their natural resources.

The highest-placed CIA whistleblower, John Stockwell, saw service in Vietnam, Angola and eventually Washington as an NSC official. As Ronald Reagan's White House developed its plans for state-sponsored terrorism in Central America in the 1980s, Stockwell protested:

It is the function, I suggest, of the CIA, with its 50 de-stabilization programs going around the world today, to keep the world unstable, and to propagandize the American people to hate, so we will let the establishment spend any amount of money on arms . . .[25]

The Cold War's ebb, the failure of the Vietnam War and Richard Nixon's policy of détente with the USSR put the hawks on the defensive. The counterattack came when Reagan replaced Jimmy Carter in 1980. People like Rumsfeld and Cheney returned to power, and embarked on a new arms race with the Soviets along with a proxy war against Soviet-occupied Afghanistan.

The USSR tried to liberalize, but instead collapsed into near-anarchy. This was hailed as a victory. The relative peace and lowered military budgets under Bill Clinton saw the neocons sulking in opposition and plotting a comeback. Their most visible success was helping to derail the peace process in Israel/Palestine. They wrote a public letter to then-Prime Minister Netanyahu denouncing the Oslo accords underwritten by Washington and Moscow, encouraging him to block implementation.

With communism gone, opposition movements in various countries began to gain the sympathy of middle classes disturbed by the exponential growth of the new super-rich. By the end of the 1990s the anti-globalization movement was becoming a serious problem for the West's strategy of using "trade liberalization" to extend its economic and political influence.

THE NEW AMERICAN CENTURY

In 2000, Republican candidate George Bush declared himself a "compassionate conservative" opposed to nation-building abroad, and assuaged any worries created by the presence of Cheney on the ticket, designating relative moderate Colin Powell as eventual Secretary of State. But Cheney-overseen appointees were PNAC signatories, including Powell's deputy Richard Armitage and National Security Advisor Condoleezza Rice. (Powell's influence went into terminal decline with Bush's declaration of war immediately after 9/11.)

Bush got off to a bad start by losing the popular vote, falling back on the Supreme Court's Republican majority to secure him the presidency. Freedom of information laws in Florida allowed newspapers to count the disputed votes themselves. The unofficial Florida results would be released in the autumn.[26]

The "compassionate conservative" took office with an economy headed for recession. The stock market was headed for a major readjustment, and industry needed to lose hundreds of thousands of jobs. In the oil industry, Cheney and others worried about scarce new oilfields, while in Afghanistan the Taliban was becoming ever less cooperative as its hold on the country increased. Plans for a new energy route from Central Asia to the Indian subcontinent were floundering.

Whether by accident or design, 9/11 solved all of this. The stock market slumped, the jobs were lost and Al-Qaeda got the blame. Globally, the solution would be a new war. Samuel Huntington, another Chicago/Strauss graduate, put forward his "Clash of Civilizations" theory, suggesting that, post-Cold War, cultural identity would be the source of conflict between states. The replacement for the Red Menace was to be radical Islam; the new Cold War would be the War on Terror, sidelining the global justice movement; distracting from the recession; enabling huge increases in military spending; achieving the invasion of Iraq; overthrowing the Taliban; and casting Israel and the US together in the role of victims.

THE PRECEDENTS

How far would people in Washington go, if they have decided to operate on what Cheney called "the dark side"? Few allege that Bush gave a direct order for the murder of his own people, but could he have given approval for "something" to be done? Even if Bush and/or Cheney knew little or nothing about a Washington 9/11 plot, could they have decided to go along with it after the event? What are the precedents?

The legal authorization for America's decade-long involvement in Vietnam was Congress's Gulf of Tonkin resolution, based on President Lyndon Johnson's assurance that North Vietnam had attacked US vessels. It is now generally agreed that the incident never took place, but the ensuing war saw tens of thousands of Americans dead. There were similar disputes over Pearl Harbor, which brought the US into World War Two.[27]

Nor did presidential deception end with Vietnam. The Iran-Contra scandal in the 1980s, involving many people now in the Bush White House, saw the illegal funding of a violent insurrection against the new Nicaraguan government in defiance of a Congressional ban, via arms sold to Iran – a scam that proceeded for years, refuting arguments that such complex operations cannot be kept secret.

OPERATION NORTHWOODS

Operation Northwoods, a 1962 Pentagon plan to garner support for an invasion of Cuba, was made public through freedom of information legislation in 1997. Proposals included having 300 bogus "students" (Special Forces personnel under "carefully prepared aliases") depart from a US airport on a flight ostensibly taking them over Cuba but landing at a nearby airbase instead, to be replaced by an empty drone aircraft using the same transponder to fool air traffic controllers. Once over Cuba, a tape-recording in the drone would issue an emergency call claiming the plane was under attack by Cuba; it would then be blown up. Foreign air traffic controllers would confirm that 300 Americans had just been murdered by Fidel Castro. The Joint Chiefs of Staff concluded that the media could be fooled by bogus "relatives" produced to match the fake victims.[28]

So far, the proposal did not involve the murder of Americans. But the Pentagon planned to go further: the second part of the scheme contained various options. One was to attack a US warship; another was to create a bogus terrorist bombing campaign in Florida. The Chiefs did not absolutely specify in writing any intentions to murder people, but the proposals leave little to the imagination. Perhaps the plan was rejected because Attorney General Robert Kennedy realized that, once complicit, the White House would become a prisoner of the military – as might have happened to the Bush White House.

Some skeptics think 9/11 was similar to Operation Northwoods, but others argue there is a crucial difference: an entirely fake event would be needed to frame Cuba because Castro would never have been fool enough to be drawn into a sting operation. Osama bin Laden, on the

1. The Joint Chiefs of Staff have considered the attached Memorandum for the Chief of Operations, Cuba Project, which responds to a request of that office for brief but precise description of pretexts which would provide justification for US military intervention in Cuba.

2. The Joint Chiefs of Staff recommend that the proposed memorandum be forwarded as a preliminary submission suitable for planning purposes. It is assumed that there will be similar submissions from other agencies and that these inputs will be used as a basis for developing a time-phased plan. Individual projects can then be considered on a case-by-case basis.

3. Further, it is assumed that a single agency will be given the primary responsibility for developing military and para-military aspects of the basic plan. It is recommended that this responsibility for both overt and covert military operations be assigned the Joint Chiefs of Staff.

wave of national indignation.

4. We could develop a Communist Cuban terror campaign in the Miami area, in other Florida cities and even in Washington.

8

Annex to Appendix
to Enclosure A

UNCLASSIFIED

TOP SECRET — SPECIAL HANDLING — NOFORN

support chartering a non-scheduled flight.

a. An aircraft at Eglin AFB would be painted and numbered as an exact duplicate for a civil registered aircraft belonging to a CIA proprietary organization in the Miami area. At a designated time the duplicate would be substituted for the actual civil aircraft and would be loaded with the selected passengers, all boarded under carefully prepared aliases. The actual registered aircraft would be converted to a drone.

b. Take off times of the drone aircraft and the actual aircraft will be scheduled to allow a rendezvous south of Florida. From the rendezvous point the passenger-carrying aircraft will descend to minimum altitude and go directly into an auxiliary field at Eglin AFB where arrangements will have been made to evacuate the passengers and return the aircraft to its original status. The drone aircraft meanwhile will continue to fly the filed flight plan. When over Cuba the drone will being transmitting on the international distress frequency a "MAY DAY" message stating he is under attack by Cuban MIG aircraft. The transmission will be interrupted by destruction of the aircraft which will be triggered by radio signal. This will allow ICAO radio

10

Annex to Appendix
to Enclosure A

Operation Northwoods would have manufactured a fake airline tragedy over Cuba, complete with 300 bogus "victims".

other hand, by all accounts vain and by some accounts a stupid man, would be far more open to manipulation.

FALSE-FLAG TERRORISM IN EUROPE

In Europe during the Cold War, there were many instances of terrorism eventually linked with covert state involvement. Well-known examples include the 1980 railway bombing in Bologna, Italy, killing eighty-five people, and a series of random killing sprees in Belgian supermarkets in the 1980s known as the "Brabant massacres".

As the Cold War wound down, various right-wing groups confessed and, in some cases, boasted publicly that they had been behind many terrorist attacks. It emerged that, fearing a Soviet invasion, NATO had organized a series of so-called "stay-behind" networks recruited from the extreme right, as covert forces ready to fight a potential communist occupation. These groups were responsible for some or all of the terrorism, much of which was blamed on the left at the time.[29]

The hidden hand was exposed in Italy when magistrates investigated Licio Gelli, who turned out to be the grandmaster of the "Propaganda 2 Masonic Lodge" (official Freemasons disavowed any connections). Its membership included senior politicians, key figures in the military and intelligence services and suspected participants in the Bologna bombing. A committee of Italian MPs concluded in 2000 that "those massacres, those bombs, those military actions, had been organized, or promoted, or supported . . . [by Italians and] . . . by men linked to the structures of United States intelligence."[30] The enquiry also cited the *US Army Field Manual*, which seemed to advocate the use of this sort of false flag terrorism as a policy.[31]

A Belgian Senate enquiry in 1991 found that US Special Forces and Belgian secret services had attacked police barracks in the town of Vielsalm in 1984, killing a policeman and stealing guns. The incident was blamed on terrorists.

NORTHERN IRELAND

Shortly after the 1998 Good Friday Agreement promising peace in Northern Ireland, the process was threatened by the Omagh bombing, a slaughter of innocent people by a group called "The Real IRA". The *Sunday Herald* concluded that the bombing could have been stopped, citing three different sources: "Both republican and intelligence sources say the [Royal Ulster Constabulary] did not act on the information as one of the Omagh bombing team was a British informer."[32]

A fourteen-year-long police enquiry led by Sir John Stevens reported in 2003, after years of obstruction, that British security forces had colluded with Loyalist paramilitaries.[33] Stevens's report should have been a bombshell, but the Blair government and the media virtually ignored it. Kevin McNamara, formerly Labour's official spokesman on Northern Ireland, made the following comments to Parliament:

> The Stevens report's stark message is that successive British Governments have sanctioned murder – that they have employed agents and given them a licence to kill. Agents have acted above the law, without the law and with impunity . . . there was collusion in both murders and the circumstances surrounding them. [Stevens] says: "The unlawful involvement of agents in murder implies that the security forces sanction killings."[34]

Later, double agent Kevin Fulton explained the logic of the situation: "How can you pretend to be a terrorist and not act like one? You can't. The only way to beat the enemy was to penetrate the enemy and be the enemy." His handlers told him: "This goes the whole way to the Prime Minister. The Prime Minister knows what you are doing."

The problem with the "be the enemy" strategy is that perhaps the enemy would not exist at all without the help of powerful security forces infiltrating it. Suppose Fulton's handlers had simply arrested his fellow terrorists instead of "monitoring" them?[35]

9/11 SCENARIOS

The official 9/11 story was adopted within an hour or two of the attacks on the word of officials who professed to have had no warnings, by a media asking few questions and by senior Washington politicians who already shared the perception that the US was at war with Al-Qaeda. Precedents point to many possibilities, from a cold-blooded Operation Northwoods-type mass murder plot to an intelligence sting gone terribly wrong.

For most scenarios conspirators will fall into four subgroups: A, B, C and X Teams. The A-Team comprises the ringleaders, who know the general scope of the plot. There are very few of them, but they are in key positions – perhaps political, perhaps operational. Their main weapon is

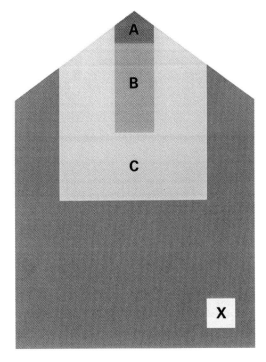

Four possible categories of teams in a 9/11 plot scenario.

the paralysis of US defences, principally the CIA, FBI and Pentagon. If things go wrong, their basic defence is incompetence ("intelligence failures") or naiveté ("nobody could have imagined such attacks").

The X-Team's task is to take the necessary steps to ensure the success of the attacks, say, tracking genuine hijackers and clearing their path, possibly also tailing them with aircraft to shoot them down should they go off course. In an outright fakery operation like Northwoods, the X-Team would be rather large, encompassing fake relatives, controllers of drone aircraft, etc.

The B-Team, mostly senior officials, have played a major part in one or other segment of the plot but are one step away from the plotters. B team members might suspect something dishonest is afoot and decide to keep silent, either out of military discipline or political loyalty, or because they are fully supportive but outside the narrow "need to know" circle. It might be an innocent component of the plot (e.g. conducting surveillance on the hijackers) and only start to suspect the truth later. The C-Team is on the periphery, suspecting a plot only after the event, and unable to do much then. It does not possess evidence, and is bound by rules obliging it to secrecy.

A-Team members are the plot's beneficiaries; they would only betray it late in an investigation, to save themselves. X-Team members would be fiercely policed and would risk being murdered if they started to talk (there are precedents[36]). The B- and C-Teams are the vulnerable points. If enough people bring forth their small shreds of evidence, investigators could fit them together and solve the case.

As time passes, the C-Team would grow considerably. Since 9/11, many people who fit the C-Team profile as described have spoken out – they are the core of the truth movement – but they have little effect, with the media and the FBI in lockdown (as we shall see later). C-Team members lack anything like a smoking gun, so can also rationalise doing nothing.

The A-Team can use routine systems of secrecy within government to protect the X-Team, which would be given a high-security classification and compartmentalized.

When it comes to protecting the plot from discovery after the event, the A-Team would be aware of the key psychological factors at play:

shock, fear and tribal loyalty. Shock increases suggestibility, while fear and tribal loyalty propel people towards leaders. Bush's approval ratings rose to over 90 per cent after 9/11. Knowledge of social psychology and perhaps expertise gained from CIA operations abroad could help plotters confidently predict public reaction. So long as the media can be co-opted, the public will buy virtually any story. One oft-heard basis for doubting that 9/11 was a plot – that it was on too big a scale – is precisely the reason that it would be more likely to succeed.

Humans are tribal animals. We are disturbed but not altogether surprised to hear that our leaders have connived in the torture and murder of those designated as enemies in faraway Iraq, but are vastly more reluctant to believe that the familiar figures we see daily on TV could be complicit in a plot to murder *us*.

THE THEORIES EVOLVE

The theories have evolved over time. At first the authorities gave the false impression that, in the words of Condoleezza Rice, "no one could have imagined" the nature of the attacks, while the vast majority of US skeptics raised the issue of foreknowledge, wondering whether Washington had allowed the attacks to happen. As it became clear that many warnings had been ignored, skeptics began suspecting greater US control over the attacks: a blank cheque to Al-Qaeda might have meant planes diving into nuclear power stations.

Skepticism also mounted over the collapse of the towers. Photos circulated showing the very limited damage to the Pentagon wall before it collapsed. Radical suspicions were fed by authorities' refusal to take normal investigative steps like checking the plane part numbers, unlikely claims that the black boxes were not recovered from Ground Zero (witnesses said they were) and threats against air traffic controllers if they talked to anyone about the hijackings. Some skeptics, aware of Operation Northwoods, suspected the fakery possibility.

For others, the subsequent Al-Qaeda attacks in Bali, Madrid, London and Iraq, and the Moussaoui trial in 2006, seemed to confirm that there

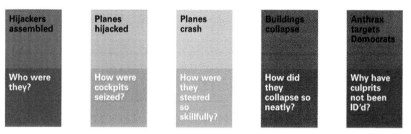

Hijackers assembled	Planes hijacked	Planes crash	Buildings collapse	Anthrax targets Democrats
Who were they?	How were cockpits seized?	How were they steered so skillfully?	How did they collapse so neatly?	Why have culprits not been ID'd?

9/11: Five key phases and crucial questions never fully resolved.

were indeed people prepared to sacrifice their lives in suicide attacks. However, Moussaoui's deranged personality seemed to confirm that the other presumed 9/11 hijackers were not highly trained operatives. These other Al-Qaeda bombings seemed to have the same confusing aspects as the 9/11 attacks, with obviously inexperienced terrorists supposedly displaying professional skills and elusive ringleaders with links to intelligence services.

Hence the theory that intelligence-agency moles manipulated the hijackers, who might have either been genuinely suicidal, intending to take the planes back to the airports, or some sort of double agents.[37]

Skeptics have also raised the possibility that the collapse of the Towers and of WTC 7 were add-ons to the attacks, not spontaneous occurrences.

The official line that the post-9/11 anthrax attacks were perpetrated by persons unknown in the US has also generated skepticism: the anthrax letters were made to appear to come from Muslim extremists, and Democratic senators objecting to Bush's post-9/11 plans were the targets. (Operation Northwoods also called for a follow-on, low-level terrorist campaign.)

The essential questions, given the authorities' refusal to release even the most basic evidence, are: Who were the people who boarded the planes? What were their intentions? Why did the planes crash? Were suicide pilots in full control of the planes? The details seem to contradict this assumption, but even if it is accurate, there are still important issues: Who usurped the identity of the incompetent Hani Hanjour, who allegedly flew Flight 77 into the

Pentagon? How did the terrorists escape detection and arrest? Were they patsies?

There are three approaches to the 9/11 attacks:

The Official Story, As Reported

The attacks were entirely the work of Al-Qaeda. Due to institutional failure, officials failed to respond to warnings at all stages from FBI field offices to planes flying off-course on the day. The only help Al-Qaeda received from Washington was incompetence or negligence. (Many Bush-haters hold to this theory).

The Official Story, Partly True

Planes full of passengers hit the buildings/crashed/were shot down, but plotters in Washington either made this happen or made *sure* it did. (As skepticism has mounted and received media attention, this widely held approach is nonetheless ignored. Many skeptics suspect a disinformation ploy.) There are several possibilities:

- *Wilful paralysis.* One or more defences, from the FBI to NORAD, were paralysed by the A-Team, but only with the vague hope something would happen. No cover story would be needed beyond gross incompetence.
- *Complicity.* An X-Team cleared a path for the hijackers and monitored them closely (perhaps through a double agent/ ringleader); X-Team planes probably trailed the jets to shoot them down if plans went awry, with a cover story prepared that a sting operation went wrong and the planes were expected to return to the airports.
- *Active manipulation.* The "moles and patsies" theory holds that the ringleaders might have been double agents, drug dealers, hijackers or some other type of patsy, who might never even have boarded the planes. The other "muscle" hijackers could have been genuine or actors in the anti-hijack exercise finally confirmed in 2006. The high speed targeted crashes were the

result, not of good luck by amateur pilots but were engineered by doctored flight computers or remote control overrides. (After 9/11, officials suggested such technology might be introduced in future; but it was already developed.) Some or all of the dramatic phone reports from the planes, which as we shall see do not make any sense, could have been faked by a small X-Team using voice-morphing techniques announced by the Pentagon in 1999. A cover story could have held that the planes were slated for the exercise and something went terribly wrong – e.g. the team in charge of remote guidance went rogue.

There Were No Hijackings

Operation Northwoods, Mark Two. If planes full of passengers ever took off, they landed and were replaced by empty drones or guided by remote control/autopilot into the buildings, with no passengers aboard. The alleged hijackers were Special Forces personnel laying an evidence trail. The case depends on the huge gaps in the evidence, there has yet to be any irrefutable evidence to support this scenario, like passengers turning up alive, proof of planes landing quietly at airports, etc.

Part 2
The Evidence

3
The Investigations

How would any 9/11 plotters hope to get away with it, to survive the inevitable enquiries? The possibility that the media might, on its own initiative, reject the story is dealt with later. This chapter looks at the official enquiries, or lack of them.

In the shock and panic, with anthrax attacks in train and another attack judged inevitable, the White House took the line that this was no time for recriminations. There would be no enquiry; there were more important things to do. A previously unthinkable threat had to be addressed. The priority was to deal with Al-Qaeda.

The man in charge of the FBI's investigation was Assistant Attorney General Michael Chertoff, a Bush ally appointed in June 2001. The FBI unyieldingly asserted its right to seize evidence, keep it secret and insist on witnesses' silence. Air traffic controllers, firefighters who believed the Towers were brought down with explosives, an emergency phone operator who took a Flight 93 call implying the plane had been shot down, and Atta's Florida associates said they had been aggressively warned not to talk to the media.[38]

CONGRESS STYMIED

Eventually, the White House made the concession it probably always planned to make: a limited enquiry would be held, based on the assumption that, at worst, this was an institutional and intelligence failure. The Senate and the House intelligence committees held a joint investigation and reported in spring 2002, producing little new information.

Meanwhile, investigations into how the Towers collapsed, and what had happened at the Pentagon, proceeded under the auspices of the independent-sounding National Institute for Science and Technology (NIST) and the Federal Emergency Management Agency (FEMA). Both part of the executive, they ultimately reported back to the White House. Had the administration wished, it could have involved independent bodies like the Federation of American Scientists or the Government Accountability Office, the investigative arm of Congress.

In April 2002, Congresswoman Cynthia McKinney finally put the question every journalist should have asked on Day One: What did the administration know about the attacks, and when did it know it? She was greeted with a storm of outrage. A national effort by Republicans, allied with her district's newspaper, ensured she lost her Congressional seat.[39]

The Washington media, theoretically the eyes and ears of democracy, acted instead as goons for the White House. Senator Frank Torricelli advocated a real enquiry and reminded the Senate that after Pearl Harbor "we had a board of enquiry. We found those responsible, we held them accountable, and we instituted the changes". Within

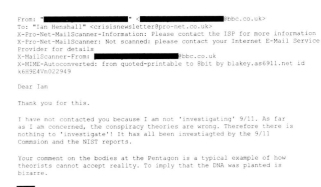

One BBC reporter felt no need to consult skeptics before writing a disparaging report about "conspiracy theorists". His reasoning? The 9/11 Commission had resolved any doubt.

weeks, the press was hounding Torricelli on corruption charges he had already answered. Nothing new turned up, but Torricelli lost his seat in 2002.[40]

Part of the cover-up included spectacular payments made to the relatives of the deceased, an average of $1.8 million each, far higher than the payments to the victims of the 1995 Oklahoma City bombing, a comparable act of terrorism. This generosity did not extend to rescue workers at Ground Zero, many of them unpaid volunteers who later suffered debilitating lung problems. To obtain compensation, relatives forfeited the right to initiate legal action.[41]

THE 9/11 COMMISSION

The joint intelligence enquiry outraged FBI officers, who disagreed with the line taken by Bureau headquarters that there had been no specific warnings of the attacks. In Minneapolis, agents had arrested Moussaoui before the attacks, but were prevented from examining his

---

TITLE VI—NATIONAL COMMISSION ON TERRORIST ATTACKS UPON THE UNITED STATES

6 USC 101 note. **SEC. 601. ESTABLISHMENT OF COMMISSION.**

There is established in the legislative branch the National Commission on Terrorist Attacks Upon the United States (in this title referred to as the "Commission").

6 USC 101 note. **SEC. 602. PURPOSES.**

The purposes of the Commission are to—
(1) examine and report upon the facts and causes relating to the terrorist attacks of September 11, 2001, occurring at the World Trade Center in New York, New York, in Somerset County, Pennsylvania, and at the Pentagon in Virginia;
(2) ascertain, evaluate, and report on the evidence developed by all relevant governmental agencies regarding the facts and circumstances surrounding the attacks;
(3) build upon the investigations of other entities, and avoid unnecessary duplication, by reviewing the findings, conclusions, and recommendations of—
(A) the Joint Inquiry of the Select Committee on Intelligence of the Senate and the Permanent Select Committee on Intelligence of the House of Representatives regarding the terrorist attacks of September 11, 2001, (hereinafter in this title referred to as the "Joint Inquiry"); and
(B) other executive branch, congressional, or independent commission investigations into the terrorist attacks of September 11, 2001, other terrorist attacks, and terrorism generally;
(4) make a full and complete accounting of the circumstances surrounding the attacks, and the extent of the United States' preparedness for, and immediate response to, the attacks; and
(5) investigate and report to the President and Congress on its findings, conclusions, and recommendations for corrective measures that can be taken to prevent acts of terrorism.

USC 101 note. **SEC. 603. COMPOSITION OF COMMISSION.**

Although it could have investigated a Washington plot, the law setting up the 9/11 Commission assumed that the "terrorist attacks" came from outside. Its starting point was the FBI investigation supervised by Michael Chertoff. The report became a forest of footnotes referring mostly to the FBI's reports, which were secret. Despite the explicit mention of the Pentagon, the Commission failed to provide any hard evidence that Flight 77 had impacted there.

laptop by headquarters on spurious grounds. Special Agent Coleen Rowley published a devastating memo, which propelled her to national status. Together with the brief "Bush Knew" media meltdown, it led to the formation of the 9/11 Commission, active in late 2002 after protracted Congressional debate. Its remit: to prepare a complete account of the circumstances surrounding 9/11; nevertheless, it pretended there were no questions from any skeptics that needed attention. The commissioners soon made it clear that they had decided not to blame any individual for anything.

The White House nominated Henry Kissinger to chair a "bipartisan" lineup of Washington insiders. But the man who is accused of orchestrating the bloody CIA-backed coup in Chile on 11 September 1973 was too much even for the cowed American public to accept. After a storm of protest he declined the job, to be replaced by little-known Republican Thomas Kean, who had links to the oil industry and was a board member of the National Endowment for Democracy, a set-up tasked with spreading US influence abroad.[42]

Vice Chairman Lee Hamilton, nominally a Democrat, was in charge of the 1987 Congressional Iran-Contra investigation, in which he granted immunity to key suspects, undermining the Special Prosecutor. He worked closely with his Republican colleague on the House Committee – Cheney.

After the 9/11 report came out, Hamilton was ambushed on Canadian radio by a surprisingly well-informed interviewer who asked questions like: "What did the Commission make of the payment from the ISI [Inter-Services (Pakistani) Intelligence] to Mohamed Atta of $100,000?" His responses were a succession of "I don't recall"; "I don't know anything about it"; "We may have, but I don't recall it". Hamilton could "not recall" a crucial piece of testimony that the Commission had nixed, even though he conducted the questioning himself.[43]

Perhaps the most flagrant appointee was Executive Director Philip Zelikow; it would hardly have been possible to choose a more partisan person to take control of the day-to-day investigations. A close associate of Condoleezza Rice, Zelikow was appointed Counselor when Rice became Secretary of State in 2005. He was involved in the Bush transition team's security appointments, and

1

"WE HAVE
SOME PLANES"

TUESDAY, SEPTEMBER 11, 2001, dawned temperate and nearly cloudless in the eastern United States. Millions of men and women readied themselves for work. Some made their way to the Twin Towers, the signature structures of the World Trade Center complex in New York City. Others went to Arlington, Virginia, to the Pentagon. Across the Potomac River, the United States Congress was back in session. At the other end of Pennsylvania Avenue, people began to line up for a White House tour. In Sarasota, Florida, President George W. Bush went for an early morning run.

For those heading to an airport, weather conditions could not have been better for a safe and pleasant journey. Among the travelers were Mohamed Atta and Abdul Aziz al Omari, who arrived at the airport in Portland, Maine.

1.1 INSIDE THE FOUR FLIGHTS

Boarding the Flights

Boston: American 11 and United 175. Atta and Omari boarded a 6:00 A.M. flight from Portland to Boston's Logan International Airport.[1]

When he checked in for his flight to Boston, Atta was selected by a computerized prescreening system known as CAPPS (Computer Assisted Passenger Prescreening System), created to identify passengers who should be subject to special security measures. Under security rules in place at the time, the only consequence of Atta's selection by CAPPS was that his checked bags were held off the plane until it was confirmed that he had boarded the aircraft. This did not hinder Atta's plans.[2]

Atta and Omari arrived in Boston at 6:45. Seven minutes later, Atta apparently took a call from Marwan al Shehhi, a longtime colleague who was at another terminal at Logan Airport. They spoke for three minutes.[3] It would be their final conversation.

1

The opening of *The 9/11 Commission Report* reads like a cheap crime thriller and betrays the superficial approach of the investigation.

was now investigating people he had helped to select only nine months before 9/11.

Investigative reporter Peter Lance, who developed a source in the Commission through FBI and Justice Department contacts, suggested that Democrats and Republicans had got together and agreed up front to follow a limited investigation of events, that by late 2003 only one of eight teams had issued subpoenas – "evidence was being cherry-picked in order to fit the limited story the Commission staff was prepared to tell". Key investigators were people from Justice and the FBI responsible for monitoring Al-Qaeda in the first place.[44]

It was too much for Commissioner Max Cleland, who resigned. The *Washington Post's* Bob Woodward, he complained, had better access to White House documents:

> This is the most serious independent investigation since the Warren Commission . . . the Warren Commission blew it. I'm not going to be part of that. I'm not going to be part of looking at information only partially . . . This is serious.[45]

Special Agent Rowley, named *Time's* "Woman of the Year", and whose testimony had been instrumental in creating the Commission, was given no more than a footnote in the final report. FBI translator Sibel Edmonds was ignored after spending hours explaining to investigators where in the FBI files to find corroboration of her allegations of gross incompetence and infiltration of the US government by criminal networks.[46]

Decorated hero William Rodriguez, the building manager who saved many and nearly died in the attacks, delivered eloquent testimony as one of many eyewitnesses who believed they had seen and heard explosions prior to the Towers' collapse – he did not even make it into a footnote. In its only attempt to explain the collapse, the report described the forty-seven interlinked steel columns comprising the Towers' massive central core as a "hollow shaft". The collapse of WTC 7 received no mention at all.

The final blow to the Commission's credibility came in 2005 with the Able Danger scandal, examined in detail later. The case was taken up by Congress in 2005. Even right-wing columnist Mark Steyn was appalled:

> Maybe we need a 9/11 "commission commission" to investigate the 9/11 commission. A body intended to reassure Americans that the lessons of that terrible day had been learned – instead of engaging in what, at best, was transparent politicking and collusion in posterior-covering and, at worst, was something a whole lot darker and more disturbing.[47]

COVER-UPS

The list of what we do *not* know is awesome. The evidence black hole covers events from the moment Atta boarded his flight from Portland to Boston until the last steel beams were removed from Ground Zero.

Why did the 9/11 Commission fail to reveal the contents of the Northeast Air Defense Sector (NEADS) tapes that showed that NORAD's hijacking exercise confused operators struggling with up to twenty-six apparent hijackings? What were the "other important matters" that preoccupied the NMCC for over twenty minutes at the peak of the crisis? Has the executive simply slapped a top-secret classification over everything important, as suggested by whistleblower Lauro Chavez (on whom more later), who reported that the day's exercises were so classified for no apparent reason?

Despite two dozen apparent phone calls from four planes, we have no idea how the terrorists could have taken over the cockpits with no hijack warning from any of them. We have no idea whether they used knives, guns, mace, bombs, box cutters or plastic cutlery, most of which should have been detected at check-in; no clear photos showing them checking in or boarding; no clear statement from any airline staff that they were checked in at all; and no manifests ever published beyond apparently faked ones circulated anonymously on the Internet (details later).

While the media blithely assures the public that the hijackers' remains were confirmed at the crash sites, the most anyone would confirm was that one or two unnamed individuals had been identified at one or another unspecified site. Although it is technically feasible that some or all of the passenger phone calls were faked, perhaps as part of the exercises, the 9/11 Commission does not even specify whether the calls were from mobiles or Airfones.

Testimony from air traffic controllers has been ruthlessly suppressed. A manager recorded the New York controllers' accounts (on the leaked tapes, they seem to have doubted the hijackings were real) but then destroyed the record by shredding the tapes and depositing the scraps in different wastebins. He said this was to protect the personal interests of the controllers themselves.

Photographic evidence from New York confirms large aircraft parts were recovered. Why did the FBI later deny that there were any large parts recovered at the landfill site? Why did investigators not take the routine step of matching the parts to the hijacked planes and announcing the results clearly? The only confirmation on the public record that the ID numbers on these parts were checked is in the form of a brief quote from a rescue worker published in *Popular Mechanics*.[48]

CREDIT: Andrea Booher/FEMA

9/11 Commissioner Richard Ben-Veniste, in comments that did not find their way into the Commission's report, described how the Pentagon withheld the NEADS tapes and then claimed they were unreadable. The Commission reclaimed the tapes using an independent outside contractor, raising the possibility of evidence tampering. NEADS and the FAA used the same radar system, but the limited FAA data that has been released makes no clear mention of the hijacking exercise, additionally raising the possibility that the FAA tapes might have been tampered with or censored.

Immense pressure has been put on witnesses. April Gallop narrowly escaped death in the Pentagon, crawling out through the debris. She became the centre of a bitter tug-of-war after saying she had seen no evidence of a plane.[49] Atta's girlfriend Amanda Keller was pressured to deny her acquaintance with him. Others were similarly threatened: "They called me a liar, and told me to keep my mouth shut," said landlord Charlie Grapentine. Neighbour Stephanie Frederickson got regular visits from the FBI:

> . . . They told me I must have been mistaken in my identification. Or they would insinuate that I was lying. Finally they stopped trying to get me to change my story, and just stopped by once a week to make sure I hadn't been talking to anyone.[50]

This does not imply that there was a massive conspiracy involving the entire FBI. Once the Bureau takes a line in a criminal case, it is institutionally hostile to people who might become defence witnesses and undermine it. The story that embarrassing information needed to be withheld would be sufficient for most situations; a small X-Team could have been placed to respond quickly to any smoking-gun evidence or well-informed witnesses emerging.

THE UNOFFICIAL ENQUIRY

This book is an unofficial enquiry, filling the gap until an enquiry is set up with a brief to investigate *all* evidence, wherever it leads. This section looks at issues any investigation would have to address. Obstacles lying in the path of a rational enquiry include:

- *Denial.* In Britain and the US, the adversarial culture permeating the political and legal systems tends to create a dialogue of the deaf, each side addressing a cartoon version of its opponent. Instead of addressing an opponent's best argument, emphasis is directed instead to their worst argument.
- *Burden of proof.* Presumption of innocence until proved guilty beyond a reasonable doubt is not appropriate at this stage. It is right for defendants actually on trial, but a preliminary enquiry, starved of information, can only look at probabilities. It is a matter of opinion what level of probability justifies a call for a major criminal investigation. Given the seriousness of the allegations, the terrible cost of the wars spawned by the official 9/11 story and the dishonesty of the investigations to date, most people without a vested interest would demand one on quite a low probability.

- *Evidence or proof.* There is confusion over these two critical words. Some skeptics say they have proof when they mean evidence; mainstream journalists say there is no evidence, when they mean no proof. Sensible 9/11 skeptics propose that there is an array of evidence, no single piece of which amounts to proof, but which, taken together, makes a strong case.

9/11 events have a massive evidence trail despite the cover-ups, ranging from the paper trail in Congress to debris photographed at the Pentagon crash site. To evaluate it all, there are generally recognized categories of evidence and a body of knowledge in place.

- *Eyewitnesses.* Supporters of the official story emphasize eyewitnesses at the Pentagon who believe they saw Flight 77 fly into it, while ignoring eyewitnesses at the Towers who believe they heard explosions, and vice versa. The media likes eyewitnesses because they have immediate visual and emotional impact on camera and because they can be presented selectively. However, psychologists and lawyers agree that eyewitness testimony is often unreliable. People recount not what they saw but what they think they saw, and are therefore liable to misjudgement or suggestion.
- *Experts.* Experts can be wrong, and often say less than the advocates using them claim. Experts used to support the spontaneous-collapse theory for the Towers and WTC 7 have genuine scientific credentials, but have been starved of evidence and can only say what *might* have happened.
- *Material witnesses.* Sibel Edmonds has promised that if she is allowed to testify, her evidence alone should lead to criminal charges against prominent individuals.
- *Forensic evidence.* 9/11 truth activists have collectively put a massive effort into seeking out publicly available photographs. One researcher writes that of an estimated 1,000 pictures he has examined of the Pentagon attack, not one shows a plane seat. It is hard to interpret negative evidence like this. It also appears odd that none of the supposedly hundreds of people who saw Flight 77, nor any fixed camera, managed to produce a clear image of it.

▦ *Paper trail.* This has proved the best avenue for skeptics so far. While there are no smoking-gun confessions, statements from FBI agents point to a pattern of obstruction going well beyond incompetence or bureaucratic inertia. Memoirs from officials and investigations like the 9/11 Commission inevitably reveal more than intended.

▦ *Circumstantial evidence.* One suspicious coincidence – e.g. the hijacking exercise on the morning of the "real" hijackings – can be explained away as just that. But if more appear and fit a pattern, then the defence must find a common explanation, too. The most favoured explanation is the cockup or incompetence theory.

THE COCKUP THEORY

There are several variants of the incompetence theory, each emphasizing different elements of the following proposition: Although, with hindsight, the attacks might have been stopped, key institutions – particularly the FBI – were not structured to forestall an attack like this. Therefore, they generally failed to collate the warnings. Where warnings ended up on the same individual's desk, he or she failed to join the dots. On 9/11, the system was overwhelmed by the enormity and unforeseen nature of what was happening, and automatically went into paralysis. The cockup theory has major problems, say skeptics.

▦ The 9/11 Commission section on the NORAD failures is titled "Improvising a Homeland Defense", but there were protocols already in place for dealing with hijackings, and regular exercises to test them. The supposed institutional tendency of the FBI to wait for a crime to occur has been argued, but for decades the FBI has infiltrated organized-crime networks to prevent future harm.

▦ The media, politicians and officials must maintain good working relations, and all have an interest in playing down malfeasance in favour of incompetence. They are consequently blind to evidence contradicting the incompetence theory.

- The evidence suggests deliberate paralysis and even proactive behaviour as opposed to only incompetence.
- Why was nobody even quietly moved from key posts? Apparently incompetent officials were *rewarded*. If the White House believed stories about Al-Qaeda getting hold of nuclear bombs or that more attacks were imminent, the nation was put at further risk. This departure from the norm suggests there was more than incompetence to be hidden.

The other side of the cockup coin is the argument that conspirators could never have succeeded because either the plot would have gone wrong or leaked, as governments cannot keep secrets. Skeptics say:

- Technical fixes are far in advance of what many scientifically ill-informed people imagine. (One professor of constitutional law assured a *Guardian* journalist that a controlled demolition requires miles of cabling.) For instance, doctored computers on the planes could have achieved the 9/11 strikes with no suicide pilots on board.
- The media is incompetent too, a government-friendly cartel. So long as there is nothing too glaring, it will practise self-censorship, especially at a time of hysteria and war. A big lie is harder to expose than a small lie.
- A "moles and patsies" scenario does not require a complex plot, just a few relatively minor adjustments to the agreed story: the FBI is blocked; one ringleader is a double agent or simply a patsy; a small X-Team is tasked to run the patsies; a flight computer is tampered with. A big result does not need a big conspiracy. A small conspiracy does not need a big cover-up.
- Plotters have already been beset by cockups like exposure of the anthrax attacks and widespread disbelief in the official story, but they have calculated that members of the establishment, many of whom may have vaguely guessed the truth, will hold firm to prevent the general discredit that an admission at this stage would entail. Plotters calculate that at worst they might have to confess to some level of criminal negligence.

The idea that governments cannot keep secrets from the media is false. History shows they can, at least for as long as it matters. The Manhattan Project involved thousands of people and was kept secret, for instance.

The Iran-Contra scam was only foiled when a plane crashed abroad and White House plotters could not suppress the news. Even then, they got away with a handful of light sentences and an acquittal for the organizer. Recently, Daniel Ellsberg – who leaked the "Pentagon Papers" (the official secret history of US involvement in Vietnam) to the *New York Times* – said:

> It is a commonplace that "you can't keep secrets in Washington" or "in a democracy", that "no matter how sensitive the secret, you're likely to read it the next day in the *New York Times*". These truisms are flatly false. They are in fact cover stories, ways of flattering and misleading journalists and their readers, part of the process of keeping secrets well . . . The reality unknown to the public and to most members of Congress and the press is that secrets that would be of the greatest import to many of them can be kept from them reliably for decades by the executive branch, even though they are known to thousands of insiders.[51]

4
The CIA and
Al-Qaeda

"I had no knowledge of these attacks, nor do I consider the killing of innocent women, children and other humans as an appreciable act," bin Laden told the Urdu newspaper *Ummat* shortly after 9/11. Weeks later, in Pakistan's *The Dawn*, he claimed the right to attack Americans. Bin Laden was allegedly filmed during a private meeting, admitting the attacks but an "official" Al-Qaeda video in December 2001 showed a haggard bin Laden who did *not* admit responsibility.[52]

The "confession tape" was apparently acquired by the Coalition after the invasion of Afghanistan, but the man it depicts hardly looks like bin Laden.

By comparison is this image, generally accepted as genuine and taken during approximately the same period.

Bin Laden in a video released just before the 2004 US election. His nose is wider, his eyes less slanted; there is little sign of his having aged during years on the run. Some skeptics believe it was fabricated to ensure Bush's re-election.

Bin Laden released his first video in over two years during the 2004 US election, in which he accepted responsibility for ordering the 9/11 attacks.[53] But to skeptics it seemed odd that the 2004 video was such poor quality, and that bin Laden looked different. The tape could have been produced with voice cloning technology[54] and an actor. Why couldn't Al-Qaeda use a decent camera, and how had bin Laden survived three years on the run without looking any older?

Skepticism about the video's origins even crept into the mainstream. Broadcasting doyen Walter Cronkite commented: "I'm a little inclined to think that Karl Rove, the political manager at the White House . . . probably set up bin Laden to this thing."[55]

There are grounds to suspect bin Laden was more patsy than mastermind. His early denial of responsibility might have been, strictly speaking, true – and certainly prudent for someone seeking to avoid both extradition and appearing the aggressor.

Journalist Robert Fisk, who interviewed bin Laden, noticed increasing signs of vanity as bin Laden's legend began to take shape in the West.[56] Afghan militia commander Abdul Rasul Sayyaf disputes his old ally's image: "He was a simple man. I think the media made him a huge man. He was not at that level. He's a stupid man and he's created problems for Afghanistan."[57]

SOURCES

This checklist contains the main sources used in the following chapters. All except Tarpley and Jan assume the official story is true. The final-column summary is, inevitably, an oversimplification.

Author	Title	Sources mainly from	Critical of
Jason Burke	*Al-Qaeda*	Arabist, Afghanistan correspondent	Neglect of Afghanistan
John Miller, Michael Stone, Chris Mitchell	*The Cell*	FBI	CIA
Peter Lance	*Triple Cross*	FBI, court transcripts	FBI, Justice Department
Gerald Posner	*Why America Slept*	CIA	FBI, Clinton White House
Ron Suskind	*The One Per Cent Doctrine*	CIA, Bush White House	No particular target
Mike Scheuer	*Imperial Hubris*	CIA operations	Washington culture
Richard A. Clarke	*Against All Enemies*	White House, CIA, Israel	FBI, Bush principals
Steve Coll	*Ghost Wars*	CIA, Washington	Washington culture
Yosri Fouda, Nick Fielding	*Masterminds of Terror*	Alleged Al-Qaeda operatives	No particular target
Webster Tarpley	*Fake Terror*	Press reports	Washington plotters
Pervez Musharraf	*In the Line of Fire*	Pakistani elite	No particular target
Abid Ullah Jan	*From BCCI to ISI*	Skeptic; press reports	Washington plotters

WHAT IS AL-QAEDA?

Al-Qaeda is, officially, a vast terrorist network dating from the early 1990's when the US lost interest in Afghanistan; earlier cooperation with bin Laden there is deemed a mistake, the threat he posed then unrecognized. Afghanistan experts often hold another version. Jason Burke says Al-Qaeda was a small, potent network that operated some years prior to 9/11, and is now mostly rolled up, though the occupation of Iraq has created a second wave. The third view sees Al-Qaeda as small in number but running continuously since the late 1980s. The 2006 publication of *Triple Cross*, Peter Lance's researches into the FBI and the US agent Ali Mohamed, produced a mountain of evidence for this view.

The story starts in 1980s Afghanistan, where bin Laden appears as a sort of Saudi pinup, the privileged offspring of a rich family sacrificing comfort to support Islamic freedom. Burke believes bin Laden's stories of heroism, though Steve Coll calls them embellishments from one campaign, bin Laden was otherwise an armchair general sipping tea and scheming in Pakistan. There are rumours he received training in the US under the alias "Tim Osman".[58] The CIA denies training or funding radical Arab brigades in Afghanistan. Milt Bearden, CIA station chief in Pakistan in the 1980s, was defensive after 9/11: "I think there's a belief . . . that we trained Arabs. We didn't do it. It didn't make sense . . . We trained the Afghan people."[59]

But Pakistan's ISI, Coll says, was acting as CIA cutout. He describes Washington micromanaging the war with "Congressional staff flying into Islamabad to examine the books kept by the CIA station *and the ISI* to determine which commanders got which weapons". (our emphasis)[60]

General Hamid Gul, ISI boss at the time, says bin Laden "was fondly nurtured by the CIA: they admired him . . . I used to hear all about him from all the CIA people here – operators, officers. They were always inviting him to garden parties at the embassy."[61] Pakistan's President Pervez Musharraf agrees: "The CIA and . . . ISI were encouraging and helping them along."[62]

The late former British foreign secretary Robin Cook wrote in the *Guardian*, presumably based on intelligence reports he saw: "Al-Qaida, literally 'the database', was originally the computer file of the

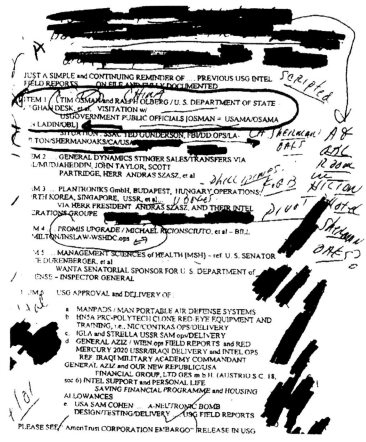

Did bin Laden (aka "Tim Osman") receive CIA training in the US? This document could be a forgery but other evidence points in the same direction.

thousands of mujahideen who were recruited and trained with help from the CIA to defeat the Russians."[63] Former French military intelligence agent Pierre-Henry Bunel confirmed that view in 2004:

> In the mid-1980s, Al Qaida was a database located in a computer and dedicated to the communications of the Islamic Conference's secretariat. Al Qaida remained the database of the Islamic Conference . . . When Osama bin Laden was an American agent in

Afghanistan, the Al Qaida Intranet was a good communication system through coded or covert messages. Al Qaida was neither a terrorist group nor Osama bin Laden's personal property.[64]

Pakistan-based Palestinian radical Abdullah Azzam, described as bin Laden's mentor, ran an international support network for the Afghan Arabs called the Office of Services (*Makatab al-Khidamar*, or MAK), with branches all over the world. The main US branch was the al-Kifah Refugee Services Center in New York. As the USSR disintegrated and the Afghanistan war ebbed, a split occurred: Azzam wanted to help rebuild Afghanistan, bin Laden to widen the war and attack secular governments in the Arab world. Azzam was assassinated in 1989; Musharraf and others suspect bin Laden.[65] Coll believes it unlikely, but agrees that he was the beneficiary: he assumed control of MAK, the organization linked to the database, evolving it into Al-Qaeda.[66]

New York MAK leader Mustafa Shalabi was a supporter of Azzam. In 1990, Egyptian radical Omar Abdel-Rahman (aka "the Blind Sheikh") arrived in New York. He soon fell out with Shalabi. In 1991, Shalabi was murdered too, whereupon militant control of the New York office became complete. John Miller *et al* write: "Why Abdel-Rahman, a known terrorist and fugitive, was even allowed to enter the US remains a mystery." Astonishingly, his "visa was signed by a CIA officer stationed at the Sudanese consulate, and one theory advanced by FBI agents is that the agency sponsored his immigration".[67] Along with others from MAK he would later be convicted for the 1993 World Trade Centre attack.

An article in the *New Yorker* fingered the Blind Sheikh as a CIA asset.[68] Miller *et al* suggest the CIA wanted to exchange favours with the Islamist movement as an insurance policy: "The CIA . . . may have wanted to nurture its ties to Egyptian fundamentalists in order to avoid a replay of Iran in 1999 when the overthrow of the Shah left US intelligence out in the cold."[69]

In 1990, Rabbi Meir Kahane's assassination uncovered a second CIA connection to the New York MAK. Arresting culprit El Sayyid Nosair, detectives found training manuals from the US Army's Special Warfare Center at Fort Bragg and, say Miller *et al*, "copies of teletypes that had been routed to the Secretary of the Army and the Joint Chiefs of Staff."[70]

The militants were professionally trained by Ali Mohamed, a onetime Egyptian army major then with the army's Special Forces school.[71]

Lance, attempting to unravel Mohamed's story, quotes two retired officials: FBI Special Agent Jack Cloonan, who handled the case leading to Mohamed's arrest in 1998, and Lieutenant-Colonel Robert Anderson, Mohamed's commanding officer at Fort Bragg. Cloonan explains that Mohamed was recruited by the CIA in 1984, but officially dropped. However, no explanation has been produced for his subsequent moves. Mohamed obtained a US visa shortly thereafter. "Everyone in the community knew he was working as a liaison between the CIA and the Afghan cause," says Ali Zaki, a California neighbour in 1985. Anderson says: "You or I would have a better chance of winning the . . . lottery than Ali Mohamed getting assigned to a Special Forces unit at Fort Bragg."[72]

Ali Mohamed was in the US special forces unit at Fort Bragg while training the New York terrorist cell, linked to bin Laden's MAK, that would go on to carry out the 1993 World Trade Centre attack.

CREDIT: US Army

Mohamed led a charmed life for more than ten years, training Al-Qaeda personnel, writing at least one Al-Qaeda handbook and helping bin Laden move from Sudan to Afghanistan. While still in the US Army, Mohamed travelled to Afghanistan and to New York, where he trained the MAK cell on weekends.[73] The discovery of the secret documents from Fort Bragg was met with swift action. Miller interviewed the case officer Eddie Norris, who claimed that while he was at lunch "the FBI removed Nosair's 16 boxes of files from Norris's squad room . . . the evidence was about to enter a black hole".[74]

The FBI used informant Emad Salem to infiltrate the New York MAK, but dropped him (at least officially) in July 1992. The story of the World Trade Center bombing, in February 1993, was deeply contested in a way that has many parallels with 9/11.[75] *Time* reported: "Defense Attorney William Kunstler accuses [Salem] of concocting the whole plot and entrapping the other defendants in it as a money-making venture – there are reports that the FBI is paying him as much as $500,000."[76] The bombmaker, Ramzi Yousef (nephew of presumed 9/11 mastermind Khalid Sheikh Mohammed), was arrested in Pakistan in 1995.

THE NEXT PHASE

In retrospect, 1995 and 1996 were landmark years in the evolution of the "war on terror". The so-called "Bojinka" plan was discovered in Yousef's laptop in Manila shortly before his arrest. Bojinka conjectured blowing up several airliners simultaneously, with a small, explosives-laden plane flying into CIA headquarters. Lance has discovered that the 9/11 plot was also in Yousef's laptop, and cites three separate sources, including Filipino police, who interviewed Yousef's partner Abdul Hakim Murad. (One source was aggressively threatened by US officials.) This makes one official post-9/11 claim – that nobody could have imagined such attacks – all the more scandalous.[77]

The official story recounts how, after falling out with the Saudis, bin Laden was operating from a new base, in Sudan. Like a venture capital fund manager, he would listen to proposals from Islamic militants, confer with his advisors and decide whether or not to offer support. To any intelligence agency concerned about radical Islam, his method

– hearing all the plans and rejecting most of them – would have screamed out potential for a sting operation. But supposedly this never occurred to the CIA.

By 1995 Khartoum was keen to get off the State Department list of supporters of terrorism. The CIA station chief there was Cofer Black, later the Agency's counterterrorism chief by September 2001. Sudan handed the notorious Carlos the Jackal to the French; as for bin Laden, extraordinarily, the US just pushed for expulsion to Afghanistan.

Sudanese intelligence offered "thick files, with photographs and detailed biographies of many of his principal cadres, and vital information about al-Qaeda's financial interests in many parts of the globe," reported journalist David Rose, who broke the story in the *Observer* and *Vanity Fair*. He cited documents, CIA sources and the former US ambassador to Sudan, saying that Washington "lost access to a mine of material on Bin Laden and his organization."[78] In his 2007 book CIA director Tenet simply denied all knowledge of the offer, saying "I am unaware of anything to substantiate that" and that UBL left Sudan "apparently of his own accord".[79]

Richard Clarke, self-proclaimed early prophet of the Al-Qaeda threat, confirms the offer was made, and admits that bin Laden could have been indicted in the US.[80] FBI sources, record Miller *et al*, were bewildered: "As a final option, the Sudanese recommended leaving bin Laden in Khartoum and offered to keep close tabs on him . . . But the White House wanted no part of an extended arrangement with Sudan . . . its first priority was getting him out . . . and away from his business and operational infrastructure."[81]

This incident is damning evidence that bin Laden was still a US asset in 1996. Instead of arresting him or running surveillance, Washington arranged a safe haven for him in Afghanistan. Al-Qaeda would be a more valuable asset there, straddling the Indian subcontinent and the new Central Asian republics. Coll explains, in a slightly different context, that the CIA compartmentalized material that could identify "key paid agents . . . at a level of top secret classification so high that hardly anyone at the State Department knew of its existence". This could explain the bewilderment of FBI officials and perhaps Tenet's unlikely disclaimer, too.

One key agent was Ali Mohamed, who, Lance discovered, trained bin Laden's personal bodyguard around this time and helped arrange the exodus to Afghanistan. Lance, noting that Al-Qaeda was suspicious of Mohamed as an American spy, concludes he was a triple agent.[82]

In 1996, the CIA created a Washington-based virtual CIA station known as "Alec Station", focusing on bin Laden. Coll portrays it as a harmless collection of analysts, though based in leased premises that would be harder to trace to the CIA. *The 9/11 Commission Report* records that "the new Bin Ladin unit" was a medium-sized CIA station with a dozen staff. By 9/11 this had risen to between forty and fifty.[83]

Mike Scheuer, head of Alec Station, was later to write his blood-curdling book calling for "brutal and, yes, blood-soaked offensive

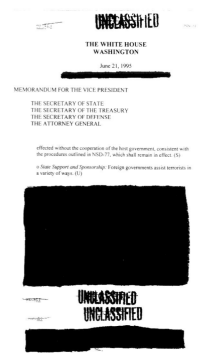

Many sections of Clinton's 1995 Directive on terrorism are still secret. It included instructions to the CIA to undertake "an *aggressive* program of foreign intelligence collection, analysis, counterintelligence and *covert action*". (our emphasis)[84]

C. *Enhancing Counterterrorism Capabilities:* The Secretaries of State, Defense, Treasury, Energy and Transportation, the Attorney General, the Director of Central Intelligence and the Director, FBI shall ensure that their organizations' counterterrorism capabilities within their present areas of responsibility are well managed, funded and exercised. (U)

D. *Lead Agency Responsibilities:* This directive validates and reaffirms existing lead agency responsibilities for all facets of the United States counterterrorism effort. Lead agencies are those that have the most direct role in and responsibility for implementation of U.S. counterterrorism

military actions until we have annihilated the Islamists who threaten us . . . that they recognize continued warmaking on their part is futile."

The decision to set up a bin Laden unit while arranging refuge for him in Afghanistan may have something to do with Clinton's landmark Presidential Directive in June 1995, most of which remains classified but, according to Clarke, "called for both offensive and defensive actions in order to reduce terrorist capabilities".[85] The unclassified version mentions only deterrence. Could the secret offensive actions, confirmed by Coll, be linked with new plans for bin Laden in Afghanistan? The location of Alec Station in the Directorate of Operations suggests so.

ON THE SAME SIDE

In the 1990s, in the conflict-ridden Balkans, radical bin Laden-supported Islamists from Afghanistan fought with Bosnians against the Serbs.[86] It was reported that during the Kosovo crisis, bin Laden was again involved. One Canadian diplomat confirmed the presence of Al-Qaeda in Kosovo as an indirect ally of NATO.[87]

In 1996, Britain's MI6 plotted with Al-Qaeda to assassinate Libyan leader Muammar Gaddafi, revealed MI5 whistleblower David Shayler. Cell leader Anas al-Liby was paid over £100,000, according to a leaked

MI6's Libyan ally Lib Anas al-Liby tipped off Al-Qaeda "triple agent" Ali Mohamed that Mohamed faced arrest. How did he discover that?

CREDIT: FBI

MI6 document. Shayler expected his disclosures to lead to an enquiry, but instead faced legal proceedings and a stonewall of denial.[88]

Lance reports that Mohamed trained al-Liby in Peshawar in 1992, and that they took surveillance photos for the 1998 Kenya/Tanzania bombings (discussed below). Al-Liby tipped off Mohamed in 1998 that he was a suspect in the bombings; did al-Liby's contacts in MI6 inform him?[89]

By 1997, with help from Al-Qaeda and backed by Pakistan, the Taliban controlled most of Afghanistan. Al-Qaeda was fulfilling US goals there; discussions were underway with Texas-based Unocal to build a gas pipeline from Turkmenistan to Pakistan. In December 1997, a Taliban delegation visited Unocal headquarters, then Washington: "The US government, which in the past . . . branded the Taliban's policies against women and children 'despicable', [appeared] anxious to please the fundamentalists to clinch the lucrative pipeline contract", observed a reporter from the *Daily Telegraph*.[90]

Bin Laden had befriended Taliban leader Mullah Omar and his fighters were a major tactical asset in the takeover of Afghanistan. However, by the end of the decade some more prescient Taliban politicians disliked Al-Qaeda and so did many in Pakistan, increasingly concerned about domestic terrorism. As a gesture to Pakistan and the US, the Taliban agreed to suppress opium production in 1999-2000 – successfully, according to UN figures.[91]

Some skeptics believe suppressing opium was the Taliban's biggest mistake, earning the enmity of the Western underworld, the ultimate beneficiaries of drug money. A year later, the invasion would see the opium trade restored, under Taliban foes the Northern Alliance. By 2007 British troops in southern Afghanistan were effectively protecting the booming trade in their efforts to win hearts and minds in a new war against the resurgent Taliban.

In February 1998, bin Laden announced the launch of the World Islamic Front and issued his notorious *fatwa* against "Jews and Crusaders", a turning point as significant as the move from Sudan. That June he was finally indicted by New York's district attorney – kept so secret, says Gerald Posner, virtually nobody outside a tight circle of FBI agents knew about it: "afraid of leaks, the officials did not even tell people like Sandy Berger, Clinton's national security advisor, or Richard Clarke . . ." Here is yet another indication of a hidden agenda concerning bin Laden.[92]

In August 1998 bombs exploded outside the US embassies in Tanzania and Kenya, killing over 200 people. Apparently the CIA and the FBI had taken their eyes off the ball. They believed they had disrupted the East African Al-Qaeda cell, but phone intercepts made it clear it remained intact, and there were warnings from Kenyan intelligence. Miller *et al* conclude: "No one can seriously argue that the horrors of August 7, 1998 couldn't have been prevented."[93]

Clinton's "response" to the African bombings with missile strikes against Afghanistan and Sudan was a public-relations and military disaster. Bin Laden and his top aides were unharmed, while the "chemical weapons factory" targeted in Sudan turned out to be innocently producing cheap pharmaceuticals.

Former National Security Advisor Zbigniew Brzezinski wrote in 1997:

As America becomes an increasingly multicultural society, it may find it difficult to fashion a consensus on foreign policy issues . . . except in the circumstances of a truly massive and widely perceived direct external threat . . . the public supported America's engagement in World War II largely because of the shock effect of the Japanese attack on Pearl Harbor.[94]

Well before Bush came to power, Washington strategists were beginning to think they needed a new enemy to replace communism. That enemy was going to be "terrorism".

THE DELENDA PLAN

"Retaliating . . . is all well and good, but we've gotta get rid of these guys once and for all," Clinton told Clarke in 1998. The ensuing Clarke-crafted Delenda Plan (from the Latin for "to destroy") followed a major reorganization of counterterrorism that saw Clarke sitting at Cabinet level, effectively in charge of policy. He writes: "We all knew we had to destroy the organization and had set out to do so."[95]

Could Clarke have masterminded any 9/11 plot? Some of Coll's CIA sources "attributed to Clarke the unseen powers of a Rasputin"; he thrived on "an air of sinister mystery". Information on Delenda is scant. According to the 9/11 Commission, it was merely a plan to bomb Al-Qaeda bases in Afghanistan more effectively. But things were afoot at the CIA, too. "In fall 1999, DCI Tenet unveiled the CIA's new Bin Ladin strategy. It was called, simply, 'the Plan'."[96]

Tenet told the Senate Intelligence Committee in 1998 that a key element of CIA strategy would be to "recruit or expose" Al-Qaeda operatives.[97] In a 1999 secret briefing, Coll records, Cofer Black "wanted to develop liaison operations specifically aimed at agent recruitment".[98] Terrorism expert Paul Bremer, in charge of a Congressional anti-terrorism panel (and later to be the US viceroy in occupied Baghdad), also concluded that the CIA needed "to recruit terrorists as informants", reports Miller *et al.*[99] Tenet's 2007 book confirms this but adds little detail except to say that "by September 11 Afghanistan was covered in human and technical operations".

Mohamed was arrested in 1998. He has never been put on trial, and as of 2007 seems to be in a permanent witness-protection programme. Lance rationalizes that he was such an embarrassment to federal prosecutors that they preferred to let him go free for years. However, this does not fit the facts. Another bin Laden aide, Wadih El-Hage, who made fools of the FBI and ran the East Africa cell, is currently serving life without parole. More likely, Mohamed was a spent force as Washington's man in Al-Qaeda because his role became too apparent to too many people. As his American wife told Lance: "He's done a lot for the government, some day you'll know it all, but I can't discuss it."[100]

Al-Qaeda's three known plans at the time – simple, "traditional" bomb attacks – failed due to incompetence. Its only real success prior to 9/11, apart from East Africa, would be the October 2000 attack on the USS Cole in Yemen, organized (as was 9/11) at a terrorist planning session, the January "Malaysian summit". The CIA's handling of the summit provides strong evidence it knew plenty about the 9/11 plot even then, and froze out the FBI. The summit took place under the close attention of the Malaysian Special Branch, the CIA, the National Security Agency (NSA) and even the White House. Khalid al-Mihdhar and Nawaf al-Hazmi, later identified as 9/11 hijackers, were there, and also, by some accounts, presumed 9/11 organizer Khalid Sheikh Mohammed. Black told Coll the CIA was watching, "not close enough to hear what they're actually saying . . . but we're covering, taking pictures, watching their behaviour . . . they're acting kind of spooky . . . going up to phone booths making lots of calls".[101]

The 9/11 Commission refers to "the original NSA reports on the planning for the meeting". Journalist James Bamford, who has excellent contacts at the NSA, says reports went immediately to the highest intelligence levels including the White House, where "updates were circulated to senior officials".[102] It seems highly unlikely that the CIA knew nothing about the vital content of the meetings either through NSA surveillance or informants. Moreover, al-Mihdhar's travels were flashed to eight CIA offices and six intelligence services, and he had a multiple re-entry visa to the US – but the FBI was somehow not informed, and the CIA "forgot" to put him on the State Department watch list.[103]

Al-Qaeda operative al-Mihdhar was known to the CIA, which went to considerable lengths to keep the FBI in the dark. Al-Mihdhar's presence on the Flight 77 manifest meant the White House could point the finger at Al-Qaeda when the attacks happened.

Returning to form, Al-Qaeda bungled its first attempt at attacking a US ship. Operatives filled their boat with so many explosives that it sank. Although warnings had been received, the USS Cole was a sitting duck. The second attempt – which could have sunk the ship – achieved limited success, damaging it and killing seventeen servicemen. Clarke and his ex-Special Forces colleague Mike Sheehan were incensed by Clinton's failure to retaliate. "What's it gonna take, Dick?" Sheehan asked. "Does Al-Qaeda have to attack the Pentagon to get their attention?"[104]

NEW PRESIDENT, SAME POLICY

Clarke records in his 2004 book that Clinton, exiting office, "put in place the plans and programs that allowed America to respond to the big attacks when they did come, sweeping away the political barriers to action". In other words, Washington was ready for "the big attacks" before Bush came to power – a notion starkly contrasting Clarke's earlier statement to the press that there was no plan.[105]

Newly President, Bush planned to wreck the Kyoto treaty on climate change and proposals for an International Criminal Court; invade Iraq; and put into action the PNAC policy of US global supremacy.

Iraq was at the top of Bush's agenda in January 2001, *before* 9/11; Treasury Secretary Paul O'Neill and Clarke both confirmed it. Ron Suskind mentions "dozens of reports generated inside the Defense and State Departments about a possible invasion of Iraq" in spring/summer 2001.[106] Nevertheless, mainstream media pundits routinely call the Iraq invasion plan a reaction to 9/11.

Iraq dominated Bush's first NSC meeting, in January 2001. Insiders included Rice, Rumsfeld, Cheney and Tenet. Outsiders – everyone else – included Powell, Clarke and O'Neill. The insiders come over as sinister, secretive and conspiratorial, even to other White House staffers. Clarke writes: "As one Republican columnist told me, 'these guys are more inbred, secretive, and vindictive than the Mafia'."[107] Secrecy was the watchword at all levels. According to one report, at the start of Bush's presidency White House staffers were provided with cellphones monitored to prevent leaks.[108] A 9/11 plot run by this mafia would not have leaked, say skeptics.

THE NATIONAL
SECURITY STRATEGY
OF THE
UNITED STATES
OF AMERICA

SEPTEMBER 2002

The United States has long maintained the option of preemptive actions to counter a sufficient threat to our national security. The greater the threat, the greater is the risk of inaction—and the more compelling the case for taking anticipatory action to defend ourselves, even if uncertainty remains as to the time and place of the enemy's attack. To forestall or prevent such hostile acts by our adversaries, the United States will, if necessary, act preemptively.

The United States will not use force in all cases to preempt emerging threats, nor should nations use preemption as a pretext for aggression. Yet in an age where the enemies of civilization openly and actively seek the world's most destructive technologies, the United States cannot remain idle while dangers gather.

National Security Strategy 15

The Bush White House confirmed to the 9/11 Commission that it knew the "big attacks", confidently predicted by Clarke and planned under CIA surveillance at Al-Qaeda's summit, were essential to win over US public opinion for Washington's new global military doctrine of pre-emptive attack.

One of the Bush team's first acts was to reappoint Tenet and Clarke. Recalling officials from the hated Clinton administration was unprecedented, though understandable if a 9/11 plot were already in place. Why else would Tenet, with his plan to "recruit" Al-Qaeda operatives, be invited to join the White House mafia? Clarke was not in the magic circle, presumably because he did not know the real plans or did not want to use the confidently expected "big attacks" to invade Iraq.

According to the 9/11 Commission, Delenda was reconfirmed, and the invasion of Afghanistan became a near-certainty in March 2001. Bush declared that he wanted the US to "stop swatting at flies". He told the 9/11 Commission "he had concluded that the United States must use ground forces for a job like this".[109]

There was a major problem with the elimination strategy. As Rumsfeld testified to the Commission, it was not only the military that was reluctant to invade Afghanistan; there was no public support. The 9/11 Commission reported:

President Bush told us that before 9/11 there was an appetite in the government for killing Bin Ladin, not for war . . . The problem, he said, would have been how to do that if there had not been another attack on America . . . Both civilian and military officials of the Defense Department state flatly that neither Congress nor the American public would have supported large-scale military operations in Afghanistan before the shock of 9/11.[110]

Nevertheless, the plans for the invasion of Afghanistan and Iraq proceeded. Reports confirm that the US also gave the Taliban one last chance to cooperate; according to one account, Afghan diplomats were told: "Either you accept our offer of a carpet of gold, or we bury you under a carpet of bombs."[111] The confidently expected "big attacks" from Al-Qaeda – unable to fill a boat with explosives in 2000 without sinking it – were now an essential component of White House global strategy.

THE PAKISTAN CONNECTION

We have seen the leaks suggesting the secret new policy involved proactive moves like recruiting Al-Qaeda operatives. Where better to start than Pakistan, with its long, deep relationship with Afghanistan, the Taliban and Al-Qaeda? Strong circumstantial evidence suggests top Pakistanis cooperated with the CIA in a sting operation targeting Al-Qaeda that evolved, perhaps in an unintended way, into 9/11.

At first the Taliban and Al-Qaeda had tacit US support as ostensibly the best way to generate stability for a new Central Asian energy route. Against them was the Northern Alliance, led by charismatic warrior Ahmed Shah Massoud along with legendary *jihadist* Rasul Sayyaf. However, the 9/11 Commission, perhaps unaware of the implications, recounted that "freelance terrorist" and alleged 9/11 mastermind Khalid Sheikh Mohammed was, as late as 1998, allied not with bin Laden but with Massoud.[112]

Sheikh Mohammed committed himself to bin Laden only in early 1999, finally convincing him to support the 9/11 plan first conceived as part of Operation Bojinka. Even afterwards, he maintained contact with Sayyaf. Described as an ISI agent, Sheikh Mohammed must have been a prime candidate for the role of Al-Qaeda infiltrator sought by Washington, the man who could create the "big attacks". But in that case (or that of any other ISI-supplied mole), Washington would need to liaise closely with Pakistan. As it happens, it *did*.

In October 1999, General Mahmoud Ahmad, then a commander in Rawalpindi, acted as kingmaker in the struggle between Musharraf and Nawaz Sharif. As a reward, Ahmad was appointed Director-General of the ISI. Musharraf and Ahmad shared the increasing frustration of the Pakistani elite with the Taliban.[113]

Coll says the CIA already had a "passing acquaintance" with Ahmad. After the coup, there was much diplomatic activity between Musharraf, Ahmad and the CIA, providing ample room for the planning of an Al-Qaeda sting operation. Clarke's deputy Michael Sheehan visited Pakistan in January 2000; Clinton visited in March, pulled Musharraf aside and "offered him the moon" to neutralize bin Laden. In April, Ahmad visited Washington, meeting with diplomats and CIA officials; in May, he went to Kabul with the US demand that the Taliban produce "immediate results" on the bin Laden question.[114]

Here the official story branches off sharply from reality. Coll records that after Ahmad's return from Washington, he became a radicalized Muslim and cut off contact with local CIA officers. This looks more like cover for a Washington-hatched plan to deal with Al-Qaeda. The 9/11 Commission records that after Ahmad's May warning to the Taliban, a senior State Department official flew out for another meeting with Musharraf. A June meeting between Tenet, Musharraf and, presumably, Ahmad saw "Musharraf [agree] to create a counter-terrorism working group to coordinate efforts between Pakistani agencies and the CIA".[115]

Then the paper trail goes cold until 2001. Coll says Tenet made a "secret visit" to Ahmad in "spring 2001" and "came and went" quickly. In May, Powell's deputy Richard Armitage and Tenet visited India and Pakistan, with "an unusually long meeting" reported in the Indian media between Tenet, Musharraf and, presumably, Ahmad. The visit was seen in connection with attempts to broker a deal between India and Pakistan, but Clarke reports that in April Armitage said he saw Al-Qaeda as "a major threat and countering it as an urgent priority".[116]

In the weeks before 9/11, the pace was frenetic. In late August 2001, the chairmen of the House and Senate Intelligence Committees, Representative Porter Goss and Senator Bob Graham, along with Senator Jon Kyl, were on a top-level mission in Islamabad, ignored in the US media. Meetings were held with Musharraf and Ahmad. On 4 September 2001, Ahmad arrived in Washington for a series of high-level meetings.[117]

The day before 9/11, the *Dawn* in Pakistan commented:

> One can safely guess that the discussions must have [included] Osama bin Laden . . . That this is not the first visit by Mahmood in the last three months shows the urgency of the ongoing parleys.[118]

The writer feared something was going to go "topsy-turvy". As the planes hit the towers, Ahmad was at a breakfast meeting at the Capitol with Graham and Goss. Asked about this meeting in 2002, Condoleezza Rice said: "I have not seen that report, and he was certainly not meeting with me." White House and CNN transcripts of the press conference omitted the reference to "ISI chief". (The transcript states that "inaudible" was in Washington.)[119]

A few weeks after 9/11, Musharraf announced that Ahmad had taken early retirement; Ahmad abruptly departed from public life. The official story, expressed in a despatch from Associated Press, hints that after 9/11 Ahmad was too sympathetic to Al-Qaeda, but evidence for this does not add up. Virtually ignored in the Western media was a report that mortally threatened the official 9/11 story and provides more evidence for the alternative possibility of a sting operation run by the ISI on behalf of the CIA.[120]

In the aftermath of the attacks, there was much talk about following the paper trail. Brian Ross, ABC's chief investigative reporter, said: "Federal authorities have told ABC News that they've now tracked more than $100,000 from banks in Pakistan to . . . suspected hijack ringleader Mohamed Atta." The *Guardian* reported that "the man at the centre of the financial web is believed to be Sheikh Saeed, also known as Mustafa Mohammed Ahmad".

CNN identified "Ahmad Umar Syed Sheikh, whom authorities say used a pseudonym to wire $100,000 to suspected hijacker Mohamed

Atta". There should not have been much doubt over this identification; *Newsweek* reported that the FBI had video footage of the mysterious Mustafa Mohammed Ahmad at a bank. Then the bombshell struck.

The *Times of India* alleged that US authorities sought General Ahmad's removal after

> confirming the fact that $100,000 was wired to WTC hijacker Mohammed Atta from Pakistan at the instance of General Mahmoud. Senior government sources have confirmed that India contributed significantly to establishing the link between the money transfer and the role played by the dismissed ISI Chief . . . including [Ahmad Umar Syed] Sheikh's mobile phone number, [helping] the FBI in tracing and establishing the link.[121]

A bit of Indian-media troublemaking, perhaps motivated by dislike of the ISI or jealousy of Pakistan's post-9/11 relationship with the US? Unlikely; the report was confirmed by Agence France-Presse:

> A highly-placed government source told AFP that the "damning link" between the General and the transfer of funds to Atta was part of evidence which India has officially sent to the US. "The evidence we have supplied to the US is of a much wider range and depth than just one piece of paper linking a rogue general to some misplaced act of terrorism," the source said.[122]

The Indian newspaper *Daily Excelsior* quoted FBI sources, saying: "Gen. Mehmood Ahmed, the FBI investigators found, fully knew about the transfer of money to Atta."[123]

In a series of press leaks in the US/UK media soon afterwards, the story gradually underwent a U-turn. The name of Syed Sheikh, Pakistani, morphed report by report, based on anonymous sources, into a completely different individual: Mustafa Ahmed Alhawsawi, Saudi. But Syed Sheikh, a jetsetting British national with a degree from the London School of Economics, was jailed in Pakistan a few months after 9/11, accused of murdering the *Wall Street Journal's* Daniel Pearl, who had attempted to track the money trail.[124]

In 2006, Musharraf stated Syed Sheikh was an MI6 agent, radicalized and possibly recruited by MI6 when he went to fight in Bosnia. *The Times* and the *Daily Mail* reported that British officials offered Syed Sheikh amnesty in 1999 to betray his links with Al-Qaeda. He reportedly refused, but was seen in London in 2000 and 2001.[125]

It hardly seems likely that, if Washington had nailed Ahmad as an Al-Qaeda godfather, it would simply have accepted his quiet resignation. As ISI director, Ahmad was well-placed to supply nuclear materials to Al-Qaeda. Even Iraq-obsessed neocons, ever haunted by the nightmare of nuclear terrorism, would have wanted to hang around a bit longer in Afghanistan to capture bin Laden and eradicate Al-Qaeda.

The notion that plotters in Washington enlisted the ISI and Saudi intelligence has been given unwitting support by Posner, who says he received a CIA leak: Abu Zubaydah, reportedly one of Al-Qaeda's top operatives, was captured in 2002. Tortured, tricked into believing he had been moved to Saudi Arabia and under truth drugs, he offered the details of five key officials, Al-Qaeda allies, in Saudi Arabia and Pakistan.

Posner names Prince Turki-al Faisal bin Abdul Aziz, longtime Saudi intelligence chief before resigning two weeks before 9/11, and Prince Ahmed bin Salman bin Abdul Aziz, publisher and racehorse enthusiast. It is preposterous to suggest that two of the most Westernized of the Saudi royal family would be secret agents for Al-Qaeda. Coll describes Prince Turki, eventually ambassador to London and Washington, as "educated at Georgetown and Oxford . . . one of the royal cabinet's most obviously pro-American princes".[126]

Posner's evidence, if true, confirms the sting possibility: Zubaydah gave away the 9/11 chain of command, which ran through pro-Western Saudi and Pakistani intelligence services to the CIA and perhaps MI6.

THE GREAT ESCAPE

Bin Laden spent far more time as ally than enemy. His fuzzy video image, according to CIA analysts, was intended to deliver the 2004 election to Bush.[127] It cannot be ruled out that bin Laden, reportedly suffering from kidney disease in 2001, is either dead or captured, and the video faked. According to Musharraf's detailed description of Al-Qaeda's command structure – invisible leadership despatching messages in one direction only – it is even possible that the setup is by now entirely controlled by the CIA or ISI.[128]

The French newspaper *Le Figaro* reported that in July 2001 bin Laden received kidney treatment at the American Hospital in Dubai, and that his many well-connected visitors included the local CIA station chief, who travelled to Washington the day after bin Laden left hospital.[129] The reports remain unconfirmed, but veteran journalist Anthony Sampson had the source as French intelligence.[130] According to CBS News, bin Laden was back in hospital on 10 September in Pakistan.[131] Both hospitalizations could have been diplomatic covers for last-minute discussions. Some skeptics believe these meetings prove bin Laden was a US agent – but they could also have been negotiations between adversaries.

In November, bin Laden was trapped in Tora Bora, in eastern Afghanistan. Suskind reports that exasperated CIA briefer Henry Crumpton warned Bush that bin Laden was in a position to escape.[132] The CIA's Gary Berntsen said in 2005 he'd had definitive intelligence: "He was there".[133] Rumsfeld's troops never arrived.

According to Suskind, whatever the complexities of the relationship between bin Laden, Sheikh Mohammed and the US, following 9/11 the US got the better of Al-Qaeda. The Delenda Plan worked. He describes the massive array of computer power deployed as Al-Qaeda tried to regroup, identifying money flows, tapping phones and tracking emails. At one stage the CIA ran one of Al-Qaeda's banking facilities in Pakistan. A high-level agent supposedly betrayed Sheikh Mohammed and received a massive payoff. Many cells were tracked down while bin Laden and his entourage retreated to the hills.[134]

Buzzy Krongard, retired as the CIA's Number Three in 2004, suggested the US is "better off" with bin Laden at large. Reporting this, *The Times* added: "Several US officials have privately admitted that it may be better to keep Bin Laden pinned down on the border of Afghanistan and Pakistan rather than make him a martyr or put him on trial. But Krongard is the most senior figure to acknowledge publicly that his capture might prove counter-productive."[135]

5
The Warnings: Paralysis at the FBI

As the 9/11 warnings flooded in, how did the White House, the Justice Department and the leadership of the FBI and CIA react? Was their reaction rational, demanding extra vigilance by the FBI – the lead agency for antiterrorist measures within the US? Did they fail to respond adequately, showing incompetence or negligence? Or was their behaviour so bizarre that there must have been some other agenda at work?

At first, the White House said the attacks had been unthinkable, that no specific warnings had been received, that no one expected an attack in the US. By the time of the 9/11 Commission, this line had been quietly abandoned. It was explained that the operative word in the denial was "specific". By 2006, Peter Lance's research showed that even this was wrong: the specific 9/11 plot was known to the CIA since the arrest of Ramzi Yousef in 1995.

The Russian newspaper *Izvestia* reported, on 12 September 2001: "According to . . . sources, Russian intelligence agents know the organizers and executors of these terrorist attacks . . . Moscow warned Washington a few weeks in advance."[136] According to the *Daily Telegraph* four days later, two senior Mossad experts were sent to Washington in August 2001 to alert the CIA and FBI, and passed two specific names to the US.[137]

In an article in New York's *Village Voice* subheaded "My Not-So-Secret Life as an FBI Informant", a journalist describes how she tipped off the FBI following the attacks that an Egyptian friend had left New York in July 2001, telling her: "I have gotten e-mails from people I know saying that Osama bin Laden has planned big terrorist attacks for New York and Washington", and specifying "late August or early September". The man was arrested by the FBI but soon released because "the information he had shared . . . that July morning was simply common knowledge in the Arab world".[138]

There were many other reports that seemed to imply prior warnings, which would be good leads for a genuine investigation but could also be put down to coincidence. *Time* reported that Pentagon generals cancelled their flights on 9/11, and the Mayor of San Francisco was quoted as saying he was warned by security sources at the airport not to fly that day, though the FAA denied issuing any warnings. Israeli Prime Minister Sharon cancelled a visit to New York, while the US/Israeli Odigo messaging service received an unspecific warning to avoid New York on the day of the attacks. The radio programme *Democracy Now* reported that a breakfast meeting at the Windows on the World restaurant at the top of the World Trade Center saw the majority of its guests cancelling at short notice.

Then-Press Secretary Ari Fleischer told the media in May 2002: "The President did not – not – receive information about the use of airplanes as missiles by suicide bombers. This was a new type of attack that was not foreseen." However, he admitted the President *was* warned that Al-Qaeda might be planning hijackings.[139] One expert explained: "The idea that Al-Qaeda was going to use a routine hijacking tactic . . . never made sense. It's an organization that sought to kill large numbers of people dating back a decade . . . [they] should have immediately deduced that they would try to kill everyone on board."[140]

At the July 2001 G8 summit in Genoa, security concerns had Bush sleeping aboard an aircraft carrier[141]:

> U.S. and Italian officials were warned in July that Islamic terrorists might attempt to kill President Bush and other leaders by crashing an airliner into the Genoa summit of industrialized nations . . . Italian officials took the reports seriously enough to prompt extraordinary precautions . . . including closing the airspace over Genoa and stationing antiaircraft guns at the city's airport . . .[142]

Further evidence that US officials were aware of the risk comes from a spate of newspaper articles in 2004. The *Boston Globe* noted: "Concerns that terrorists might use hijacked airliners as missiles date back to the 1996 Olympic Games in Atlanta, when jets were placed on patrol to guard against such a threat."[143] *USA Today* reported: "In the two years before the September 11 attacks the North American Aerospace Command conducted exercises simulating what the White House says was unimaginable at the time: hijacked airliners used as weapons to crash into targets and cause mass casualties. One of the imagined targets was the World Trade Center."[144]

TOP OFFICIALS EXPECT ATTACK, BUSH IN THE DARK

Chapter eight of *The 9/11 Commission Report*, "The System Was Blinking Red", recounts:

> On June 25, Clarke warned Rice and Hadley that six separate intelligence reports showed Al-Qaeda personnel warning of a pending attack . . . Clarke wrote that this was all too sophisticated to be merely a psychological operation to keep the United States on edge, and the CIA agreed. The intelligence reporting consistently described the upcoming attacks as occurring on a calamitous level, indicating that they would cause the world to be in turmoil.[145]

The Commission said warnings concerned attacks abroad; in that case, why did key officials say the opposite at the time? Clarke convened with officials from twelve different federal agencies in July 2001. The *Washington Post*, citing two people present, quotes Clarke: "Something really spectacular is going to happen here, and it's going to happen soon."[146] Clarke recalls: "I asked the agencies to cancel summer vacations and official travel for the counterterrorism response staffs. Each agency should report anything unusual, even if a sparrow should fall from a tree. I asked FBI to send another warning to the 18,000 police departments."[147]

The 9/11 Commission account is quite different:

> Attendees report that they were told not to disseminate the threat information they received at the meeting. They interpreted this direction to mean that although they could brief their superiors, they could not send out advisories to the field.

Why not? Who told them? Not Clarke, according to his account. The Commission's footnote suggests it questioned peripheral agencies attending the meeting, but not the key agency that was to fail so disastrously – the FBI.

FBI counterterrorism chief Dale Watson told the National Governors' Association on 12 July: "[We are] headed for an incident inside the United States."[148] On 16 July, CBS noticed that Attorney General John Ashcroft had started flying on private jets: "Neither the FBI nor the Justice Department, however, would identify what the threat was, when it was detected or who made it." Asked if he knew anything about the threat, Ashcroft replied: "Frankly, I don't. That's the answer."[149]

The new administration demoted Clarke to the Deputies Committee, but Tenet was present most mornings as Bush's CIA briefer went through the President's Daily Brief (PDB). In contrast, according to Posner, "in his two years as director of the CIA, [James] Woolsey had only two semi-private meetings with Clinton".[150]

In 2004, after one of Washington's longest wrangles – beginning with Ari Fleischer's misleading statements in 2002 – the 9/11 Commission finally obtained the PDB for 6 August 2001 that had become the focus of two years of intense speculation: "Bin Ladin Determined to Strike *in* US"

36. President Bush and Vice President Cheney meeting (Apr. 29, 2004). For Rice's reaction to the August 6 PDB article, see Condoleezza Rice testimony, Apr. 8, 2004.

37. The CTC analyst who drafted the briefing drew on reports over the previous four years. She also spoke with an FBI analyst to obtain additional information. The FBI material was written up by the CIA analyst and included in the PDB. A draft of the report was sent to the FBI analyst to review. The FBI analyst did not, however, see the final version, which added the reference to the 70 investigations. Barbara S. interviews (Apr. 12, 2004); Joint Inquiry interview of Jen M., Nov. 20, 2002. Because of the attention that has been given to the PDB, we have investigated each of the assertions mentioned in it.

The only information that actually referred to a hijacking in this period was a walk-in to an FBI office in al

Who lied to the President? Somebody gave Bush false information that the FBI was active on the antiterrorism front. The Commission discovered it was an unnamed analyst from the CIA's counterterrorism centre, the department failing to pass vital information to FBI field offices.

(our emphasis); the very title destroys a key plank of the official story:

> We have not been able to corroborate some of the more sensational threat reporting, such as that from a [-] service in 1998 saying that Bin Ladin wanted to hijack a US aircraft to gain the release of "Blind Shaykh" 'Umar 'Abd al-Rahman and other US-held extremists. Nevertheless, FBI information since that time indicates patterns of suspicious activity in this country consistent with preparations for hijackings or other types of attacks, including recent surveillance of federal buildings in New York. The FBI is conducting approximately 70 full field investigations throughout the US that it considers Bin Ladin-related.[151]

The PDB included an explicit reference to hijackings. The mention of New York also stood in glaring contrast to Condoleezza Rice's statement under oath to the Commission when the document was still secret: "But I can also tell you that there was *nothing in this memo* that suggested that an attack was coming on New York or Washington, DC . . . This was not a threat report to the President." (our emphasis)[152]

The CIA's claim that the FBI was conducting seventy bin Ladin investigations was false. FBI spokesman Ed Coggswell said the Bureau tried "to ascertain how the number 70 got into the report . . . many were criminal investigations, which terrorism experts say are not likely to focus on preventing terrorist acts".[153] There were only a handful, in fact, which were strenuously blocked by senior FBI officials. The Commission discovered that this false information was added by a CIA analyst at Cofer Black's counterterrorism centre.[154]

The following is the text of an item from the Presidential Daily Brief received by President George W. Bush on August 6, 2001.[37] Redacted material is indicated by brackets.

Bin Ladin Determined To Strike in US

Clandestine, foreign government, and media reports indicate Bin Ladin since 1997 has wanted to conduct terrorist attacks in the US. Bin Ladin implied in US television interviews in 1997 and 1998 that his followers would follow the example of World Trade Center bomber Ramzi Yousef and "bring the fighting to America."

After US missile strikes on his base in Afghanistan in 1998, Bin Ladin told followers he wanted to retaliate in Washington, according to a [—] service.

An Egyptian Islamic Jihad (EIJ) operative told an [—] service at the same time that Bin Ladin was planning to exploit the operative's access to the US to mount a terrorist strike.

The millennium plotting in Canada in 1999 may have been part of Bin Ladin's first serious attempt to implement a terrorist strike in the US. Convicted plotter Ahmed Ressam has told the FBI that he conceived the idea to attack Los Angeles International Airport himself, but that Bin Ladin lieutenant Abu Zubaydah encouraged him and helped facilitate the operation. Ressam also said that in 1998 Abu Zubaydah was planning his own US attack.

Ressam says Bin Ladin was aware of the Los Angeles operation.

Although Bin Ladin has not succeeded, his attacks against the US Embassies in Kenya and Tanzania in 1998 demonstrate that he prepares operations years in advance and is not deterred by setbacks. Bin Ladin associates surveilled our Embassies in Nairobi and Dar es Salaam as early as 1993, and some members of the Nairobi cell planning the bombings were arrested and deported in 1997.

Al-Qa'ida members—including some who are US citizens—have resided in or traveled to the US for years, and the group apparently maintains a support structure that could aid attacks. Two al-Qua' da members found guilty in the conspiracy to bomb our embassies in East Africa were US citizens, and a senior EIJ member lived in California in the mid-1990s.

A clandestine source said in 1998 that a Bin Ladin cell in New York was recruiting Muslim-American youth for attacks.

We have not been able to corroborate some of the more sensational threat reporting, such as that from a [—] service in 1998 saying that Bin Ladin wanted to hijack a US aircraft to gain the release of "Blind Shaykh" 'Umar 'Abd al-Rahman and other US-held extremists.

Nevertheless, FBI information since that time indicates patterns of suspicious activity in this country consistent with preparations for hijackings or other types of attacks, including recent surveillance of federal buildings in New York.

The FBI is conducting approximately 70 full field investigations throughout the US that it considers Bin Ladin-related. CIA and the FBI are investigating a call to our Embassy in the UAE in May saying that a group of Bin Ladin supporters was in the US planning attacks with explosives.

Bush's briefing for 6 August 2001. Contrary to what the White House had been saying for three years, it confirmed that the coming Al-Qaeda attack was likely to be in the US.

The Commission picked up a sinister detail when it examined the Senior Executive Intelligence Briefing (SEIB), the version of the PDB for top officials like FBI managers:

Although the following day's SEIB repeated the title of this PDB, it did not contain the reference to hijackings, the alert in New York, the alleged casing of buildings in New York, the threat phoned in to the embassy, or the fact that the FBI had approximately 70 ongoing bin Ladin-related investigations.[155]

Was this false information deliberately inserted by plotters to mislead Bush, or permit him deniability?

Rice assured the Commission that, in July 2001: "The F.B.I. tasked all 56 of its U.S. field offices to increase surveillance of known suspected terrorists and to reach out to known informants who might have information on terrorist activities."[156] Commissioner Tim Roemer

Rice testified that in summer 2001 the FBI had increased terrorist surveillance, but the Commission could find little evidence of this.

© Getty Images/Mario Tama

later retorted: "We've gone through literally millions of pieces of paper. To date, we have found nobody . . . at the FBI who knows anything about a tasking of field offices. Nothing went down the chain to the FBI field offices."[157]

Thus, with the system "blinking red" (as the Commission termed it), Rice and Bush were fully aware of a possible Al-Qaeda attack in the US, perhaps involving hijackings; the CIA's vital presidential briefing, kept secret for over two years, contained false information that the FBI had investigations going when, in fact, it had few if any; and Rice's statement to the Commission contained incorrect information that all FBI field offices were alerted when few, if any, were.

FBI counterterrorism chief Dale Watson, Clarke at the White House and Tenet at the CIA were in daily contact with each other. So it does not take Sherlock Holmes to see that something is very wrong with the information flow, from the FBI to Bush and Rice, from Watson to the FBI offices and more importantly (see below) from the offices back up to Watson. The incompetence theory holds that the FBI is stuffed with risk-averse managers, but that hardly explains these problems. Someone was being highly proactive, seriously misleading Bush and Rice – or giving them cover.

Could overworked middle managers have obstructed the reaction at the FBI, hoping their budgets would increase if things went wrong? If so, these few individuals successfully withstood massive pressure from the top down to task the field offices and equally massive pressure from the bottom up to let the field offices take action, and persuaded investigators they had done nothing wrong. The case for a hidden agenda is already strong.

THE WALL

Clarke, with customary apparent blunt honesty, said the CIA and FBI "had specific information about individual terrorists from which one could have deduced what was about to happen . . . it apparently did not even make it up the FBI chain to Dale Watson".[158]

Set up around the time of Clinton's terrorism directive in 1995, the Wall was an integral part of the new strategy, most of which is still secret. Information gathered for intelligence purposes could not automatically be shared with criminal investigators. FBI agents on the intelligence side of the Wall were effectively under the control of the CIA. By defining an investigation as intelligence, FBI operatives on the wrong side of the Wall could be excluded.

The success of 9/11 against all odds was simple: for reasons that have not been explained people on the intelligence side used the Wall to paralyse the FBI. The explanation of the pro-CIA lobby for the "failures" of the FBI is an outrageous piece of buck-passing. The FBI was not institutionally incapable of stopping the terrorists; it was the CIA and its allies on the FBI's intelligence side who, for some reason, never allowed the FBI a chance. Thus it seemed surprising that Jamie Gorelick, who had erected the Wall as Deputy Attorney General, should be appointed as a 9/11 Commissioner.[159]

Clarke and Watson were well aware that Al-Qaeda might strike in the US – but that was the one place where law enforcement was being paralysed. The 9/11 Commission records: "In late June, the CIA ordered all its station chiefs to share information on Al-Qaeda with their host governments and to push for immediate disruptions of cells."[160] And later: "There was a clear disparity in the levels of response to foreign

44. CIA cable, "Activities of Bin Ladin Associate Khalid Revealed," Jan. 4, 2000. His Saudi passport—which contained a visa for travel to the United States—was photocopied and forwarded to CIA headquarters. This information was not shared with FBI headquarters until August 2001. An FBI agent detailed to the Bin Ladin unit at CIA attempted to share this information with colleagues at FBI headquarters. A CIA desk officer instructed him not to send the cable with this information. Several hours later, this same desk officer drafted a cable distributed solely within CIA alleging that the visa documents had been shared with the FBI. She admitted she did not personally share the information and cannot identify who told her they had been shared. We were unable to locate anyone who claimed to have shared the information. Contemporaneous documents contradict the claim that they

Here, buried deeply in one of hundreds of footnotes, *The 9/11 Commission Report* details one of the key moments when the CIA blocked the FBI from doing its job.

versus domestic threats."[161] Thus Al-Qaeda was being corralled into attacking the US mainland; as usual, this aroused no suspicions.

Presumed hijacker al-Mihdhar played a vital role in the official 9/11 story, and was the Wall's most spectacular beneficiary. Uncharacteristically, the Commission conducted a relatively thorough investigation into al-Mihdhar and discovered a series of what it called "day-to-day gaps in information sharing".

Al-Mihdhar had a US visa and participated in the 2000 "Malaysian summit" (travelling to Los Angeles afterwards), but the CIA failed to put him on the State Department watch list until a few weeks before 9/11. Cofer Black assured the 2002 Congressional enquiry that "CTC [Counterterrorism Center] officers detailed to the FBI kept the FBI updated through verbal briefings" on the terrorist summit.[162] Verbal briefings hardly seem appropriate for informing the leading antiterrorist agency of an operation so significant that reports were going directly to the White House – but they are conveniently deniable. The Commission noted: "We were unable to locate anyone who claimed to have shared the information."[163]

The CIA alerted nobody when al-Mihdhar's visa was renewed. When New York FBI investigators handling the USS Cole case started asking questions about al-Mihdhar, they were stonewalled at a vital meeting in June 2001. CIA agent "Dave" from Alec Station was there. The Commission found: "No one at the meeting asked 'Dave' what he knew; he did not volunteer anything. The New York agents left the meeting without obtaining information that might have started them looking for Mihdhar."[164]

However, Miller says: "The CIA officers stonewalled them, claiming the intelligence was too sensitive to be shared, and the meeting

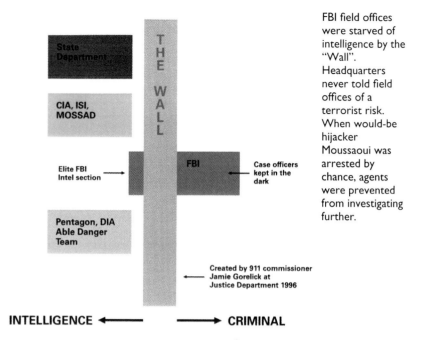

FBI field offices were starved of intelligence by the "Wall". Headquarters never told field offices of a terrorist risk. When would-be hijacker Moussaoui was arrested by chance, agents were prevented from investigating further.

INTELLIGENCE ← → CRIMINAL

degenerated into a shouting match."[165] Lance says: "The so-called shouting match nearly turned into something more, Bongardt gets so angry he almost goes over the table."[166]

The Alec Station officers, perhaps to cover themselves after that angry scene, were told to look into al-Mihdhar again, but managed to spend weeks getting nowhere – even though he was living openly and the FBI's database contractor Choicepoint could have located him at the click of a mouse. They put out an alert, but only on the lowest, "routine" level. They headed off a further enquiry from the USS Cole team by invoking the Wall, even insisting the New York agents destroy a memorandum they received.[167]

MOUSSAOUI ARRESTED

In her angry 2002 memo, Special Agent Rowley detailed how FBI headquarters had spiked Minneapolis's investigation into Zacarias

The likely fifth hijacker on Flight 93, Moussaoui's grossly unrealistic behaviour at flight school led to his arrest. FBI headquarters aggressively blocked Minneapolis agents' investigations.

CREDIT: FBI

Moussaoui. She believed it involved more than incompetence and omission. Agent Harry Samit told the Moussaoui trial in 2006 that it was due to "obstructionism, criminal negligence and careerism".[168] Rowley extensively briefed the 9/11 Commission, but her story – which had contributed to the creation of the Commission – never made it into its report.[169]

Moussaoui was arrested for overstaying his visa following a tip-off from a flight school that he might be a potential hijacker. Agents agreed. They wanted a search warrant to examine his laptop. FBI headquarters instructed Minneapolis not to open a criminal investigation – the case was now on the wrong side of the Wall. Then headquarters blocked the warrant, saying the case was too weak.[170]

In Rowley's words:

> FBIHQ personnel . . . continued to, almost inexplicably, throw up roadblocks and undermine Minneapolis' by-now desperate efforts to obtain a FISA search warrant . . . HQ personnel brought up almost ridiculous questions in their apparent efforts to undermine the probable cause . . . HQ personnel never disclosed to the Minneapolis agents that the Phoenix Division had, only approximately three weeks earlier, warned of Al-Qaeda operatives in flight schools seeking flight training for terrorist purposes![171]

Instead, HQ produced spurious legal arguments to block the warrant request. The Minnesota office contacted the CTC to see if it had anything on Moussaoui, but instead was "chastised" for this, reports Rowley.[172] Samit testified that he was warned: "This was just the kind of thing that would get FBI agents in trouble."[173] The Commission noted: "Tenet told us that no connection to Al-Qaeda was apparent to him at the time."[174] But FBI agents contacted French intelligence, which was absolutely clear that Moussaoui was a dangerous terrorist belonging to Al-Qaeda.[175]

The French had tracked Moussaoui for years, including his time in Al-Qaeda training camps, and even knew he had planned to fly a hijacked Air France jet into the Eiffel Tower in 1994. FBI headquarters replied that the French must have been mistaken, and argued that the Paris phone directory must contain many Moussaouis. Rowley objected:

> The Supervisor's taking of the time to read each word of the information submitted by Minneapolis and then substitute his own choice of wording belies to some extent the notion that he was too busy . . . Why would an FBI agent deliberately sabotage a case?[176]

In another contradiction, Tenet can be seen on video saying, much later: "We knew who Moussaoui was all the time."[177] This all stands in spectacular contrast to the statement by Watson to a national conference of FBI field office supervisors early in 2000, as reported by Clarke: "[Al-Qaeda] are the FBI's number one priority in terrorism. You will find them. If you have to arrest them for jaywalking, do it. If the local US attorney won't prosecute them, call me. If you can't get your FISA wiretap approved by Justice, call us, don't just sit out there and sulk." But in this case it was different.

Special Agent Rowley was called "flippant" for suggesting there might be a Robert Hanssen-type Al-Qaeda spy at FBI headquarters. Hanssen (not to be confused with serial killer Robert Hansen) was a highly effective Soviet spy. Why did official investigations fail to consider this possibility, given the unlikely success of the attacks? Ali Mohamed was precisely such a mole, according to the official story.

CREDIT: FBI

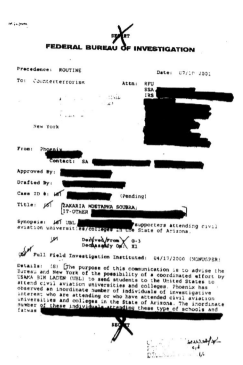

Shortly before FBI headquarters blocked the Minneapolis office's investigation of Moussaoui, the Phoenix office warned headquarters it suspected terrorists were taking flying lessons.

The Minneapolis office circulated over seventy memos to government agencies warning that Moussaoui was dangerous, and taking flying lessons. Samit later told an internal enquiry he was told by headquarters: "You will not question the unit chief and you will not question me. We've been through a lot. We know what's going on."[178] Rowley provides telling evidence suggesting that the 9/11 plot was protected by counterterrorism officials – not by incompetence but by design. On 11 September the agents made yet another attempt to open Moussaoui's laptop. The supervisor refused again, saying they "might 'screw up' something else going on elsewhere in the country".[179]

A year after 9/11, Chicago-based FBI Special Agent Robert Wright approached the conservative public-interest group Judicial Watch, saying his Al-Qaeda-linked investigation was also blocked by FBI headquarters. Judicial Watch came up with a more serious accusation than mere incompetence:

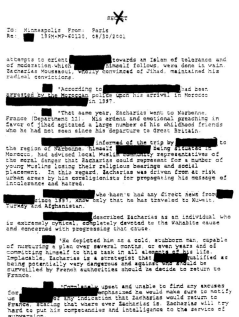

Tenet told the Commission the CIA had no awareness of Moussaoui's Al-Qaeda connections. But the French knew all about him.

SA Wright alleged FBI intelligence agents lied and hid vital records from criminal agents for the purpose of obstructing his criminal investigation of the terrorists in order to protect their "subjects" and prolong their intelligence operations. SA Wright was stunned to learn recently that some of the FBI intelligence agents that had stalled and obstructed his criminal investigations of terrorists in Chicago had also lied to the judges of the FISA Court in Washington, DC.[180]

Wright told ABC News in December 2002:

The supervisor who was there from headquarters . . . started yelling at me: "You will not open criminal investigations. I forbid any of you. You will not open criminal investigations against any of these intelligence subjects."[181]

Intelligence investigations were harder to get warrants for, but were ultimately controlled by the CTC.

No alarm bells rang at the FAA either. The Commission reported that half the FAA's daily intelligence summaries over six months before 9/11 mentioned Al-Qaeda.[182] Few mentioned risks inside the US, so inaction here can be explained by inertia. Harder to explain is the change in regulations introduced in July 2001 forbidding pilots to carry guns. The rule had been in force for forty years.[183]

BEHIND THE SCENES

What was going on in the impenetrable area between intelligence chiefs protesting they were on full alert and people on the ground being aggressively blocked? *Newsweek* reported one clue in March 2004: In summer 2001,

> a federal judge severely chastised the FBI for improperly seeking permission to wiretap terrorists; as a result . . . the Justice Department curtailed a highly classified program called "Catcher's Mitt" to monitor Qaeda suspects in the United States.[184]

Clarke later said that a highly classified programme had been closed down. But shutting it down could not have been the only option. Who made the decision? This incendiary story was never followed up and completely escaped the Commission.

Perhaps the programme was shut down by Michael Chertoff. In June 2001, FBI Director Louis Freeh resigned after ten years on the job, and Chertoff arrived as Assistant Attorney General in charge of the Criminal Division. Under the 1995 Presidential Directive, the FBI was the lead agency for counterterrorism; if anyone should have insisted that those on the intelligence side of the Wall stop blocking criminal FBI investigations, it was Chertoff.

Chertoff was US Attorney in New Jersey at the time of the 1993 World Trade Center bombing. Shortly before taking the new job, as an expert in terrorist funding, he helped defend Dr Magdy Elamir from accusations of diverting health-fund money to Al-Qaeda. In 2001, Chertoff assumed charge of the 9/11 investigation. He helped introduce the US Patriot Act, and advised the CIA on the legality of torture methods.[185]

Michael Chertoff, Assistant Attorney General in June 2001 – when FBI agents were blocked from investigating suspects – and later in charge of the FBI's 9/11 investigation.

CREDIT: US Department of Homeland Security

The man ultimately in control of the FBI was Ashcroft, widely seen as a close ally of the Bush inner circle. Special Agent Wright went public in 2002, but his attorney David Schippers was alerted to both the Chicago and New York blocks *before* the attacks. He got word to Ashcroft, and was contacted by someone described as a deputy who replied: " . . . we don't start our investigations at the top . . . I'll have somebody get back to you right away." No one ever did.[186]

It would appear that the bureaucracy was operating under Ashcroft's orders. Thomas Pickard, acting FBI director in the summer of 2001, testified to the Commission: "Pickard told us that after two such [terrorist threat] briefings Ashcroft told him that he did not want to hear about the threats anymore. Ashcroft denies Pickard's charge." The Commission adds that Ashcroft "did not ask the FBI what it was doing in response to the threats and did not task it to take any specific action".[187]

What about Tenet, whose officers failed to alert the State Department or the FBI to al-Mihdhar, blocked FBI demands for help in New York and perhaps pulled the strings in the Moussaoui case? The CIA chief was extremely evasive about his dealings with Bush during the vital days in August when the plot might still have been foiled. Tenet gave false information under oath to the Commission. Three times,

Commissioner Roemer asked Tenet when he met with Bush that August. Each time, Tenet denied he did.[188]

Within hours the CIA issued a correction: "Tenet flew to Texas to brief Bush on Aug. 17, 2001, and briefed the president again on Aug. 31 when Bush returned to Washington, a spokesman for Tenet said later in the day."[189] A CIA spokesman said: "It's not accurate . . . He momentarily forgot."[190] Tenet apparently forgot taking a plane journey down to Texas even though Commissioners were suggesting he *should* have been talking to Bush. (Earlier in the hearing he had been criticized for misleading the Commission, suggesting that the August briefing was at the CIA's request rather than at the President's.)

Was Tenet covering up something else? If Bush is to be believed, the CIA was still wrong even with its correction – because there was another meeting at the ranch too, on 24 August. Keen to dispel press stories that he was spending too long vacationing, Bush let slip on 25 August:

> The CIA briefings, I have on our porch, the end of our porch looking out over the lake. When Tenet came up, that's where we visited, out there . . . We got back here at about 11:30 a.m. and met until 5:15 p.m. I think they left. That's the longest meeting I've had in a long time, on a very important subject . . .[191]

Q   You've done some work out of here. Has it been more difficult to work out of here or --

THE PRESIDENT: No, it's just the same. You know, when you pick up the phone and you call de la Rua to talk to him about Argentina, it's -- it may be a different hookup, but it's the same voice.

Yesterday -- as a matter of fact, in some ways, this place is better for work. Yesterday, we spent -- well, they arrived at 10:00 a.m. It took a while to get the press conference. We got back here at about 11:30 a.m. and met until 5:15 p.m. I think they left. That's the longest meeting I've had in a long time, on a very important subject. And so it gave us a chance to sit back and relax. It was a much less hectic schedule.

Therefore, we had a good chance to talk about a really important subject, which is our military strategies. And so in some ways, it lets -- this place allows for more in-depth discussions. Condi and I spend a lot of time just sitting around visiting about our foreign policy matters.

You know, Andy Card and I talked for a while yesterday. Josh is around. Karen Hughes was here. We spent a good deal of time with Karen talking about the fall and what we'll try to communicate in the fall.

I had a good visit with Vicente Fox on the phone. You know, we're working on immigration policy. And although I haven't been in the meetings, I have been in communications with Margaret LaMontagne is heading up that task for us. And I think we'll make some pretty good progress there.

Q   When you have those business meetings, like the Joint Chiefs briefing, do you like to keep it separate from the living quarters on the ranch?

THE PRESIDENT: Actually, you know, what we call the governor's house, the place where you all came out during the -- that's where we went. Condi and Karen Hughes stayed there. And right across the street from that is a -- it's a nice looking government doublewide. (Laughter.) And that's where the mil aide, the nurse, the WHCA head, the doc, they stay.

The CIA briefings, I have on our porch, the end of our porch looking out over the lake. When Tenet came up, that's where we visited, out there.

You know, everybody wants to see the ranch, which I'm proud to show it off. So George Tenet and I -- yesterday, we piled in the new nominees for the Chairman of the Joint Chiefs, the Vice Chairman and their wives and went right up the canyon.

Tenet's meeting with Bush at the President's Texas ranch would have been entirely secret, but for some casual remarks to the press by Bush. Tenet denied meeting Bush at all in August 2001 to the Commission. Was this a final planning meeting for Operation 9/11?

The "very important subject", some skeptics believe, was the planning meeting for 9/11, safely away from prying eyes in Washington, at the end of the porch out of reach of any recording devices. The Commission did not ask about the mysterious 24 August meeting. In his 2007 book (p. 159). Tenet acknowledges the meeting and describes it as a follow up to the 6 August briefing. He fails to explain why he denied it to the 9/11 Commission, how long it was and what the Chiefs of Staff were doing there. The Commission did, however, refer people in the Pentagon and CIA to their internal disciplinary process: investigation by the departments' Inspector Generals (IG).

Tenet, who mentioned the mysterious "The Plan" and appeared to give incorrect information to the Commission, used 9/11 to push through a billion-dollar budget rise and obtain the biggest increase in CIA power in the Agency's history. James Pavitt, whose Operations Directorate was responsible for the overall failure, saw his department boosted to levels not seen since the days of Vietnam. Cofer Black, who oversaw the secret bin Laden unit that failed to report vital information from the Malaysian summit to the FBI, pushed successfully for Bush to sign off on new policies of "extreme interrogation" and putting "heads on sticks" – in other words, torture so shameless that FBI officers refused even to be present.[192]

The IG report was "scathing . . . The report, delivered to Congress this week, recommends punitive sanctions . . . What is at stake for them is personal honor . . .".[193] But Tenet fought back with scarcely veiled threats:

> Until now, Mr. Tenet has kept silent about what Mr. Bush knew and when he knew it . . . Mr. Tenet himself may go public to defend his reputation. The $4.5 million book offer may soon be back on the table, and this time Mr. Tenet might take it.[194]

This version of Tenet's book never appeared, and the IG report was never published.

6
The Hijackers: Terrorists or Patsies?

"I was stunned, not that the attack was Al-Qaeda but that there were Al-Qaeda operatives on board aircraft using names the FBI knew were Al-Qaeda." According to Clarke, the news was in by about 10.30 a.m. on the morning of the hijackings. Watson of the FBI, who had warned publicly weeks earlier of a US-based "incident", reported personally to Clarke on a secure line that the FAA had checked the flight manifests of the hijacked planes, and found the names of two known Al-Qaeda operatives.

CNN already had the story by about 9.30, probably briefed by Clarke or an aide. The extraordinary failings of the CIA and its FBI allies on the intelligence side of the Wall ensured not only that the operation succeeded, but had the Washington media announcing the case solved before midday.

Other intelligence professionals saw it differently, as suggested by a widely circulated quote from journalist Seymour Hersh: "A former high-level intelligence official told me, 'Whatever trail was left was left deliberately – for the F.B.I. to chase'."[195]

This trail could equally be signalling a false-flag operation. The apparent use of suicide hijackers was an indication of Arab terrorism, but they could have been manipulated by elements like Israel's Mossad – famous for its false-flag operations – or, as strenuously argued by Cheney and others, by Saddam Hussein's Iraq.

The dossier promised by Powell proving bin Laden was responsible was delayed. Investigators simply could not agree on the story. The FBI view, eventually upheld by the Commission, was that the suicide teams were simply lucky. Hersh quotes an official: "In your wildest dreams, do you think they thought they'd be able to pull off four hijackings? . . . Just taking out one jet and getting it into the ground would have been a success. These are not supermen."[196]

Most of the Washington media went with an alternative story, the one that fitted the plans to attack Afghanistan and Iraq: "Another view, centered in the Pentagon and the CIA, credits the hijackers with years of advance planning and practice."[197] This chapter looks at the confusion that still persists over the identities of the hijackers; additional evidence that the hijackers may have been under surveillance; and multiple reports contradicting the assumption that the lead hijackers in each plane were capable pilots set on suicide.

WHO WERE THEY? THE FUZZY IDENTITIES

The presumed hijackers' behaviour was a very long way from that of religious devotees about to martyr themselves. Can we be sure of the identities of the people who boarded the planes? Hersh reported four weeks later: "The F.B.I. is still trying to sort out the identities and backgrounds of the hijackers. The fact is, the official acknowledged, 'we don't know much about them'." This contrasts with the official view that all the alleged hijackers, using their real identities, were identified correctly within about three days.

```
23.GUADAGNO  R.SFO  YV**        19A A              ET BM  O
24.GLICK     J SFO  YK**        11A A              ET  M      S
25.GRANDCOL\L SFOYXY**          11D A              ET
26.JARRAH    Z SFO  FF**        O1D A              ET        O S
27.KUGE      T SFO  YL**        1SA A              ET  M  O
)28.MARCIN   H SFO  YT**        17C A              ET BM   S
```

The "original flight manifests" were leaked in an attempt to bolster the official story. However, the *Boston Globe* was told: "FBI agents, reviewing flight manifests, found a Ziad Jarrahi – the 'i' in the last name a possible misspelling." The FBI at first named Jarrah as Jarrahi. The otherwise convincing Flight 93 "manifest" looks like a forgery. The FBI has refused to answer questions about the manifests.

```
G*L77/11SEPIAD/ON
AA    77 11SEP    IAD D26   81OA  757 ON LIST          F15Y43
HANJOUR        HANI      F  LAX  1E-F RB SC LF CLUE TKT
2  EOOTH       KJ        F  LAX  1E-F  Q DE 8C LF ET
                                       AUTH EMPL PS
```

The *Washington Post* explained the absence of Hani Hanjour from the first FBI list of hijackers because he was not on the flight manifest. But this "manifest" for Flight 77 has him clearly on it. Once again, it looks like a skilful forgery.

The list of passengers released to the media did not include any of the alleged hijackers, an omission that fuelled 9/11 skepticism from the start. Apparently faked documents purporting to be the original flight manifests appeared on the Internet in 2006. The forgeries, quite convincing but for the press reports contradicting them, raise the question of who would have the means and the motive to produce them. Perhaps significantly, the genuine manifests are not among the documents produced at the 2006 Moussaoui trial.

The 9/11 Commission reported that Al-Qaeda had a false-passport factory in Afghanistan. Of the four recovered passports, definitely two and probably at least half the others had been "doctored". This assessment was based on photocopies, record-checking, etc., the Commission explained. In 2006, then-UK Chancellor Gordon Brown, arguing for national identity cards, said: "One 11 September hijacker used 30 false identities to obtain credit cards and $250,000 . . . Since then the problem has . . . worsened . . . Over the last few years the

American Airlines #77
Boeing 757
8:10 am departed Washington Dulles for Los Angeles
9:39 am crashed into the Pentagon

1) **Khalid Al-Midhar** - Possible residence (s) : San Diego, California and New York, New York; Visa Status: B-1 Visa, but B-2 Visa had expired.

2) **Majed Moqed** - No information available.

3) **Nawaq Alhamzi** - Possible residence (s) : Fort Lee, New Jersey and Wayne, New Jersey and San Diego, California.

4) **Salem Alhamzi** - Possible residence (s) : Fort Lee, New Jersey, and Wayne, New Jersey.

5) **Hani Hanjour** - Possible residence (s) : Phoenix, Arizona and San Diego, California. Believed to be a pilot.

American Airlines #11
Boeing 767
7:45 am departed Boston for Los Angeles
8:45 am crashed into North Tower of the World Trade Center

1) **Satam Al Suqami** - Date of birth used: June 28, 1976; Last known address: United Arab Emirates.

2) **Waleed M. Alshehri** - Dates of birth used: September 13, 1974/January 1, 1976/ March 3, 1976/ July 8, 1977/ December 20, 1978/ May 11, 1979/ November 5, 1979; Possible residence (s) : Hollywood, Florida/ Orlando, Florida/ Daytona Beach, Florida; Believed to be a pilot.

3) **Wail Alshehri** - Date of birth used: July 31, 1973; Possible residence (s) : Hollywood, Florida, and Newton, Massachusetts; Believed to be a pilot.

4) **Mohamed Atta** - Date of birth used: September 1, 1968; Possible residence (s) : Hollywood, Florida/ Coral Springs, Florida/ Hamburg, Germany; Believed to be a pilot.

5) **Abdulaziz Alomari** - Date of birth used: December 24, 1972 and May 28, 1979; Possible residence: Hollywood, Florida; Believed to be a pilot.

United Airlines #175
Boeing 767
7:58 am departed Boston for Los Angeles
9:05 am crashed into South Tower of the World Trade Center

1) **Marwan Al-Shehhi** - Date of birth used: May 9, 1978; Possible residence: Hollywood, Florida; Visa Status: B-2 Visa; Believed to be a pilot.

2) **Fayez Ahmed** - Possible residence: Delray Beach, Florida.

3) **Ahmed Alghamdi** - Possible residence: Delray Beach, Florida.

4) **Hamza Alghamdi** - Possible residence: Delray Beach, Florida.

5) **Mohald Alshehri** - Possible residence: Delray Beach, Florida.

United Airlines #93
Boeing 757
8:01 am departed Newark, New Jersey, for San Francisco
10:10 am crashed in Stony Creek Township, Pennsylvania

1) **Saeed Alghamdi** - Possible residence: Delray Beach, Florida.

2) **Ahmed Alhaznawi** - Date of birth used: October 11, 1980; Possible residence: Delray Beach, Florida.

3) **Ahmed Alnami** - Possible residence: Delray Beach, Florida.

4) **Ziad Jarrahi** - Believed to be a pilot.

Three days after 9/11 the FBI released a list of the alleged hijackers, with more pilots than necessary on Flight 11 – apparently naming innocent Saudi pilots by mistake. It would be over a week until the pictures were released. Several of these are still in dispute.

major terrorist suspects arrested, typically, have had up to 50 false identities each."[198]

A spate of media reports seemed to suggest that up to seven hijackers were still alive. The *Washington Times* quoted an FBI spokesman in 2003: "There are a lot of people with the name of John Smith, but they're not the same person . . . We checked the flight manifests, their whereabouts in this country, and we interviewed witnesses who identified the hijackers." However, there was no doubt that several Saudis were still alive who had the same names, places and dates of birth as the alleged hijackers. The *Washington Times* and BBC thought, respectively, that Wail and Waleed al-Shehri, whose photos were on the FBI website, were still alive.[199] To alleged hijacker Abdul Aziz al-Omari was ascribed the picture of living pilot Abdul Rahman al-Omari.[200]

The oddities of the fake manifests, the slight name changes and the contested identities, the absence of Hani Hanjour – the most problematic pilot – from the earliest list, the fact that too many pilots were allocated to Flight 11 and only Hanjour, belatedly, to Flight 77, all add up to a deeper deception than merely Al-Qaeda manipulating IDs for people they could not get into the US legally.

Most of the Saudis, if genuine, should not have been given visas in the first place. The neocon *National Review*, perhaps motivated to blame Saudi intelligence for 9/11, reported:

> According to expert analyses of the visa-application forms . . . all the applicants among the 15 reviewed should have been denied visas under then-existing law. Six separate experts who analyzed the simple, two-page forms came to the same conclusion: . . . *even allowing for human error*, no more than a handful of the visa applications should have managed to slip through the cracks.[201] (our emphasis)

Michael Springmann, head of the US embassy visa section in Jeddah, Saudi Arabia, in the 1980s, commented after 9/11: "I issued visas to terrorists recruited by the CIA and its asset, Osama bin Laden." He

Abdul Aziz al-Omari   Wail al-Shehri   Wail al-Shehri

INNOCENT. Al-Omari and al-Shehri identified by the FBI as suicide pilots remain on the list. But according to media reports, these are innocent living pilots with the same names. Eventually the FBI named Atta as the pilot of Flight 11.

HIJACKERS' TRUE NAME USAGE
2001

NAME	NAME USED	DATE	ITEM	GX NUMBER	BATES NUMBER
Al-Omari, Abdul Aziz	Abdul Aziz Al Omari	6/29/2001	INS I-94 entry document	OG01019P	M-LBP-00008711
Al-Shehhi, Marwan	Marwan Yousef Mohamed R. Lekrab AlShehhi	1/18/2000	U.S. DOS printout entitled Non-Immigrant Visa Applicant Detail (no original visa application available)	OG01119P	M-LBP-00006681
Al-Shehhi, Marwan	Marwan AlShehhi	5/2/2001	U.S. Customs Form 6059B, Customs Declaration	M-LMP-00004494-9
			INS I-94 entry document	OG01011P	M-LBP-00009263
Jarrah, Ziad	Ziad Samir Jarrah	5/25/2000	U.S. visa issued in Berlin showing dob 5/11/75, nationality Lebanese, passport # 1619505 (no original visa application available).	OG01108P	M-LBP-00000982
Al-Haznawi, Ahmad	Ahmad Ibrahim Al Haznawi		U.S. non-immigrant visa application showing KSA passport #B991866; dob 10/11/190 in USA		
Moqed, Majed	Majed Moqed	6/27/2001	U.S. visa & VA ID card, Application for Delivery of Mail through Agent.	FO00261P	M-LBP-00005756-61
U.S. INS & CUSTOMS FORMS					
Atta, Mohamed	Mohamed Mohamed Elamir Atta	5/18/2000	Copy of U.S. visa, #34137932, from Mail Boxes, Etc. In Hollywood, FL (no original visa application available).	OG01114P	M-MMA-00021371
Atta, Mohamed	Mohamed Atta	1/10/2001	INS I-94 entry document		

The FBI checked the original visa applications, except in the case of alleged pilots Atta, Jarrah and al-Shehhi. Each of these was missing. Did the US embassy in Berlin lose its copies? With no originals ever recovered, how could the FBI be so sure these people were not impostors?

wondered if the Agency had helped clear a path for terrorists again. Travel agents might "simply send a package of passports and visa applications over to the Consular's section. And because they came from a reputable source, people didn't look too closely at it, I guess." This was "an old agency [CIA] ploy".[202]

There are signs the Commission was troubled by the legend of the hijackers. While its discussion of "intelligence failures" has huge gaps, and while it barely mentions the warnings of an imminent attack received at the diplomatic level, several chapters of its report are devoted to an exhaustive rehearsal of the activities of the alleged hijackers, based on unspecified phone, credit card, car hire records and witness identifications. Unless the surveillance powers of US authorities have achieved truly Orwellian, unguessed-at proportions, anyone could have been occupying these identities. Witness identification is hardly reliable – photographs of the alleged hijackers have been flashed endlessly in the media. In Portland, many people said they had seen Atta there in the previous weeks, while the FBI believed he had never been there before.

The presumed hijackers at Dulles Airport: this is the only direct evidence that the people whose photographs the FBI released were the same people who boarded the planes.

© AP/PA Photos

It is hard to find an innocent explanation for the evidence black hole at the airports. Some of the busiest and most security-sensitive international airports in the US were apparently unable to produce anything more than one non-standard, undated, unclear piece of CCTV footage (from Washington/Dulles, released three years later) of the four parties of presumed hijackers.

Surely the presumed hijackers were at least identified by airline personnel who checked them in? The Commission records that of the nineteen presumed hijackers no fewer than ten triggered the Computer-Assisted Passenger Prescreening alert, which singled their bags out for an extra explosives check. The nearest the Commission

One airline staff member identified Mohand al-Shehri (right) as either Ahmed al-Ghamdi (centre) or Hamza al-Ghamdi (left) who are supposedly brothers.

got to a positive ID was when check-in assistant Gail Jawahir remembered two people of the same name boarding flight 175 – presumably the al-Ghamdi brothers – but identified Mohand al-Shehri who did not look like either of them.[203]

If the hijackers were mostly unknown and identified initially from names on the flight manifests, why was Flight 93's Ziad Jarrah, Lebanese, assumed to be a hijacker and Flight 11 passenger Waleed Iskandar, Lebanese, above suspicion? Iskandar was admittedly seated back in row 31; however, Flight 77's Majed Moqed was not in first class either, but row 12.

THE LUCKY FINDS

Three key pieces of evidence confirmed the official story in the first hours. The first, mentioned earlier, was the apparent presence of known Al-Qaeda operatives al-Mihdhar and al-Hazmi on Flight 77. The

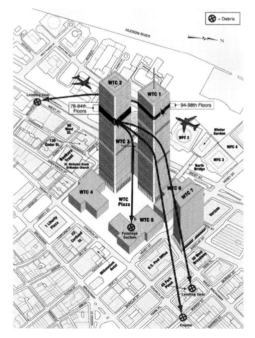

This plan, drawn up by the FEMA investigation, shows how it thinks the debris emerged. The passport discovery was in Vesey Street, near WTC7 and it came from the impact with WTC1, so it had to blow back out through the fireball to get there.

CREDIT: FEMA

The passport of alleged hijacker Satam al-Suqami supposedly survived the inferno, floating down to the ground. It was released in evidence at the Moussaoui trial in 2006.

GOVERNMENT
EXHIBIT
WT00001
01-455-A (ID)

second was the lucky find of the passport of another alleged hijacker, Satam al-Suqami, reportedly discovered at Ground Zero. The passport was not, as originally reported, Atta's, nor was it from Flight 175, which emerged partially after hitting the South Tower. It came from Flight 11, which ploughed into the North Tower.

Susan Ginsburg, senior Commission counsel, said: "A passer-by picked it up and gave it to an NYPD detective shortly before the World Trade Center . . . collapsed."[204] It seemed odd that in the chaos of New York on that morning a mere passport could have survived the inferno, to be discovered by a member of the public and identified as being from one of the hijackers, all within a few hours.

The other evidence concerned Atta, alleged ringleader and lead pilot. A photo apparently showing Atta boarding his flight flashed around the world, while the contents of his bag, with its apparent confession, intrigued newspaper readers the following weekend. However, skeptics noticed that the photo actually showed him boarding a connecting flight early that morning. Why did Atta take an unnecessary flight that could have been cancelled or delayed? It looked more like a setup, said skeptics, and why wasn't there any video from Boston/Logan, showing even one of the ten hijackers?

Fast Green ATM
9/10/01

8:41 pm

UNO's Restaurant Parking Lot
280 Maine Mall Road
South Portland, ME

These pictures were presented by the FBI to show Atta and al-Omari in Portland on the evening before the attacks, and on their way to the connecting flight. Al-Omari does not much resemble official FBI photos of him (see p. 93).

CREDIT: FBI

In 2006, former FBI agent Warren Flagg declared that a hitherto unknown second bag of Atta's was discovered in Boston. It was from this "Rosetta Stone", gushed *Newsday*, that the FBI obtained

Arab-language papers revealed the identities of all nineteen hijackers involved in the four hijackings, as well as information on their plans, backgrounds and motives . . . "How do you think the government was able to identify all 19 hijackers almost immediately after the attacks?" Flagg asked. "And that's how it was known so soon that al-Qaida was behind the hijackings."[205]

Nevertheless, the FBI has given its explanation for how it identified the alleged hijackers so quickly, because they all used their own IDs. This looks like a shoddy attempt to shore up the official story. *Newsday* did not state that Flagg had any firsthand knowledge of the matter, and those who did refused to comment. The story contradicts Al Jazeera journalist Yosri Fouda's account of meeting alleged ringleaders Khalid Sheikh Mohammed and Ramzi bin al-Shibh (discussed later), who explained that everyone had obscure codenames based on ancient Arab heroes.[206]

The ill-founded revelation from Flagg only highlights the mystery of Atta's Portland flight and his highly suspicious bag, which contained pepper spray, a videocassette for a Boeing 757 flight simulator, a folding knife – according to the Commission – and a pilot's uniform, according to some reports at the time. There were also the confessional last-minute instructions described as Atta's testament, which also showed up in another hijacker's bag. Robert Fisk, the highly regarded Middle East expert, described this document as "fearful, chilling, grotesque – but also very, very odd . . . men who murdered more than 7,000 innocent people believed in a very exclusive version of Islam – or were surprisingly unfamiliar with their religion".[207]

Atta had attracted attention from immigration officials on his recent June re-entry to the US; surely this highly suspicious collection of surplus hijacking equipment could, if found at check-in, have at the least caused a fatal delay in his connection at Logan – itself an unnecessary risk. The media explained that Atta arrived late, that this was somehow why the bags did not make it on the plane. But the Commission records he arrived a full hour before takeoff. Why did the bags get lost?

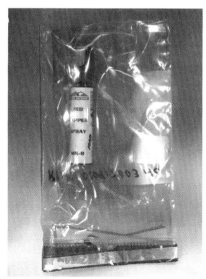

Pepper spray from Atta's baggage, which never made it onto the plane in Boston. It was taken as evidence for the official story, but why did Atta have this in his baggage? It would be of no use in the hold of the plane and, if his bags were opened, might (along with the confession, knives, flight tape and pilot's uniform) lead to disaster. Why not just leave them in the car boot at Portland? Skeptics suspect the bag was somehow planted to establish the story early on.

CREDIT: FBI

Somebody seems to have tried laying down a trail, and in this instance, at least, it could not have been Al-Qaeda unless it had an agent in the baggage room. This cannot be explained as bin Laden wishing to leave a discreet signal that Al-Qaeda was responsible. How could anyone but an insider have arranged for Atta's bag to be kept off the plane to be "discovered" in time for the evening news bulletins?

THE PILOTS

It is essential to the official story that Al-Qaeda was able to find willing and capable suicide pilots. Pilots Atta, al-Shehhi and Jarrah seem unlikely to have had the inclination or the skill for such a plot, while pilot Hanjour certainly lacked the skill.

The story of Atta, Jarrah and Hanjour (little is known about Marwan al-Shehhi other than that he was Atta's frequent companion), of angry young men brainwashed by extremists in Hamburg and choosing to martyr themselves, is a very long way from the evidence.

According to his father, Atta was a quiet, effeminate boy with a fear of flying who was somehow tricked by Mossad. Burke, in his widely praised book, believes Atta never had a girlfriend.[208] But Fouda identifies a significant relationship: in 1994 he fell in love with a Syrian woman, and marriage was considered.[209] Atta's father was secular; women in his family never wore veils, did not attend the local mosque and wore Western dress, according to neighbours who spoke to Western reporters.[210]

It therefore seems odd that in 2005 CNN interviewed Atta's father, claiming to be Arab journalists. The man was now a convinced *jihadist*: he was proud of his son, a brave Muslim fighter in "a 50-year religious war".[211] *One* version of Atta's father was surely wrong – and the first version had been reported many times. If the new version is true, Atta's father would be risking a visit from Egypt's feared secret police – notorious for disliking *jihadists*. Was the event staged, Atta's father intimidated into cooperating?

After Atta moved from Germany to the US, he, Jarrah and Marwan al-Shehhi seemed more typical of another South Florida type, well-known to the FBI and CIA though less familiar to the general public:

the successful, middle-ranking drug dealer. According to reports by Florida-based investigative journalist Daniel Hopsicker, Atta and Jarrah chose to learn to fly in an area that was a veritable hotbed of CIA-linked activities and drug trafficking. One executive at the small airport in Venice, Florida, where the pilots trained, told Hopsicker: "Early on I gleaned that these guys had government protection. They were let into this country for a specific purpose. It was a business deal."[212]

Hopsicker interviewed Amanda Keller, briefly Atta's girlfriend. Her story was reported in the German tabloid, *Bild Zeitung*, but ignored in the US. Keller apparently noticed multiple passports in different names and observed Atta speaking fluently in several languages. According to her, Atta and his (non-Muslim) German friends would indulge in cocaine binges and visit strip clubs and bars. Some of this was confirmed in the mainstream media. After 9/11, London's *Observer* reported:

> [Atta] spent Friday afternoon drinking with Marwan al-Shehri [*sic*] and a third man in Shuckums Oyster Pub and Seafood Grill in Hollywood, a small town 30 miles from Miami. Patricia Idrissi, a waitress, remembered that . . . Atta and al-Shehri sat drinking and arguing. Al-Shehri drank rum and coke; Atta knocked back five Stolichnaya vodkas with orange juice.[213]

A local paper in Jacksonville reported Jarrah's affinity for strip clubs – and the unwillingness of anyone to allow their names to be used.[214] The *New York Times* reported in November 2001 that "while the leaders seemed to be Islamic zealots, the muscle did not, indulging often in pornography and liquor." But reporters following up the stories in Saudi Arabia emerged with tales of men at least some of whom appeared to be typical *jihadist* recruits, pious Muslims from small towns or rural backgrounds. The FBI called them the "muscle hijackers" because the role was apparently to enforce the takeover of the planes and little else.[215] There was speculation that these people did not know they were going to die.

The Commission observed: "Even with the benefit of hindsight, Jarrah hardly seems a likely candidate for becoming an Islamic extremist." Hopsicker reports that nobody at Jarrah's flight school, who found him sociable and had shared beers with him, could believe he was a suicidal terrorist. This view, confirmed by other media reports, was corroborated by reports from Germany that Jarrah – who had attended a Christian boarding school in Beirut – did not even attend prayers. Multiple media reports confirm that Jarrah's cousin in Germany and family in Lebanon expressed utter disbelief in the official story. The *Boston Globe* said Jarrah would have had to have lived "a double life worthy of a first-rate spy".[216] His family still believes he did not board Flight 93.[217]

Authorities said Jarrah's suicide plan was confirmed in a letter to his fiancée Aysel Senguen, but she denied this. The letter contained no more than the mention of a big event. She said there was nothing unusual in his last call.[218]

It appears there were two different people blurring into the Ziad Jarrah identity. While the real Jarrah lived in Germany in 1995-6, a

Jarrah 1: the official photograph released by the FBI.

Jarrah 2: Jarrah from his US visa. Can this really be the same person? It would be interesting to know if this is a German or a Lebanese passport. The original visa application, presumably granted in Berlin, was never given to the FBI.

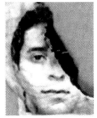

Jarrah 3: This was recovered from the Flight 93 crash site.

Three Jarrah photographs, with the widths equalized to take account of any mechanical errors in reproduction. They still look like three different people.

This still is from the "soundless confession" video apparently featuring Jarrah and Atta that emerged in 2006.

© The Sunday Times/NI Syndication

"Ziad Jarrahi" lived in New York.[219] Again, in January 2001, Jarrah was in two places: one was with his family while another was being questioned in Dubai on his way back from Afghanistan. CNN cited multiple sources saying this was at the CIA's behest.[220] Three reports confirm that Jarrah or Jarrahi was travelling in the US on a German passport.[221] The German embassy in London refused to give me any information about either figure, but German nationality rules dictate

The official photograph of Atta, looking ten years older than in the "soundless confession" video – if it is Atta. Given his reported drug and alcohol binges in Florida, perhaps this is possible.

that if Jarrah, a Lebanese national, was travelling on a German passport, it can only have been provided specially or been a fake.

In 2006, new video footage was released showing Atta and Jarrah sitting together, each wearing a beard. If authentic, this was the first clear evidence that Atta and Jarrah knew each other. The video was said to confirm the FBI timeline that placed Jarrah, contrary to the evidence of his family, in Afghanistan in January 2001. In it, the two chat and laugh in a relaxed way, then become serious as they deliver speeches. The videos are far crisper than normal "Al-Qaeda productions". Jarrah appears genuine, but "Atta" has aged by about ten years in the space of a few months.

The video had a murky history; reports said the Pentagon had had it since 2001. The FBI says it does not feature 9/11 on its bin Laden wanted poster because it does not have proof he was responsible for it. But this video, supposedly shot at a bin Laden camp in Afghanistan, should represent that proof. There are more questions than answers here: how was the soundtrack lost? Why could lipreaders not manage to decipher what these people were saying? Why would the most precious asset of these two recruits – their lack of any connection to Islamic radicalism – be risked by a visit to Afghanistan? Even if genuine, there is little here to undermine the "moles and patsies" or double-agent theories.[222]

Marwan al-Shehhi, apparently the pilot of flight 175 who pulled off a split-second banking manoeuvre to strike the corner of the South Tower, is a little-known figure, described as outgoing and frequently seen by witnesses in Atta's company. Hopsicker describes him as Atta's bodyguard, based on witness reports from Florida and the testimony of Keller, who thought they were business partners.[223]

Beyond the fact that he drifted from flight school to flight school, showing little talent for flying and leaving a trail of worried instructors, little is known of Hanjour. He went on the FBI hijackers list a day later than the others, perhaps replacing the "Mosear Caned" CNN named in a hastily transcribed report a day earlier. Abulrahman Hanjour, his brother, told a reporter: "We are in shock, we thought that he liked

Hanjour, as agreed by his family   Alleged hijacker "Hanjour" on security camera

The real Hanjour seemed to have very poor flying skills. Is the man in the official photograph the same as the alleged hijacker caught on a security camera? Do the ears look the same?

The prosecution at the Moussaoui trial presented this red bandanna, apparently recovered unharmed from Flight 93. But Milt Bearden, the retired Pakistan CIA station chief, was doubtful:

How do we know Osama bin Laden is the man? Everybody has simply agreed that that's it. Colin Powell and President Bush have said he is a prime suspect. I believe that Osama bin Laden is a component of all of this, there's no question of that. But was Osama bin Laden the evil genius behind what happened on Tuesday in New York and Washington? I'm not sure . . . Three of the hijackers on the flight that went down in Pennsylvania were wearing red headbands . . . that is a uniquely Shi'a Muslim adornment. Sunnis are by and large most of the people following Osama bin Lad[e]n.[225]

the USA." Hanjour was a little over five feet tall and described as meek. He had lived on and off in the US for about five years.[224]

The personalities and motives of the hijackers are also fuzzy, particularly the ringleaders. We have Jarrah, the master spy who kept up a perfect pretence of planning to marry his girlfriend, even buying a new suit. Atta must have undergone a radical personality disintegration, from the boyish "Afghanistan" photos to the FBI "cocaine" mugshot. The hard-living image reported by the media (at first), and confirmed by Hopsicker, would corroborate this – but we are a long way from the master operative that the official story requires.

Atta looks more like a patsy. After the Florida drinking session, reports the *Observer*, there was a major scene:

"You think I can't pay my bill?" Atta shouted. "I am a pilot for American Airlines. I can pay my fucking bill." Then he peeled out a note from a thick wad of $50 and $100 bills, leaving a $2 tip.[226]

THE INVISIBLE RINGLEADERS AND THE HAMBURG CELL

The main evidence produced for the hijackers' fanaticism comes not from the US but Germany, with the legend of the Hamburg cell, which

Detainee Interrogation Reports

Chapters 5 and 7 rely heavily on information obtained from captured al Qaeda members. A number of these "detainees" have firsthand knowledge of the 9/11 plot.

Assessing the truth of statements by these witnesses—sworn enemies of the United States—is challenging. Our access to them has been limited to the review of intelligence reports based on communications received from the locations where the actual interrogations take place. We submitted questions for use in the interrogations, but had no control over whether, when, or how questions of particular interest would be asked. Nor were we allowed to talk to the interrogators so that we could better judge the credibility of the detainees and clarify ambiguities in the reporting. We were told that our requests might disrupt the sensitive interrogation process.

We have nonetheless decided to include information from captured 9/11 conspirators and al Qaeda members in our report. We have evaluated their statements carefully and have attempted to corroborate them with documents and statements of others. In this report, we indicate where such statements provide the foundation for our narrative. We have been authorized to identify by name only ten detainees whose custody has been confirmed officially by the U.S. government.[2]

The Commission relied almost entirely on one man's second-hand evidence for its account of the plot – a man whose statements were almost certainly extracted under torture.

has changed radically over the years. The cell's alleged masterminds were Ramzi bin al-Shibh and Khalid Sheikh Mohammed. But here is, again, a complex, ambivalent tale with little clarity. The main sources are *The 9/11 Commission Report*, trial transcripts for Hamburg cell prosecutions in Germany, and Sheikh Mohammed's and bin al-Shibh's interview with Fouda before they were arrested.

The Commission cites Sheikh Mohammed almost exclusively for its narrative of the plot, relying on his second-hand statements literally scores of times. Bin al-Shibh, who unlike Sheikh Mohammed was in contact with Atta, is barely mentioned. In 2007, it was reported that the detainees had been moved to Guantánamo Bay.

According to the first version of the official story, Hamburg was a hotbed of Islamic radicalism that sucked the pious Atta and feckless Jarrah into its deadly vortex. In the aftermath of 9/11, German police rounded up large numbers of people alleged to be terrorists, and the legend of the Hamburg cell was constructed on the statements of suspects under threat of long-term imprisonment for knowing Atta, al-Shehhi and Jarrah. They knew whom to arrest because US investigators *already knew*, according to leaks in the German media. US investigators had a great deal of information about the cell that they had not shared with their German colleagues – more evidence that the alleged plotters had been closely monitored all along. There was even a report in the German magazine *Focus* that while in Germany, Atta, under close surveillance by the US, had been followed as he purchased ingredients for explosives.[227]

CIA Berlin station chief David Edger "directed both military and civilian U.S. intelligence programs in Germany" according to a citation at Oklahoma University, where Edger has taught since retiring in June 2001.[228] His post there was arranged by university president David Boren, the former Senate Intelligence Committee Chairman who gave George Tenet his first big job in Washington (and, coincidentally or not, was having breakfast with Tenet on 11 September 2001). Also coincidentally – or not – Moussaoui lived at the university dormitory for several months in 2001.[229]

During a February 2002 address to a meeting in Oklahoma, Edger confirmed that the CIA monitored the Hamburg cell. The local paper reported:

> He said although officers knew members of the cell and some of what they were doing, they had no idea that they would meet in London and go to different parts of the U.S., where they would learn to fly planes to crash into the World Trade Center. "In that case, we failed," Edger said.[230]

However, they must have known that Atta, Jarrah and al-Shehhi had been granted US visas. As discussed, the FBI said it was not given visa

The CIA Berlin station chief David Edger.

applications for these three, although it was for the other presumed hijackers.

After the arrests of bin al-Shibh and Sheikh Mohammed in 2002 and 2003, the Hamburg cell legend changed. Germany was the only country prosecuting anyone for direct involvement in 9/11, but even though German courts are prepared to travel anywhere and take evidence in secret, the CIA still refused to produce the alleged ringleaders. Instead, the State Department sent a statement supposedly from bin al-Shibh that the cell had never existed and that key defendant Mounir al-Motassadeq was not involved in 9/11. The constitutional court ordered his release, but prosecutors had convinced themselves of the official CIA story and obtained incriminating statements from people caught up in the dragnet. They brought more charges, and by early 2007 al-Motassadeq was facing the eighth of a series of trials, appeals and retrials with no end in sight.[231]

In 2002, Yosri Fouda interviewed bin al-Shibh and Sheikh Mohammed for his book *Masterminds of Terror.* They gave many supposedly operational details of the attacks, and bin al-Shibh said he would have liked to take part in the hijackings, but his US visa was refused. There was no explanation for why he could not use an assumed identity, given Al-Qaeda's proficiency with false passports (detailed by the 9/11 Commission). Fouda thought Sheikh Mohammed had only a "shallow knowledge of religion and politics", but failed to explain what his motive might otherwise be. The two would not allow Fouda to retain any video evidence of the interview. He writes that he gave details of the meeting to senior Al Jazeera executives.[232]

Fouda's report aired shortly before 9/11's first anniversary, followed almost immediately by a shootout at a Karachi apartment resulting in the apparent capture of bin al-Shibh. Suskind, probably informed by Tenet, graphically describes bin al-Shibh resisting bitterly to the end. However, he was reportedly arrested with few, if any, injuries.[233]

Suskind asserts that bin al-Shibh kept a registry, complete with visitors' passport numbers, which included bin Laden's relatives. We are expected to believe that, with its members hunted by the CIA, Al-Qaeda would invite a potentially hostile journalist to an interview and maintain a visitors' book at the same location. More likely, perhaps,

Khalid Sheikh Mohammed, the alleged mastermind behind 9/11. As the US planned to destroy Al-Qaeda, he persuaded bin Laden to attack New York and Washington – thus guaranteeing an invasion of Afghanistan. He was believed by experts to be an ISI asset. His indictment by New York prosecutors was kept secret; no alerts were issued while he lived unmolested in Pakistan. He was delivered to Guantánamo Bay from a secret location in 2007, and his prolific confessions became the subject of ridicule.

GOVERNMENT
EXHIBIT
AQ00107
01-455-A (ID)

the CIA was receiving information from the location through another source.

Sheikh Mohammed was reportedly captured in Rawalpindi, Pakistan, on 1 March 2003 – a useful time for Bush in the run-up to the invasion of Iraq. Terrorism researcher Paul Thompson has collected a mass of conflicting news reports that, he comments, all add up to very little, except that the official story of the capture is almost certainly false. Suskind describes how agencies like the CIA often pretend someone is still free to trap their contacts, so perhaps Sheikh Mohammed was *already* captured.[234]

As mentioned, he was a possible *agent provocateur*. Lance describes how his indictment was kept secret by the FBI. Thompson cites Robert Fisk and Pakistan's former Prime Minister Benazir Bhutto as noting that Sheikh Mohammed was connected to the ISI in the 1990s.[235] Indicted, with ISI links and a "shallow knowledge of both religion and politics", he might have been a godsend for the "Plan". Perhaps he or bin al-Shibh were being used as moles by General Ahmad's new ISI-CIA liaison group – without even knowing it.

ABLE DANGER: WERE THEY IDENTIFIED?

Army Lieutenant-Colonel Anthony Shaffer went to Congress after being rebuffed by the 9/11 Commission, which judged his story insignificant. His secret data-mining project, codenamed Able Danger, involved the use of powerful computers to crunch masses of publicly available information. "We discovered two of the three cells which conducted 9/11. If that's not significant, I don't know what is," Shaffer said.

The project run by Shaffer and a colleague at Special Operations Command (SOCOM) identified Atta, al-Shehhi and the two known Al-Qaeda operatives whom the CIA went to great lengths to keep from the FBI, al-Mihdhar and al-Hazmi. Captain Scott Phillpott confirmed in testimony to Congress that Atta had been identified, and further corroboration came from James D. Smith, who had helped create a chart in 2000 that included Atta's photograph and name, posted on his office wall at Andrews Air Force Base, Maryland.[236] Defense Intelligence Agency (DIA) chiefs had ordered Shaffer *not* to warn the FBI about Atta and the other suspected terrorists on grounds that they had no right to be collecting information on "US persons" – the same pretext used to halt the Moussaoui probe in Minneapolis.[237]

Shaffer gave the details in person to Philip Zelikow in an hourlong briefing in Afghanistan, where he was stationed. Zelikow appeared to be concerned, but later the Commission cold-shouldered Shaffer and instead emphasized what it knew to be false from Shaffer and Phillpott's testimony: the assertion that Atta was not known to any US agency before the attacks.[238]

The officers could not produce original materials to prove their story; after he contacted the Commission, Shaffer's DIA superiors suspended him on suspect charges, including the alleged loss of $300 for such offences as the unauthorized redirection of his office phone to his cellphone. Then the DIA entered Shaffer's office and destroyed the evidence he had prepared.

After the Commission report came out, Shaffer began talking to Curt Weldon of the House Subcommittee on Military Research and Development. The Commission, now officially closed, was resurrected as the 9/11 Discourse Project. It first denied knowledge of Shaffer's

Lieutenant-Colonel Shaffer testified to Congress that the Able Danger project was based at SOCOM and aided by his department at the DIA. It identified Atta in 2000, but was ordered not to inform the FBI. Later, his colleagues were ordered to lie to Congress. The 9/11 Commission ignored his testimony, he was disciplined and the DIA destroyed the evidence. These excerpts are taken from his sworn testimony to Congress:

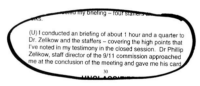

Page 7: The Defense Intelligence Agency ordered Colonel Shaffer not to alert the FBI, but their argument made no legal sense.

Page 15: Atta and others were identified by name. The information was never passed to the FBI.

Page 30: Shaffer briefed 9/11 Executive Director Zelikow personally.

Page 39: Shaffer was accused of misappropriating $300. After he was cleared, DIA officials used the disciplinary case as a pretext to seize the remaining Able Danger evidence and destroy it.

briefings. Commissioner Slade Gorton said: "Bluntly, it just didn't happen and that's the conclusion of all 10 of us."[239]

The line soon weakened in the face of overwhelming evidence. The Commission admitted it had been told, but only at the last moment, before its report came out. That, too, was false. Following Shaffer's briefing in 2003 it received two satchels of documents, in February 2004. The line changed again: Shaffer had never identified Atta. Shaffer could not disprove this, the documents having been destroyed. The

Pentagon's Inspector General, after a supposedly thorough investigation, concluded that Shaffer must have imagined Atta on the wall chart. Presumably, others who testified must have been mistaken, too.[240]

In the words of ex-FBI boss Louis Freeh:

The 9/11 Commission gets an "I" grade, incomplete – for its dereliction regarding Able Danger. The Joint Intelligence Committee should reconvene and, in addition to Able Danger team members, we should have the 9/11 commissioners appear as witnesses . . .[241]

7
The Hijackings

This chapter and the next examine the details of the hijackings to see what light they shed on the key issues: who the hijackers really were, how they were able to get control of the planes without any hijack warnings being issued, proceed without any interference from the Pentagon and steer massive planes at high speed into the right targets.

To recap the official story: Amidst a great deal of confusion, air traffic controllers gradually became aware that the pilots of the four flights had lost control, presumably to hijackers. In a departure from previous hijackings, Al-Qaeda-trained terrorists removed the pilots from their seats and steered the planes into buildings. For a few hours, news anchors asked questions that the truth movement has asked ever since: How could Al-Qaeda orchestrate such a spectacular event? Could amateurs navigate modern passenger jets hundreds of miles and steer them at high speed into targeted buildings? Why didn't the military scramble in time?

Within hours, the media found experts who explained that the operation was not hard to pull off. Some bloodthirsty people armed with knives could easily seize the pilot's seat, tamper with the plane's transponder to confuse air traffic control and, with a basic knowledge of autopilot system, navigate to within sight of the targets and into them.

THE EYEWITNESSES AND THE VANISHING CELLPHONE CALLS

The only hard evidence we have are unverified phone calls from passengers and flight attendants, transmissions from the cockpits and radar-tracking data. Some phone calls were by Airfone and some by cellphone, but the 9/11 Commission rarely makes the distinction. Only two passengers reportedly made calls from Flight 77, a few more (plus crew members) from Flights 11 and 175. Most were from Flight 93, where passengers reportedly tried to retake the plane.

Media reports first had most of the calls from cellphones, but by the time of the Moussaoui trial it was agreed that virtually all of them had

```
-------- Original Message --------
Subject: Re: Telephones in 757's
Date: Mon, 06 Dec 2004 14:17:20 -0600
From: Corp Comm <Corp.Comm@aa.com>
To: <xxxxxxx@britishlibrary.net>

xxxxxx,
AA 757s do not have any onboard phones, either for passenger or crew
use. Crew have other means of communications available.

Regards,
Tim

>>> xxxxxxxx    12/06/04 02:53AM >>>
Corp Comm wrote:
> xxxxxxx,
> American Airlines 757s do not have onboard phones for passenger
use.
> Regards,
> Tim Wagner
> AA Spokesman

Hi,

I think I asked the wrong question. What I meant was are there any
onboard phones at all on AA 757s, i.e. that could be used either by
passengers or cabin crew?

And if there are, is this all 757s or just some of them e.g. only on
aircraft used from US domestic flights?
```

American Airlines confirmed that Flight 77 was not fitted with airphones. So how did Barbara Olson make her famous calls which found their way through the Department of Justice switchboard to her husband?

come from Airfones. Even on Flight 93, "13 of the terrified passengers and crew members made 35 air phonecalls and two cell phonecalls," prosecutors told the court. Skeptics say that it is impossible to make mobile phone calls from a plane at a normal altitude. Former emeritus math professor and longtime contributor to *Scientific American*, A. K. Dewdney chartered a plane and published his results: mobile calls were highly unlikely to succeed at anything over 8,000 feet.[242]

Perhaps, under cover of the hijacking exercise, some of the calls were faked. At least two mainstream reports confirm that by 2000 the Pentagon had developed software an X-Team member could use to produce speech in a false voice. "A ten-minute digital recording" of someone's voice is all that is needed, explained William Arkin in the *Washington Post*.[243] Faking would be easier if the calls were supposed to be from cellphones. Poor sound quality masks imperfections in the system; fake relatives would be able to cut off the calls before giving themselves away. Many people who received calls reported they were broken off – predictable for cellphones but surprising for Airfones.

An X-Team could have operated as part of a group responsible for making the exercises realistic. Clarke explains anything can happen in field exercises, which are designed to be hyperrealistic:

> In a field exercise . . . counterterrorism action units actually assault targets. In the Norfolk exercise, Navy SEALs hit a boat playing the terrorist mother ship, while the FBI's hostage rescue team crashed into a house in which the sleeper cell was waiting. A special nuclear bomb squad moved in to defuse the weapon, while staff from several agencies pretended to be reporters and peppered officials with tough questions at a simulated press conference.[244]

David Ray Griffin has shown that several calls are suspicious. One Flight 93 caller greeted his mother with: "Hi, mum, it's Mark Bingham"; the call has little conversation and is punctuated with long pauses, and Bingham says: "Do you believe me? It's true", before apparently being cut off. Tom Burnett made four calls, mentions no names and says he does not wish to talk to his children. His wife assumed he used his cellphone surreptitiously, but the plane was at 40,000 ft and the Moussaoui trial record implies the calls were by airphone. His wife carefully noted the times of the calls. The first one must have been at the time the hijacking started, if not a minute earlier. But sitting in the middle of events in first class, Burnett calmly says that the hijackers have just stabbed a passenger; he reports seeing a gun that was officially determined not to be present.[245]

Barbara Olson's phone calls from Flight 77 provided key evidence for the official story at a time when mainstream sources were still unsure whether Flight 77 had hit the Pentagon. CNN assumed, and the *New York Lawyer* said later, that Olson used a cellphone; but her husband would tell the Federalist Society and the *Daily Telegraph*: "She somehow managed (I think she was the only one on that flight to do so) to use a telephone in the airplane . . . She wasn't using a cell phone, she was using the phone in the passenger seat . . . she was calling collect and she was trying to get through to the Department of Justice [his workplace] which is never very easy."[246] The Commission implies questioning American Airlines at least twice to learn that the plane had Airfones onboard, and that Olson made four calls to the Justice Department. Why did no other passengers make calls?[247]

The calls give no clear information on the vital question of how hijackers managed to seize planes from eight pilots without a clear signal reaching air traffic controllers or airline dispatchers. The hijackers' alleged weapons included bombs (Flights 11, 175, 93), guns (Flights 11, 93), knives (all planes), box cutters (Flight 77), and mace or similar (Flights 11, 175). However, the Commission reports that over half the hijackers were selected for extra screening, including four out of five on Flight 11. Could screening have been so lax as to allow long knives, guns or a bomb? Would the hijackers take such risks?

Flight attendant Amy Sweeney gave the first alert on Flight 11; her phone call was relayed and recorded at American Airlines. According to relatives who heard a secondary recording later, she reported that hijackers in first class had stabbed two flight attendants, sprayed the cabin with mace or other, menaced passengers with an apparent bomb and stormed the cockpit. A report sourced to American Airlines said Sweeney thought there were four hijackers, not five, in seats different from those of the presumed hijackers.[248] Yet, air traffic control communications records contain no drama, no sounds of struggle, no voices raised in alarm and no warning from pilots, who had several discreet ways to signal alerts – voice messages, the transponder's emergency 7500 code or the alarm button on the control yoke.

The only indication of cockpit violence came from Flight 93. According to the Commission, at almost the exact time Burnett reported the cabin seized, the pilots had just acknowledged a warning from dispatchers to secure the door. Controllers on the ground heard shouts of "Get out of here!" and "Mayday!", but no hijack warning was issued and there was no sound of a door being smashed. This is the best evidence from any flight that murderous terrorists stormed four cockpits, overpowered eight pilots, four of them ex-military, and dragged them from their seats.

Burnett and Sweeney were the only two passengers who claimed to be eyewitnesses, although Bingham on Flight 93 "probably saw what happened in the cockpit" according to a relative who said the plane was taken over by three men (the official story says four) and that Bingham mentioned nothing except a "bomb".[249]

Perhaps the most bizarre phone call came from Todd Beamer (Flight 93), who spent ten minutes on an Airfone with phone supervisor Lisa Jefferson at the GTE customer centre before joining an attempt to recapture the plane. An operator passed Beamer to Jefferson, but according to the official story the call was neither recorded automatically nor by Jefferson, who later received a Verizon excellence award. Strangely, Beamer's wife seems to have been out of the loop; she was not informed of the call until three days afterwards.[250]

Shortly before Flight 93 crashed, passenger Ed Felt called via cellphone from the toilet. He dialled the emergency number and said there had been an explosion. There was a rushing noise in the background. Unlike most of the other calls, Felt's must have been recorded. Emergency phone supervisor Glenn Cramer confirmed the call to the media. As it came from a low altitude, it may have been one of two cellphone calls confirmed by the FBI. But it does not fit the official story, implying instead that the hijackers had smuggled a bomb onboard or that the plane was shot down. Whereas authorities briefed the media on all other calls, discussion of Felt's call was forbidden and vanished from the official narrative.[251]

IN THE COCKPITS

The supposed eyewitnesses' phone calls provide no clue as to how the hijackers achieved their silent cockpit takeovers. Standard procedures instructed airline staff to cooperate with hijackers on the assumption that the plane would eventually be allowed to land. However, cooperation could not possibly extend to giving up the controls to a hijacker, who would not have the skills to pilot a heavy airliner safely. Each plane had at least one reservist or retired military man in the cockpit.

All pilots are trained to direct their planes safely away from buildings even when facing certain death. Yet, officially, air traffic control tapes for three of the planes give no indication that the pilots resisted.

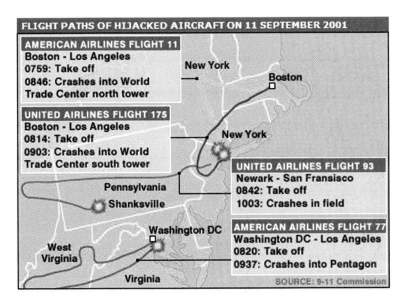

The Commission produced this map containing several oddities. Why did Flights 93 and 77 travel so far, risking interception and shoot-down? Was it a coincidence that the paths of Flights 11 and 175 crossed in real time? Flights 93 and 175 must have come quite close to each other, too. Why did Flight 77 make its U-shaped detour well before it was hijacked?[252]

CREDIT: 9/11 Commission Report

This alone demands a radical departure from the official story to make sense.

A silent takeover makes more sense if pilots, air traffic controllers or both were expecting non-routine events that morning. This would suggest some sort of crossover between the hijacking exercise and the "real" hijackings.

Perhaps warnings were issued but air traffic control tapes were scrubbed to hide embarrassing references to the exercise or explain why the FAA did not alert the Pentagon and the consequent failure to scramble planes. Still, the failure of the cockpits to respond to controllers, the alterations of transponder codes linking the planes to radar monitoring systems and, above all, the flight path changes should have immediately put the system into emergency mode. Due to the risk of collision, pilots without communications in crowded skies would not deviate from their flight path unless there was a catastrophic mechanical failure or a hijacking.

Though the FBI seized the air traffic control tapes, a version was leaked (see transcript on pages 123–4).[253] Close examination suggests the "real" planes may already have been connected to the hijacking exercise. Flight 11, first to go rogue, failed to respond to an order to climb at 8.14 a.m., followed by eleven ID requests over the next few minutes. This should have been when the hijackers began taking control of the plane, but the transponder was turned off only at 8.21. The pilots had seven minutes to warn controllers by voice, transponder or alarm signal, but there is no record they did so.

The official story assumes the pilots were overpowered straightaway, but the day after the attacks, air traffic controllers had little doubt that ex-soldier John Ogonowski or his co-pilot were in their seats most of the way. The *Christian Science Monitor* reported:

It was not clear to the listening air-traffic controllers which of the two pilots was flying the Boeing 767. What is clear is that the pilot was secretly trying to convey to authorities the flight's desperate situation, according to controllers familiar with the tense minutes after Flight 11 was hijacked. The pilot was apparently triggering a "push-to-talk button" on the aircraft's yoke, or "wheel" . . . Thus, the pilot allowed controllers to hear much of what was happening in the cockpit which also indicates that he was in the driver's seat much of the way to the plane's fiery rendezvous with the World Trade Center. "There was this voice that was threatening the pilot, and it was clearly threatening."[254]

This report contains corroborative details, but jars with the official story. Why would the hijackers leave the pilots in control, giving up the advantage of surprise? By now passengers were dead (according to phone calls from flight attendants) and removing the pilots would be even more of a problem. It is, of course, explicable in alternative scenarios such as a hijacking exercise or a plan to return the planes to the airports.

American Airlines did not react as though it was a real hijacking either. In June 2004, relatives of the victims forced the FBI to divulge the contents of Sweeney's call on a confidential basis, and were so shocked by what they heard that they broke an agreement not to talk to the media.

The *New York Observer* reported that "in Fort Worth to managers in [Systems Operations Control] was sitting beside each other and hearing it . . . they were both saying, 'do not pass this along. Let's keep it right here. Keep it among the five of us.'"[255] How could top managers think they would be able to keep secret the first US hijacking in seventeen years? Managers are quoted as saying: "What else can we find out from our own sources about what's going on?" They had only two sources, flight attendants – what others could they be thinking about? This would all make sense if Flight 11 was involved in an exercise.

At 8.37, nobody except the hijackers should have known that Flight 175 was about to be hijacked. Yet a controller at Boston air traffic control chose Flight 175 to look out for hijacked Flight 11. Following the official story, this must just be an extraordinary coincidence, as Flight 175 happened to be crossing the path of Flight 11 in real time.[256]

At 8.41, Flight 175 said to New York: "We figured we'd wait to go to your center. We heard a suspicious transmission on departure out of Boston. Someone keyed the mike and said: 'Everyone stay in your seats.'" Why did Flight 175 wait to tell the New York controller this sinister news when the Boston controller was already concerned with the emergency? The Commission records: "The same New York Center controller was assigned to both American 11 and United 175. The controller knew American 11 was hijacked; he was focused on searching for it."[257] Was this yet another coincidence, or was the New York controller involved in some hidden agenda with the ex-military pilots on the morning of a Pentagon exercise?[258]

Flight 11 was now spectacularly off-course, and out of communication for twenty minutes in one of the world's most crowded spaces. Why was the New York controller not taken off all other planes to deal with this rare emergency? Apparently it was not considered an emergency. Between 8.35 and 8.47, he has little to say about Flight 11. At 8.42, he simply says: "O.K., they said it's confirmed, believe it or not, as a thing; we're not sure yet . . ." This must be the notification that Flight 11 had indeed been hijacked. Why is he still so unsure?

At 8.53, after dealing with several other planes, the controller seems unaware that the smoke in Manhattan has anything to do with his problems, but he has noticed Flight 175 is not responding. He says: "We may have a hijack, we have some problems over here right now." A little later: ". . . Yes, that may be real traffic, nobody knows, I can't get a hold of UAL175 at all right now and I don't know where he went to."[259] The words "may be real traffic, nobody knows" make no sense at all given the official story. How could Flight 11 or Flight 175 not be "real traffic"? There is one way: if they were fake "inserts", part of the exercise. The leaked tapes stop at this point, well before the 175 crash.

It should now have been more difficult to take over Flight 175; the crew was already aware there were problems that morning. But, as with Flight 11, the cockpit was silently taken over – though passenger phone calls describe mayhem. According to the Commission:

> The hijackers attacked sometime between 8.42 and 8.46. They used knives (as reported by two passengers and a flight attendant), Mace (reported by one passenger), and the threat of a bomb (reported by the same passenger). They stabbed members of the flight crew (reported by flight attendants and one passenger). Both pilots had been killed (reported by one flight attendant).[260]

The details make little sense. Passenger Peter Hanson made three short calls, each cut off. He reported that the hijackers murdered

The air traffic control tapes leaked to the *New York Times* indicate something bizarre was going on. Why was the controller for Flight 11 left with other planes to handle? Was it just a coincidence this controller was also responsible for Flight 175?

8:40:18 R42: Point out approved.

8:40:32 UAL175: UAL175 at FL310.

8:40:37 R42: UAL 175 New York center, roger.

8:40:47 USA583: New York do a favor were you asked to look for an aircraft, an American flight about about 8 or 9 o'clock 10 miles south bound last altitude 290 – no one is sure where he is.

8:41:07 USA583: Yea we talked about him on the last frequency we spotted him when he was at our 3 o'clock position. He did appear to us to be at 29,000 feet. We're not picking him up on TCAS. I'll look again and see if we can spot him at 24.

8:40:20 R42: No, it looks like they shut off their transponder that's why the question about it.

8:41:28 UAL175: New York UAL175 heavy.

8:41:07 R42: UAL 175 go ahead.

8:41:32 UAL175: We figured we'd wait to go to your center. We heard a suspicious transmission on our departure from BOS sounds like someone keyed the mike and said everyone stay in your seats.

8:41:51 R42: O.K. I'll pass that along.

8:41:56 UAL175: It cut out.

8:42:00 R42: IGN 93 line.

8:42:01 IGN: Go ahead.

8:42:03 R42: UAL 175 just came on my frequency and he said he heard a suspicious transmission when they were leaving BOS everybody stay in your seats that's what he heard as the suspicious transmission just to let you know.

8:42:50 USA583: Center where do you place him in relation to 583 now?

8:42:55 R42: He's off about 9 o'clock and about 20 miles looks like he's heading southbound but there's no transponder no nothing and no one's talking to him.

8:43:20 DAL2315: Hello New York good morning DAL2315 passing 239 for 280.

8:43:28 R42: DAL2315 New York Center, roger.

8:43:32 DAL2433: New York center DAL2433 310.

8:43:39 R42: DAL2433 New York Center, roger.

8:43:57 USA583: center USA583.

8:44:00 R42: USA583 go ahead.

8:44:05 USA583: I just picked up an ELT (emergency locator transmitter) on 121.5 it was brief but it went off.

8:44:09 R42: O.K. they said it's confirmed believe it or not as a thing we're not sure yet so we're still trying going on another aircraft right now and there trying to see what altitude he's at –

8:44:31 R42: IGN 93 line East Texas.

8:44:36 IGN: go ahead

8:44:38 R42: can you turn that DAL2433 a little bit to the right they got that Eagle flight in there and the guy at 310 that they wanted to look at this American to see what altitude he is at can you put him on a 290 heading and stop the DAL1489 beneath him.

8:44:51 ZBW IGN: we just put DAL2433 on you we will call him again if we have him we will put him on a 290.

8:44:56 R42: I'm not talking to the Delta.

8:44:58 ZBW IGN: O.K.

8:45:00 R42: DAL2433 New York

8:45:03 DAL2433: go ahead.

8:45:05 R42: turn right heading of 290 vectors for traffic.

8:45:08 DAL2433: DAL2433 at 290 we picked up that ELT, too, but its very faint.

8:45:14 R42: O.K. make it a nice tight turn would help traffic 11 o'clock 10 miles northbound turning east-bound at 310.

8:45:21 DAL2433: O.K. we'll make it tight

8:45:51 R42: DAL2433 thank you for the turn cleared direct SBJ.

8:45:57 DAL2433: direct SBJ DAL2433.

8:45:59 R42: roger.

8:46:14 DAL1489: New York Center DAL1489 heavy out of 290 for 390.

8:46:18 R42: DAL683 contact New York Center on 134.32.

8:46:26 DAL683: 134.32 thank you.

8:46:28 R42: UAL467 contact New York Center on 133.47.

8:46:31 UAL467: 133.47 UAL467.

8:46:37 DAL1043: good morning New York DAL1043 checking in at FL390.

8:46:38 R42: DAL1043 New York Center roger.

8:47:16 R42: DAL351 contact New York Center on 134.32.

8:47:21 DAL351: 134.32 DAL351.

8:47:26 R42: DAL1489 are you on the frequency?
8:47:30 DAL1489: DAL1489 out of 310 for 390.
8:47:33 R42: DAL1489 New York Center roger cleared direct PTW.
8:47:47 DAL1489: direct PTW DAL 1489 heavy.
8:47:40 R42: roger.
8:48:50 R42: DAL2315 contact the New York Center on 134.6, have a nice day.
8:48:59 DAL2315: 134.6 DAL2315.
8:49:03 R42: 34.6 3-4-point 6.
8:49:38 USA429: USA429 leveling off at 350.
8:49:48 R42: I'm sorry, who was that?
8:49:50 USA429: USA429 leveling at 350.
8:49:51 R42: USA429 New York Center roger.
8:50:14 Unknown: anybody know what that smoke is in lower Manhattan?
8:50:17 R42: I'm sorry say again.
8:50:19 Unknown: a lot of smoke in lower Manhattan.
8:50:22 R42: a lot of smoke in lower Manhattan.
8:50:24 Unknown: coming out of the top of the World Trade Center building, a major fire.
8:50:47 R42: and which was the one that just saw the major fire.
8:50:52 DAL1489: this is DAL1489 we see lower Manhattan looks like the World Trade Center on fire but its hard to tell from here.
8:51:02 R42: DAL1489 roger.
8:51:11 DAL1489: let us know if you hear any news down there
8:51:15 R42: roger.
8:51:32 R42: DAL 1043 cleared direct PTW.
8:51:35 DAL1043: direct PTW DAL 1043.
8:51:43 R42: UAL175 recycle transponder squawk code 1470.
8:51:53 R42: UAL175 New York.
8:52:09 R42: UAL175 do you read New York.
8:52:14 R42: DAL1489 do you read New York.
8:52:16 DAL1489: DAL1489 go ahead.
8:52:20 R42: O.K. just wanted to make sure you were reading New York – United, United 175 – do you read New York?
8:52:30 R42: IGN on the 93 line Kennedy.
8:52:46 R42: IGN on the 93 line East Texas.
8:52:52 ZBW IGN: IGN.
8:52:53 R42: do me a favor see if UAL175 went back to your frequency.
8:52:58 ZBW IGN: UAL 175?
8:53:01 R42: yes.
8:53:14 ZBW IGN: he's not here East Texas.
8:53:23 R42: 10 – do you see that UAL175 anywhere and do me a favor you see that target there on 3321 code at 335 climbing don't know who he is but you got that USA583 if you need to descent him down you can nobody we may have a hijack we have some problems over here right now.
8:53:35 R10: oh you do.
8:53:37 R42: yes, that may be real traffic nobody knows I can't get a hold of UAL175 at all right now and I don't know where he went to.
8:53:51 R42: UAL 175 New York.
8:54:00 USA 583: New York 583
8:54:04 R42: USA583 go ahead.
8:54:10 USA583: yes getting reports over the radio of a commuter hitting the World Trade Center is that nordo [no radio] 76 [Boeing 767] still in the air?

passengers until the crew opened the cabin door, which must have given the crew the opportunity to press the hijack alarm.[261] But it was never activated, and the air traffic tapes contain no verbal warnings. In hindsight, this would not have helped – but these were highly trained people who worked according to standard procedures. Why would they have abandoned them?

Flight 77 was another silent takeover. The Commission reported: "At 8:54, the aircraft deviated from its assigned course, turning south. Two minutes later the transponder was turned off and even primary radar contact with the aircraft was lost. The Indianapolis ATC Center . . . failed to contact the aircraft. American Airlines dispatchers also tried, without success." Pilot Charles F. Burlingame was trained as a top Navy pilot and had worked on antiterrorism policy. "Burlingame's family says he would not have given up the cockpit without a fight," reported the *Boston Globe*.[262] A Pilots for 9/11 Truth spokesman commented: "Capt. Burlingame would have taken them where they wanted to go, but only after seeing more than a 'boxcutter' or knife. . . . We at pilotsfor911truth.org feel the same as his family in that Capt. Burlingame would not have given up his airplane."[263]

The official story says he gave up the plane without notifying the ground. Olson's apparent phone call only confuses matters. That day CNN reported: "Flight personnel, including the pilots, were herded to the back of the plane", and: "She felt nobody was in charge." Does this sound like Burlingame? Much later, the FBI claimed it had recovered his body, and that it showed he had died in a struggle.[264]

The Commission reported that the air traffic centre was in a different sector from the people dealing with Flights 11 and 175, so it never occurred to the controller that Flight 77 might have been hijacked. He chose the only other explanation – mechanical or electrical catastrophe – for the plane going off-course and out of contact at the same time. "Indianapolis Center learned [at 9.20] that there were other hijacked aircraft, and began to doubt its initial assumption that American 77 had crashed . . . There is no evidence to indicate that the FAA recognized Flight 77 as a hijacking until it crashed into the Pentagon."[265]

This account helps explain why the system failed yet again to respond, but it is absurd. Flight 11 was a suspected hijacking an hour earlier, and Flight 175 half an hour earlier; the North Tower had been in flames on every television for over thirty minutes. Flight 77 had been off-course for the past half-hour. What does it take to recognize a hijacking?

There remains the possibility that Flight 77 really did crash, and this is now being covered up. Maybe the controller's reasons for believing

The air traffic control tape for Flight 77 (abridged)266 indicates an alarm beeping almost from the moment the transponder was tampered with. By 9.09 it must have been obvious to this controller that Flight 77 was hijacked, yet the Commission says the FAA failed to recognize the hijacking until the Pentagon was hit at 9.37.

Air traffic control tape for Flight 77 (abridged)

8:56:53: Indianapolis Control: American 77, American Indy radio, check, how do you read?
8:57:35: Indianapolis Control: Override beeping.
8:57:55: Indianapolis Control: Override line beeping.
8:57:59: Controller 3: American 77, roger, maintain flight level three five zero, show that as your final.
8:58:14: AAL: American dispatch, Jim McDonnell.
8:58:19: . . . This is Indianapolis Center trying to get a hold of American 77.
8:58:23: AAL: Uh, Indys, hang on one second, please.
8:58:36: Indianapolis Control: . . . We were talking to him and all of a sudden it just, uh . . .
8:58:38: AAL: All right, we'll get a hold of him for ya.
9:00:33: AAL2493: Yeah, we, uh, sent a message to dispatch to have him come up on twenty twenty-seven, is that what you want 'em to do?
9:00:41: Indianapolis Control: Yeah, we had 'em on west side of our airspace and they went into coast and, ah, don't have a track on 'em and now he's not talking to me, so we don't know exactly what happened to him . . .
9:01:50: Indianapolis Control: Override line beeping.
9:02:07: AAL: American dispatch, Jim McDonnell.
9:02:09: Indianapolis Control: Yeah, this is Indianapolis Center, we, uh, I don't know if I'm talking to the same guy about American 77.
9:02:13: AAL: yeah I cell-called him, but I did not get a reply back from him.
9:02:28: Indianapolis Control: We have no radar contact and, uh, no communications with him, so if you guys could try again . . .
9:02:35: AAL: We're doing it.
9:02:37: Indianapolis Control: All right, thanks a lot.
9:09:00: AAL: American dispatch, Jim McDonnell.
9:09:02: Indianapolis Control: Indianapolis Center. Did you get a hold of American 77, by chance?
9:09:05: AAL: No sir, but we have an unconfirmed report a second airplane hit the World Trade Center and exploded.
9:09:10: Indianapolis Control: Say again?
9:09:11: AAL: We lost American 11 to a hijacking . . . Boston to Los Angeles flight.
9:09:17: Indianapolis Control: . . . I can't really, I can't hear what you're saying there, you said American 11?
9:09:23: AAL: Yes, we were hijacked.
9:09:25: Indianapolis Control: And it . . .?
9:09:27: AAL: And it was a Boston-L.A. flight, and 77 is a Dulles-L.A. flight, and, uh, we've had an unconfirmed report a second airplane just flew into the World Trade Center.

this have been scrubbed from the record, and the Commission is half-right: Indianapolis failed to recognize a hijacking because there wasn't one. Clarke reported that at around 10.00, the FBI told the White House: "We have a report of a large jet crashed in Kentucky near the Ohio line." This seems rather late for the hunch of one controller in Indianapolis to be echoing round. Moreover, while he mentions the other three flights, Clarke does not discuss Flight 77.

American took almost fifteen minutes to tell Indianapolis it suspected Flight 77 was hijacked, but according to the Commission the reaction at AA headquarters to the news was much faster than this implies: "At 9.00 American Airlines Executive Vice President Gerard Arpey learned that communications had been lost with American 77 . . . Shortly

ance specialists at FAA air traffic facilities. NEADS files are time-stamped clock. We also compared audio times to certified transcripts when available.

95. FAA Boston Center site visit (Sept. 22–24, 2003).

96. NORAD's mission is set forth in a series of renewable agreements b According to the agreement in effect on 9/11, the "primary mission" CN

The Commission ignored all relevant regulations, explaining *air traffic control* delays of up to half an hour by citing hearsay from a Boston *control* centre on how the system worked.

before 9.10, suspecting that American 77 had been hijacked, American headquarters concluded that the second aircraft to hit the World Trade Center might have been Flight 77."[267] Once again, American's response jars with the official story. Previously it had decided to keep the news of the Flight 11 hijacking secret – "among the five of us" – now it was jumping to the conclusion Flight 77 had raced at supersonic speed to New York in about ten minutes.

Flight 93 generated the only report of a struggle in the cabin. According to the Commission, a warning was sent to United 93 from United control (not the FAA) at 9.24 to secure the cockpit door. At 9.26, pilot Jason Dahl responded with a note of puzzlement: "Ed, confirm latest mssg plz – Jason." At 9.28 "the captain or first officer could be heard declaring 'Mayday' amid the sounds of a physical struggle in the cockpit. The second radio transmission, thirty-five seconds later, indicated that the fight was continuing." The controller "notified his supervisor, who passed the notice up the chain of command. By 9.34, word of the hijacking had reached FAA headquarters."

AMATEURS, PROFESSIONALS OR JUST LUCKY?

Do the flying skills of the presumed hijackers fit with the events? How could poorly trained pilots navigate complex passenger jets, steering them manually at high speed into specific targets? Hani Hanjour had to fly for several hundred yards, almost touching the ground, before crashing into the Pentagon. Egyptian President Hosni Mubarak, also a pilot, commented:

> I find it hard to believe that people who were learning to fly in Florida could, within a year and a half, fly large commercial airlines and hit with accuracy the towers of the World Trade Center which

Hani Hanjoor

Practice oral eval given. Student made numerous errors during performance problem including a lack of understanding of some basic concepts. The same was true during review of systems knowledge. The root cause is most likely due to the student's lack of experience. Some of the concepts involved in large jet systems cannot be fully comprehended by someone with only small prop plane experience. The lack of progress is not a question of knowledge as much as experience. Hani absorbed a great deal of information and is very intelligent, but to move beyond the comprehension level (or rote level in some cases) Hani needs more experience to reach the application level. I doubt his ability to pass an FAA oral at this time or in the near future.

Mar 9, 01
In Hani's 4th Sim session we did preflight, normal start, hot start, TO climb, dept. steep turns, stalls ILS approaches, M/A, LDGs, V, cuts, a rejected T/o and S.E. ILS. He has a rudimentary level of ability based on his limited flying time. He seemed unsure of procedures in some cases and failed to properly identify and correct a Hot StoA. Basic aircraft control was marginal. He will need much more experience flying smaller A/C before he is ready to master large jets.

216 703177

This report from a flight school, lodged by the prosecution in the Moussaoui trial, offers an assessment of Hanjour's flying skills. How could someone whose "basic aircraft control was marginal" on a small plane carry off a ground-level attack on the Pentagon in a massive passenger jet?

would appear, to the pilot from the air, the size of a pencil. Only a professional pilot could carry out this mission . . .[268A]

One skilled pilot remarked: "The author of this paper, a pilot and aeronautical engineer whose specialty is aerodynamics, challenges any pilot in the world to . . . fly the craft at 400 MPH, 20 feet above flat ground over a distance of half a mile."[268B] Another said it would be theoretically possible but extremely difficult to keep the nose down without crashing.

Hanjour, alleged pilot of Flight 77, is an unlikely ground-attack specialist. Fox News reported: "Federal aviation authorities were alerted in early 2001 that an Arizona flight school believed one of the eventual Sept. 11 hijackers lacked the English and flying skills necessary for the commercial pilot's license he already held . . . 'I couldn't believe he had a commercial license of any kind with the skills that he had,' said Peggy Chevrette, the JetTech manager."[269]

In June 2001, Hanjour tried to fly down the Hudson corridor as a trainee, but the instructor was so unnerved by his lack of skill that he refused a second run, reports the Commission. *Popular Mechanics* has a characteristically optimistic take on the Hudson corridor incident. Ignoring the comments of the many instructors, they cite the incident as evidence of Hanjour's flying skills. "It's even easier than driving a car", one expert said. "It's possible they could have seen these buildings from as far away as 50 miles", explains another.[270]

The Commission describes Hanjour in Maryland on 2001 "landing at a small airport with a difficult approach. The instructor thought Hanjour may have had training from a military pilot because he used the terrain recognition system for navigation." The report, tucked into a footnote, dates from 2004; could this be someone's memory playing tricks? A few weeks before the attacks, other instructors in Maryland again refused to rent him a plane. "He went up with two flight instructors on three occasions, but Bernard eventually refused to rent him a plane because he barely spoke English – a requirement for flight certifications – and because of his poor flying skills."[271A]

What about the other two successful attacks? Flight 11 went more or less straight into the North Tower, making the operation look simple, but tickets had been bought some days before; if it had been a windy day, even an experienced pilot might have had trouble at such speeds. As the imprint of the planes on the Towers show, the pilots had to hit objects not much wider than the planes themselves, at 555 m.p.h., meaning that five seconds before impact the plane would be nearly a mile away. An error of a few degrees of arc or a fluctuation in side wind, and the plane would miss.

Skeptics noticed that there seemed to be a "pod" on the underside of flight 175, making it look as if the plane was adapted, perhaps a drone. The pod pictures were first published in the mainstream Spanish newspaper *Vanguardia* and supported by a certificate signed by a University imaging expert. The controversy was fuelled when the FBI told Boeing they were not allowed to comment. The FBI still refused to rule this out in 2007, suggesting that either there was a pod or the authorities were trying to create confusion. The controversy certainly distracted attention from the flying skills problem. The pod was only visible because the plane was at an angle and it was only at this angle because it made an extraordinary split second high speed twist at the last moment, apparently well beyond the capabilities of Marwan Shehhi, to avoid missing the building altogether.[271B]

8
The NORAD Exercises: Empty Desks in the Chain of Command

Skeptics and believers alike raise the question of why the Pentagon, with its astronomical budget and state-of-the-art technology, was less aware of events than the average TV viewer. Given that the FAA detected the first hijacking at around 8.25 a.m., how could a rogue plane successfully attack the nation's military headquarters approximately seventy-five minutes later without a single fighter in position to intercept it?

Skeptics allege that plotters had advance knowledge of the attacks and paralysed the Pentagon and NORAD, its operational arm. The official story is that command and control systems were not in place to deal with a wholly unexpected event; that there were literally not enough planes on standby. Also, the system was paralysed because the terrorists tampered with the plane transponders, the essential air

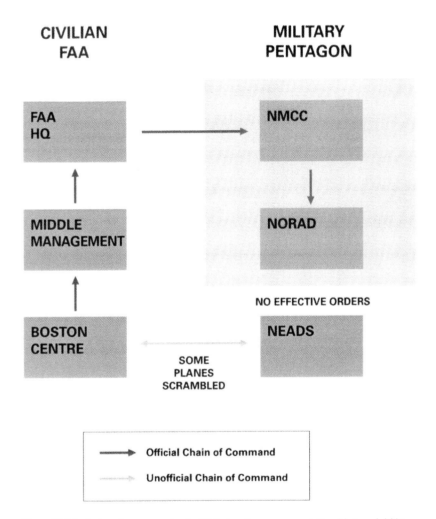

The official chain of command, via FAA headquarters and the National Military Command Center (NMCC), did not scramble planes to intercept the suspected hijackings. If personnel at the FAA had followed standing orders, all information would have been blocked at the NMCC, as happened with Flight 77 and Flight 93. The only scrambled planes arrived because Boston control centre called NEADS (Northeast Air Defense Sector) directly.

traffic control communications link. The incompetence theory factors in caution and indecision inhibiting a response.

The claim that the Pentagon had no plan to deal with an Al-Qaeda hijack – a risk highlighted in Bush's 6 August briefing – seems unlikely. However, the evidence unearthed by the 9/11 Commission, the cover-up of the hijacking exercise, the ever-changing story and the attempt to blame the stand-down on the FAA rather than the Pentagon together add up to a sinister, hidden agenda at best and a criminal plot at worst.

Ironically, the initial cause for skepticism is the least of the problems. The fact that no hijacked planes were officially shot down can be explained. First, the Air Force could not be trusted to attack the right planes: in 2007, a minor scandal arose in the UK when it emerged that a clearly marked British vehicle had been attacked in broad daylight by US pilots at the start of the Iraq war. Second, officials from Bush and Cheney down saw clearly that personal risk demanded erring on the side of caution. Third, a no shoot-down order was in place, the details of which will be examined later.

However, why did normal procedures fail to the extent that the Pentagon did not manage to intercept even one of the hijacked planes? With NORAD exercises in full swing, there were plenty of unarmed planes. The Pentagon even tried to suggest that the situation was somehow not its responsibility. Chief of Staff Richard Myers told Senators, two days after the attacks: "We had plans to deploy our fighters to defend from external threats. I never thought we'd see what we saw the last few days, where we had fighters over our cities, defending against a threat that originated inside the United States of America." Even the Commission found this excuse unsatisfactory. Commissioner Gorelick read Myers its legal mandate: "Providing surveillance and control of the airspace of Canada and the United States".

The media boosted the official Pentagon explanation – nobody told it about the hijacks in time – by reporting an exchange from the FAA tapes published in the 9/11 Commission report.[272A] After asking about Flight 93, controllers are told: "Uh . . . everybody just left the room", suggesting incompetence and vacillation. However, this was preceded by the unreported line – more telling: "They're pulling Jeff away to go talk about United 93." A course of action *was* being discussed, but beyond the range of the tape recorders.

At the centre of the story are the NORAD's NEADS tapes, the nearest thing so far to a smoking gun. They confirm that the Pentagon was running a hijacking exercise, covered up for four years, at the same time as the "real" hijackings.

THREE DIFFERENT OFFICIAL TIMELINES

When did the Pentagon scramble its planes? Where did they fly? For the first three days after 9/11, the story was that no fighters had been scrambled until after the Pentagon attack, confirmed to the *Boston Globe* by NORAD spokesman Major Mike Snyder and to the Senate by Myers.[272B] Myers said: "That order, to the best of my knowledge, was after the Pentagon was struck"; later, senators returned to this issue with some unusually sharp questions, and Myers's responses began sounding like prevarication. It was agreed to discuss the matter later in a secret session; perhaps this is when senators were informed of the hijacking exercises.[273]

The second version of events came as an unsourced leak to CBS three days after the attacks, one day after Myers's hearing. At approximately 8.45, after NEADS was first informed of Flight 11, two jets were scrambled from Otis Air Force Base in Cape Cod. Two more jets were scrambled at about 9.20 from Langley, Virginia, in search of Flight 77. This official story held for three years, confirmed in Pentagon evidence to the Commission and its own written 9/11 history.[274]

Then a Commission staffer noticed a discrepancy in the Pentagon story. The Commission, for once, made a determined effort to get the truth. It subpoenaed the tapes from NEADS. NORAD boss General Larry Arnold returned to testify, under oath. Commissioner Ben-Veniste said: "We . . . found that there were tapes . . . when you . . . were asked about the existence of tape recordings . . . you indicated that you had no such recollections . . .", to which Arnold replied that NEADS "had a tape that we were unaware of . . . what I've been told by your staff is that they were unable to make that tape run. But they were later able . . . to get that tape to run".[275] Thus the Pentagon covered up the existence of the NEADS tapes, and might have tried to scrub them.

Based on this new information, Version Three was presented to the public in the Commission's report. The second scramble was not a response to Flight 77 but to a nonexistent plane described as "phantom Flight 11". The report says:

> There was confusion at that moment in the FAA. Two planes had struck the World Trade Center, and Boston Center had heard from FAA headquarters in Washington that American 11 was still airborne. We have been unable to identify the source of this mistaken FAA information.[276]

In the following sections the source will become clear.

In 2006, Kean and Hamilton published a book revealing that the Commission had considered bringing criminal charges against Pentagon officials. Instead, it wrote privately to the Defense Department, saying the Inspector General should investigate whether "false statements made to the Commission were deliberately false".[277] This contrasted with the obsequious praise commissioners heaped on Pentagon officials in public. The new investigation was completed in 2006. Results were classified.

Senator Mark Dayton of Minnesota, member of the Senate Armed Services Committee, said NORAD officials "lied to the American people, they lied to Congress and they lied to your 9/11 Commission to create a false impression of competence, communication and protection of the American people". If the Commission was right, said Dayton, Bush "should fire whoever at FAA, at NORAD . . . betrayed their public trust by not telling us the truth".[278]

However, as NEADS chief Colonel Bob Marr said later: "I can't think of any incentive why we'd want to spin that." In one sense, Marr is right: the Pentagon essentially blamed the FAA, and the Commission bought the story wholesale. If the Pentagon was issuing false statements, was it to hide something more sinister?

Griffin points out that the story is damaging in a deeper way. The Commission's discovery implied a widespread conspiracy to hide the truth. There were many participants in the phantom Flight 11 falsehood: FAA controllers, NEADS and NORAD personnel, FBI officers who seized and reviewed FAA documents. Nonetheless, this story stood for three years. So much for the idea that a 9/11 plot would be impossible to keep secret.[279]

THE HIJACKING EXERCISE

The secret NEADS tapes were made semi-public in 2006, released apparently in full to little-known *Vanity Fair* writer Michael Bronner.[280]

Why would the US government disseminate a vital part of the historical record, documents that should be freely available to the public, as though giving a bone to a favoured dog? As it happens, Bronner was involved in the production of the 2006 film *United 93*.[281] Bronner and *Vanity Fair* were not going to rock the boat, and someone needed to defuse the deadly information in the NEADS tapes the Commission had suppressed – that the attacks happened during Pentagon hijacking exercises.

Bronner comments: "The fact that there was an exercise planned for the same day as the attack factors into several conspiracy theories, though the 9/11 Commission dismisses this as coincidence. After plodding through dozens of hours of recordings, so do I."[282] Despite his judgement that there is nothing to support "conspiracy theories" Bronner relays plenty of information indicating that he may have come to the wrong conclusion.

> [The] question "Is this real-world or exercise?" is heard nearly verbatim over and over on the tapes as troops funnel onto the ops floor and are briefed about the hijacking. Powell, like almost everyone in the room, first assumes the phonecall is from the simulations team on hand to send "inputs", simulated scenarios, into play for the day's training exercise . . .

Bronner's coincidence becomes more unlikely in the light of the bigger picture: the links between Flights 11 and 175, the failure to recognize and respond to the "real" hijacked flights, the multiple false hijack reports (see later), the comments from the controller doubting Flight 11 was "real traffic", and the five-year cover-up of the exercises.

Bronner suggests the hijacking exercise was due to start an hour later, but again this contradicts his own evidence. The NEADS operatives he cites did not know the details of the exercise, believing it might be happening simultaneously. One says at 8.43: "I've never seen so much real-world stuff happen *during* an exercise." (our emphasis) Bronner reports a NEADS operative saying of the burning buildings: "I think this is a damn input, to be honest." Moreover, in the official NORAD account of the day, General Arnold places the exercises early in the day: "As we pulled out of the exercise, we were getting calls about United Flight 93."[283]

Bronner asserts that the exercise was to be a "traditional" hijacking of only one plane but offers no evidence. If correct this would rule out the possibility that all the "real" hijacked planes were slated for the exercise. The most obvious cover story for a plot is that a traditional hijacking was expected, so most plot scenarios are compatible with Bonner's claim.

COVER-UP

The evasive behaviour of the Pentagon and the Commission suggests the exercise was far from coincidental. Given several opportunities to mention it, the Pentagon consistently failed to give full answers. The Commission, charged with giving a full and independent account, lied by omission. The Commission says the exercise "postulated a bomber attack from the former Soviet Union . . . We found that the response was, if anything, expedited by the increased number of staff at the sectors and at NORAD." Perhaps to cover itself, buried in the footnotes it also mentions a brief exchange that is meaningless without knowledge of a hijacking exercise: "Is this real-world or exercise? – No, this is not an exercise, not a test."[284]

Given the confusion demonstrated on the NEADS tapes, the Commission's claim that the response was "expedited" by the exercises is implausible. There is no record of any fighters being dispatched from the exercise to intercept hijacked planes. It also implies that without the exercises it would have taken the Pentagon *even longer* than about ninety minutes to get air cover over its own headquarters.

Norad HQ inside Cheyenne Mountain, Colorado, "keep an eye on the sky looking for threats aimed at our continent" says the caption to this military picture. It is still unclear why NORAD failed to track the airplanes.

CREDIT: US Air Force/Val Gempis

The Pentagon admitted in 2004 that at an unspecified time prior to 9/11 it conducted a hijacking exercise in which a plane crashed into a building. It still made no mention of the exercise underway on 9/11, but revealed: "The 9/11 Commission has been informed about our exercises that include hijack scenarios." The statement added: "These exercises tested track detection and identification; scramble and interception; hijack procedures; internal and external agency coordination and operational security and communications security procedures."[285] These were precisely the areas where NORAD failed so spectacularly on 9/11. In light of this admission, the Commission's bland assurance that the exercise on 9/11 helped the response looks more suspicious, and the Pentagon's claim that the hijackings were wholly unpredicted becomes more implausible.

NORAD's 2004 statement that major hijacking exercises took place about four times each year also casts light on the chances of Bronner's "coincidence".[286] Bronner has, however, uncovered the explanation for the phantom Flight 11 story. Colin Scoggins, a manager at the Boston FAA, was NEADS liaison. He told Bronner: "The problem . . . was that American Airlines refused to confirm for several hours that its plane had hit the tower. This lack of confirmation caused uncertainty that would be compounded in a very big way as the attack continued." Perhaps unaware of American's decision to keep that hijacking secret, and its impossible theory that Flight 77 turned up in New York, Bronner writes: "They routinely go into information lockdown in a crisis." It hardly seems plausible that American would

NORAD says it only had radar coverage around the perimeter of the US, but the idea that the radar was "pointing outwards" was absurd: the system was shared with the FAA. Coverage in the Northeast sector is excellent.

CREDIT: 9/11 Commission

NORAD Radar Network (CONUS) 9/11/01

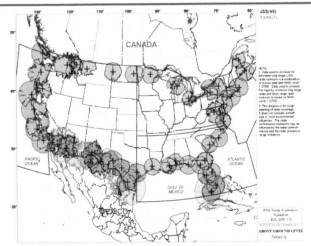

MIT Lincoln Laboratory

I-CNS-5
SRB 05/13/2002

NORAD Radar Network
With Additional 51 Interior ATC Radars

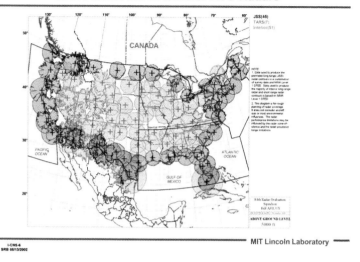

Within the mainland NORAD tapped into the FAA system, in orange.

CREDIT: 9/11 Commission

refuse to divulge vital information to authorities during a national crisis. One explanation might be that the airline was uncertain to whom it was authorized to speak after a secret operation had gone awry.

Bronner also confirms the orders to NEADS fighters: "The orders from higher headquarters are to identify by aircraft type and tail number, and nothing more. Those orders and the fact that the pilots have no clearance to shoot are reiterated by NEADS controllers as a dramatic chase towards the White House continues."

It is assumed that this was just a command exercise. Even this would have involved "inputs" or "injects" on traffic control radars, as NORAD and the FAA shared radar systems. The comments of the controller dealing with Flight 11 and those from NEADS operatives on inputs would suggest this. NEADS operators thought the exercise might also involve fake phone calls from controllers, and even television inputs on the screens. Fake phone calls from passengers were clearly also a possibility and could provide at least a partial explanation for contradictory elements in the calls. The suspicions most prominently articulated by skeptic Mike Ruppert are justified: the exercise could have functioned as a smokescreen for "real" hijackings.[287]

There are several reasons to think these were not just planned as command but as live-fly exercises, with real planes in the air pretending to be hijacked. Ruppert cites a passage in the Pentagon's history of the day, *Air War Over America*, which referred to a "Capt. Brian Nagel, who was chief of NEADS live exercises". The NORAD exercise Arnold told the Commission happened on 11 September was referred to as "Vigilant Guardian", implying command exercises only. However, according to Clarke, Myers told the White House: "We are in the middle of Vigilant *Warrior*, a NORAD exercise." (our emphasis)[288] This would be live-fly.

Live hijacking exercises were not unusual. Quoting "NORAD and defence officials", *USA Today* reported in 2004:

> In the two years before the September 11 attacks the North American Aerospace Command conducted exercises simulating what the White House says was unimaginable at the time: hijacked airliners used as weapons . . . "Numerous types of civilian and military aircraft were used as a mock hijacked aircraft . . . These exercises tested track detention and identification; scramble and interception; hijack procedures . . .".[289]

MEANWHILE, IN WASHINGTON

It may be true that NORAD only has a few scramble-ready armed jets under its direct command, and they burn a lot of fuel and cannot stay up long. However, the bigger picture is different. The exercise should have assured plenty of unarmed planes for observational purposes. The Air National Guard also had planes that could have been called despite their being outside NORAD's official command.

Washington's Andrews airbase was identified by skeptic Jared Israel within days of the attacks. According to the base's website, its mission was "to provide combat units in the highest possible state of readiness".

The "Top Brass"

SETUP	STANDS FOR	IN CHARGE OF	SHOULD HAVE	HAD LINES OPEN TO	SUCCESS RATE
FAA HQ	Federal Aviation Authority	Air traffic controllers	Requested NMCC to scramble planes	Everyone, Pentagon via military liaison officers at all levels	Medium: most information was relayed to NMCC and NSC
NMCC	National Military Command Center	Military, including NORAD and NEADS	Received information from FAA, passed on to military bases	Cheney, NORAD	Failed to order any scrambles
NSC	National Security Council based at White House Situation Room	Most government departments, but not the Pentagon	Decided policy matters, but Cheney, Bush not there	FAA, CNN, govt departments, FBI, Pentagon (but not NMCC)	Stymied by absence of Bush, Cheney, tipped off CNN Al-Qaeda was guilty
White House	Cheney in White House bunker, far from Situation Room (Rice there too)	NMCC	Oversaw military response	NMCC, Bush from time to time	Ordered Flight 77 not to be shot down over Pentagon, got cover from Andrews much later

The state of communications during the two hours of the attacks. Why did Cheney and Rice put themselves out of communication with the rest of the government in an obscure, heavily guarded bunker?

Israel noticed the website was altered after 9/11 to suggest the planes did not exist.[290]

The Andrews aspect was corroborated by the Commission:

> By 10:45 there was, however, another set of fighters circling Washington that had entirely different rules of engagement. These fighters . . . launched out of Andrews Air Force Base in Maryland . . . There is no evidence that NORAD headquarters or military officials in the NMCC knew – during the morning of September 11 – that the Andrews planes were airborne and operating under different rules of engagement.[291]

They were scrambled on Cheney's order, but why hadn't they been scrambled by the Pentagon nearly two hours earlier? What was going on in Washington, at NORAD and above all at the NMCC, which should have ordered a scramble from Andrews?

INITIATED BY	IN EFFECTIVE CONTACT WITH	NOT IN GOOD CONTACT WITH
Clarke at NSC	FAA, CNN, govt departments, FBI, Pentagon (but not NMCC)	NMCC, White House
NMCC air threat conference	Possibly NORAD HQ, possibly White House	Everywhere else
FAA	Every body except NMCC	NMCC
Boston FAA-NEADS	FAA HQ, NORAD, other FAA centres, NSC	NMCC
NORAD	NEADS, possibly NMCC	Andrews airbase, FAA, NSC

This table traces the failure of the NMCC to maintain contact with anyone except Cheney. The Commission blames the FAA for failing to intercept the rogue planes, but the only successful scramble resulted from Boston FAA contacting NEADS directly.

The phone bridge from Boston Center to NEADS headquarters was the only success of the day, though it took twenty minutes to convey the news of Flight 11's suspected hijacking. The Commission blames the FAA for the lack of response, but the evidence shows this was a travesty.

The tables above, based on the findings of the Commission, detail three top-level conferences as well as the phone bridge from Boston FAA to NEADS. The FAA testified that it adhered to correct procedures. Nonetheless, the Commission chose to believe it was the FAA's fault that the Pentagon did not know what was going on.

Ben Sliney, FAA Command Center's National Operations Manager, told the Commission: ". . . At the Command Center of course is the military cell, which was our liaison with the military services. They were present at all of the events that occurred on 9/11 . . . in my mind everyone who needed to be notified about the events transpiring was notified, including the military."[292] This was the man who gave the successful order to ground every plane in the sky while the Pentagon could not even pick up the phone to Andrews.

Monte Belger, FAA Acting Deputy Administrator on 9/11, said: "Prior to 9/11, the procedures for managing a traditional hijacked aircraft . . . were in place and pretty well tested. . . . It was my assumption that morning, as it had been for my thirty years of experience with the FAA, that the NMCC was on that net and hearing everything real-time . . . In my thirty years of history, there was always somebody listening to that net . . . it is a fact – there were military people on duty at the FAA Command Center, as Mr. Sliney said. They were participating in what was going on."[293]

After her testimony, FAA director Jane Garvey suspected what the Commission was up to and made the matter crystal clear in a memo circulated to reporters at the hearing:

The US Air Force liaison to the FAA immediately joined the FAA headquarters phone bridge and established contact with NORAD on a separate line. The FAA shared real-time information on the phone bridges about the unfolding events, including information about loss of communication with aircraft, loss of transponder signals, unauthorized changes in course, and other actions being taken by all the flights of interest including Flight 77 . . .[294]

Citing official logs, the Commission suggests the FAA started getting to work at about 9.20, and the White House at 9.25; the Pentagon cannot, therefore, have been expected to do much before then. The Commission does not cite any witnesses to support this timeline. But it is clear from Clarke's account that his meeting started around 9.03, while the FAA were in real-time contact with the military from around 8.35, according to the three senior officials.[295] For the Commission to be correct, Clarke, the three officials from the FAA and many others from the various conferences who can corroborate these accounts must all be wrong.

FALSE HIJACK REPORTS, PENTAGON FREEZES

The Commission appeared to cover up at least three important issues. First, it is clear from the air traffic control and NEADS tapes that the hijacking exercise caused confusion, leading to more delays at the management level.

Second, officials also grappled with up to twenty-six false hijacking reports. According to Clarke, Garvey told the White House videoconference at around 9.20: "We have reports of eleven aircraft off course or out of communications, maybe hijacked." Later that total rose to twenty-two. Marr told Bronner that at NEADS "we were very confused with who was what and where, what reports were coming in. I think with having twenty-nine different reports of hijackings nationwide, for us it was next to impossible to try and get back there and figure out the fidelity."[296]

Why was Marr so confused? Where were his twenty-nine false reports coming from? Panicky controllers, worried when regular planes did not respond immediately, should have sorted them out easily; none of those planes would have gone out of verbal contact, flown off-course and had transponder failure all at once. According to the Commission, the problem was that the FAA was *failing* to report real hijackings to the Pentagon. If it was also reporting *imaginary* hijacks, the Commission should have investigated and reported: any explanation connected to the hijacking exercise would mean, yet again, that the Commission's assessment that the exercises helped the response is a lie.

The exercises should have generated only a few false blips. Two dozen false blips at this stage suggest someone was hacking into the system to create extra confusion. If true, Marr's statement corroborates Ruppert's argument that the extra blips are *prima facie* evidence of a plot.

The Commission stumbled on the third important issue at the Pentagon: the flow of information through the NMCC. For instance, the controller's override started bleeping as Flight 77 went off-course at 8.56. By 9.09 the operations manager at American was warning Indianapolis of a suspected hijacking. At the FAA, Laura Brown, supported by her officials and the evidence of the White House videoconference, was sure it was passing on information on the flight deviation and the transponder failure "in real time" to the Pentagon's military liaison.

The NMCC should have known there was a problem with Flight 77 at the latest by 9.15, but the NEADS tapes confirm that the information did not reach there until 9.35. Though Marr suggests the fake hijackings were to blame for confusion, this does not explain the failure to *notify* NEADS. A similar problem applies to Flight 93. According to regulations, the NMCC should have been at the centre of the action, passing on information to NORAD, scrambling planes from Andrews, calling up those already airborne from the exercises and alerting AWACS cover.

At 8.30, Brigadier-General Montague Winfield stepped down and installed his deputy, Captain Charles Leidig, who had qualified only in August. Apparently they had no idea anything was afoot. It would be around 10.00 before Winfield returned. When Flight 175 hit the South Tower at 9.03, the Commission reports: "Inside the National Military Command Center, the deputy director for operations immediately thought the second strike was a terrorist attack . . . [he] called for an all-purpose 'significant event' conference. It began at 9:29 . . . with a brief recap."[297] What filled the twenty-six minute gap?

STATEMENT OF

CAPT CHARLES J. LEIDIG, JR.

COMMANDANT OF MIDSHIPMEN

UNITED STATES NAVAL ACADEMY

BEFORE THE

NATIONAL COMMISSION ON TERRORIST ATTACKS UPON THE

UNITED STATES

17 JUNE 2004

Leidig's testimony to the Commission was exceptionally brief and referred to a secret testimony made earlier. Asked why the NMCC was not in contact with Bush on Air Force One, he answered: "I don't recall."[298] There was no explanation for the 26 minute gap and the "other important matters" which, according to the Commission, Leidig was occupied with.

Approximately two months prior to 11 September 2001, I assumed duties as the Deputy for Command Center Operations in the J3 Directorate of the Joint Staff. In this role, I was responsible for the maintenance, operation, and training of watch teams for the National Military Command Center (NMCC). Further, I qualified in August 2001 to stand watch as the Deputy Director for Operations in the NMCC.

On 10 September 2001, Brigadier General Winfield, U. S. Army, asked that I stand a portion of his duty as Deputy Director for Operations, NMCC, on the following day. I agreed and relieved Brigadier General Winfield at 0830 on 11 September 2001.

Shortly after assuming duty, I received the first report of a plane's striking the World Trade Center. Some time after, I learned of the second plane's collision with the World Trace Center. In response to these events, I convened a Significant Event Conference, which was subsequently upgraded to an Air Threat Conference. During the Air Threat Conference, Brigadier General Winfield relieved me and reassumed duties as Deputy Director for Operations for the National Military Command Center.

The details of the Air Threat Conference are contained in the conference transcript. I was given the opportunity to review this transcript during testimony I gave to members of The National Commission on Terrorist Attacks Upon the United States staff on 29 April 2004. On that date, I recounted my actions as Deputy Director for Operations, NMCC, on 11 September 2001.

The Commission says the NMCC monitored the FAA conference only periodically, busy with "other important tasks". These unspecified "tasks" did not include getting information from the White House videoconference or setting up a link to the NMCC's own boss, Rumsfeld, then either at the videoconference or helping victims on the Pentagon lawn.

The NMCC remained out of contact with the FAA, the White House situation room and Rumsfeld. Communications at the most expensive military headquarters in the world would have embarrassed a banana republic: "The FAA was asked to provide an update, but the line was silent because the FAA had not been added to the call . . . Operators worked feverishly to include the FAA, but they had equipment problems and difficulty finding secure phone numbers."[299] What did Leidig tell the Commission in his secret testimony?

The Pentagon denied having any inkling there could be an Al-Qaeda suicide attack, but reports that exercises in the previous months involved planes crashing into buildings suggest otherwise. Moreover, in June 2001, warnings flooded in of a possible Al-Qaeda attack; the regulations governing FAA and NORAD hijacking response were reissued. General Arnold told the Commission: "We had reviewed the procedures of what it is we do for a hijacking, because we were in the middle of an exercise. So we were pretty well familiar with those procedures."[300] The June 2001 regulations expressly prohibit the use of military aircraft as "platforms for gunfire" and specify that requests for assistance be approved by the NMCC: "The NMCC will be notified by the most expeditious means by the FAA."[301] Clearly Arnold's review did not extend to ensuring that phone lines from the FAA ran into the right part of the Pentagon.

Defense Secretary Rumsfeld, specified in the newly reviewed regulations as being responsible for any shoot-down order, was apparently in two places at once – neither of them the NMCC. Clarke places him at the Pentagon's secure teleconferencing studio at approximately 9.15, and he is still there at some time after 9.45, when he tells Clarke of smoke from the Pentagon strike and complains: "I am too goddamn old to go to an alternate site." This is confirmed by Pentagon aide Robert Andrews: "The moment I saw the second plane strike 'live', I . . . ran down to our counterterrorism center . . . I was there in the Support Center with the Secretary when he was talking to Clarke on the White House video-teleconference, and to the President."[302]

The Commission had a radically different account, based on a Pentagon press statement. From his office, Rumsfeld is somehow able to make it to the other side of the Pentagon: "The Secretary was informed of the second strike in New York during briefing; he resumed the briefing while awaiting more information. After the Pentagon was struck, Secretary Rumsfeld went to the parking lot to assist with rescue efforts." In either case, Rumsfeld was a long way from the NMCC. "Secretary Rumsfeld told us he was just gaining situational awareness when he spoke with the Vice President at 10:39."[303]

9/11: WHOSE COUP?

Skeptic Thierry Meyssan caused a storm when he suggested 9/11 was a coup by the Pentagon. But Clarke suggests that Cheney, who, according to a Washington acquaintance, became paranoid after his medical problems set in,[304] suspected this as well:

> I turned the corner and found a machine gun in my face. Cheney's security detail had set up outside the vault doors, with body armor, shotguns, and MP5 machine guns. Although they knew me, they were not about to open the vault door . . . they frisked me. Condi Rice's deputy, Stephen Hadley, came to the vault door to identify me and escort me in. Inside the vault there were more MP5s and shotguns in the narrow corridor.[305]

Clarke implies that Cheney went to the Presidential Emergency Operations Centre (PEOC) shortly after 9.00, and Transportation Secretary Norman Mineta testified that Cheney was in the bunker by about 9.20. CNN reported that people began evacuating the White House at about 9.20, so it is unlikely Cheney would be left alone in his office for another fifteen minutes. Despite these sources, the Commission produced a timeline with a half-hour difference that raises yet more doubts about the official story. It says that just before 9.36, "agents propelled him out of his chair and told him he had to get to the bunker. The Vice President entered the underground tunnel leading to the shelter at 9:37".[306]

Mineta's detailed testimony contradicts the Commission timeline and confirms that the order not to fire on the rogue plane at the Pentagon came from Cheney:

> During the time that the airplane was coming into the Pentagon, there was a young man who would come in and say to the Vice President . . . the plane is fifty miles out . . . the plane is thirty miles out . . . and when it got down to the plane is ten miles out, the young man also said to the Vice President 'Do the orders still stand?' And the Vice President turned and whipped his neck around and said, "Of course the orders still stand, have you heard anything to the contrary?"[307]

Cheney's orders must have been *not* to shoot the plane down. Regulations forbade using planes as a "platform for fire"; the Commission, based on the NEADS tapes, records: "At 10:10, the pilots over Washington were emphatically told, 'negative clearance to shoot'. Shoot-down authority was first communicated to NEADS at 10:31." [308]

The Commission states that the presumed Flight 77 was first detected at 9.32 by air traffic controllers, and that they informed the Secret Service.[309] This was only five minutes before the impact on the Pentagon. In this almost impossibly tight timeline, the Secret Service, the lead agency in such a crisis, must have gone straight through to Cheney. But who was Cheney giving the orders to? The Andrews planes were not up yet, and according to the Commission's new timeline nobody in the military knew about Flight 77. Mineta's account thus provides support for the presence of an X-Team outside the normal chain of command shadowing the rogue jets. There are other reports of mysterious jets following the planes.[310]

The Commission says it was Cheney who convinced Bush not to return to Washington until the situation had stabilized. At the time the Bush people said they had received a message with the warning "Air Force One is next". Anti-Bush journalists in Washington took the view that this was a lie cooked up by White House strategist Karl

Rove to cover up the cowardly zigzag course that brought Bush to Washington only that evening. However, Webster Tarpley has dug up multiple press reports showing the story ran for several days and was repeated by different officials on different occasions. A report from Bush's plane described an atmosphere of panic as it ascended at maximum power at a forty-five degree angle until reaching very high altitude.[311]

At 9.10 that morning Bush may have been as bewildered as the rest of the world still is today, not knowing whether this was the attack by terrorists he had been warned to expect, a coup by the Pentagon, a massive cockup by rogue operatives on a hijacking exercise, a CIA plot, or something else. By the time he returned to Washington, it was all on an even keel.

THE MAESTRO REPORTED TO CHENEY

Most skeptics believe that the team running the ongoing exercises would be a good place to start for identifying the plot. Washington commentators agree that Cheney would normally be doing Bush's dirty work, if indeed there was any to be done. Suskind explains Cheney's view of how presidents "need a failsafe . . . to be able to say they had no knowledge". This was based on his lesson from Watergate: "The President should have been 'protected' from knowledge of such activities."[312]

Cheney seems to have taken on the counterterrorism brief by May 2001. Suskind says: "Intelligence collection, like much of foreign policy, had been placed in Cheney's portfolio since the first days of the administration." After 9/11 there were complaints that the Hart-Rudman Commission was ignored when it reported in January 2001 on the emerging terrorism threat. *Salon* explained, citing Bush officials: "The White House announced in May that it would have Vice President Dick Cheney study the potential problem of domestic terrorism." The May announcement referred explicitly only to "seamlessly integrated, harmonious, and comprehensive" policy for consequence management, but even taken narrowly this would clearly give Cheney oversight of anti-terror exercises.[313]

According to Major Don Arias, NORAD's public affairs officer, "it's common practice, when we have exercises, to get as much bang for the buck as we can. So sometimes we'll have different organizations participating in the same exercise for different reasons."[314]

"Tripod", scheduled for 12 September in New York and based just a few streets away from the Twin Towers, was clearly within Cheney's brief. Mayor Giuliani explained to the Commission that it involved "hundreds of people here from FEMA, from the federal government, from the state . . . and they were getting ready to drill for a biochemical attack".[315]

About ten miles from the Pentagon, reported AP, the National Reconnaissance Office was running an exercise involving a plane crashing into one of its buildings. "The NRO operates many of the nation's spy satellites . . . after the September 11 attacks most of the 3,000 people who work at the agency headquarters were sent home."[316] One can speculate that some of the "essential personnel" left behind would have been in a good position to doctor satellite data contradicting the official story. There are reports of mass-casualty exercises at the Pentagon in October 2000, May 2001 and August 2001, each of which included the scenario of a plane crashing into the building. "You know, it was kind of eerie. The scenario we had for these MASCALS was very similar to what actually happened," said medic John Felicio.[317]

Innocently or not, one can surmise that some people stayed out of the loop when disaster struck: Rumsfeld, who returned to his briefing to await further details; Bush in the Florida classroom; Winfield at the NMCC. Others found themselves surprisingly *in* the loop: Colin Scoggins at Boston FAA, Leidig at the NMCC, and Clarke, who had been demoted from the principals committee in January, and found himself chairing the key White House videoconference. Innocently or not, Cheney, charged with overseeing at least some of the exercises – perhaps the hijacking exercise too – was to be found in operational command, liaising effectively with the Secret Service, apparently issuing orders, *not* to fire on the rogue plane racing towards the Pentagon.

Not everyone had such poor reactions as Bush, the FAA Indianapolis centre, American Airlines executives or the NMCC. Television viewers and the Secret Service knew what was going on. The FAA managed to land every plane in the US without mishap. Ari Fleischer, too, was thinking fast as he held up a sign in the Florida classroom telling Bush to keep quiet. He later said of the moment when he heard a second plane had hit the World Trade Center: "We recognized right away that we were a nation that was heading to war."[318]

9
Why Did the
Towers Collapse?

There have been murmurs in the media that the White House did well out of 9/11, but cautious skeptics in the establishment shy away from the notion that a plot might have been more proactive than a sting operation gone wrong. As the approach of this book is to examine the evidence and to look at a plot as plotters would, in segments, we must now turn to a new segment: the collapse of the Towers.

Normally the scientific community would have little trouble in distinguishing between a spontaneous structural failure and the effects of multiple demolition charges which, say many skeptics, was the real cause of the collapses. But this is not a normal case: the media has made up its mind and sneers at any dissent; the evidence has mostly been destroyed, and access to what is left is refused to all but a favoured few. The small community of structural engineers specializing in high-rise construction has hijacked the debate along with the government and big businesses that pay them.

Like the rest of the official story, the version of the collapses was imposed without scientific enquiry, by media diktat, within hours of the attacks. Professor Wilhelm Frischmann of the Pell Frischmann

Group and City University, London, said: "Prior to 11 September, I scarcely believed that this icon was vulnerable."[319] Deputy Fire Chief Hayden told the Commission: "I don't think it was in our realm of thought." He expanded in *Firehouse Magazine* in September 2002: "We recognized the possibility of a collapse, but our thought process was that there was going to be a partial collapse, a gradual collapse . . . And I think everybody envisioned the idea we're going to get everybody down and back everybody out a few blocks and watch this event, the top fifteen or twenty floors fold in."[320] This is confirmed by the Commission: "Almost no one at 9:50 on September 11 was contemplating an imminent total collapse of the Twin Towers."[321]

Van Romero, demolitions expert and a former director of the Energetic Materials Research and Testing Center at NMTech, which studies the effects of explosions on buildings, told the *Albuquerque Journal*:

> My opinion is, based on the videotapes, that after the airplanes hit the World Trade Center there were some explosive devices inside the buildings that caused the towers to collapse . . . It could have been a relatively small amount of explosives placed in strategic points.

The collapse seemed "too methodical" to be the chance result of airplanes colliding with the structures. Two weeks later Romero told the same paper that after "conversations with structural engineers", he now accepted the official story. He told *Popular Mechanics* in 2006 that he had meant the collapses only *looked* like controlled demolitions. The reason for the "methodical" nature of the collapses, the astonishingly even way both towers came down, has never been explained.[322]

Eyewitness and the media reported explosions when the Towers collapsed. CNN producer Rose Arce was "about a block away" and said: "You saw the top of the building start to shake, and people began leaping from the windows . . . You saw two people at first plummet, and then a third one, and then the entire top of the building just blew up."[323]

Later accounts were similar, but peppered with phrases like "at the time I thought" or "now I realize", and even "it's been explained to

With impact damage concentrated in one corner, the South Tower at first began to topple but then went straight down. The official report does not address the even, symmetrical way the buildings collapsed.

© Getty Images/Thomas Nilsson

me". Eyewitness Richard Banaciski said: ". . . There was just an explosion. It seemed like on television when they blow up these buildings. It seemed like it was going all the way round like a belt, all these explosions." Eyewitness Timothy Hoppey said: "At that point I was thinking it was a secondary explosion. It looked to me like it was much lower than where the planes had gone in."

Why did experts claiming it was almost inevitable the buildings would collapse fail to share their wisdom until 12 September? The official "spontaneous collapse" theory implies the structural engineering community is incompetent. Since the Empire State Building was hit by a plane in 1945, the effect of such an impact was hotly debated both when the Towers were built and after the 1993 attack. World Trade Center chief engineer John Skilling designed the building to withstand an impact with a Boeing 707, comparable to a 757 or 767. A report at the time said the building design had been "investigated and found to be safe in an assumed collision with a large jet airliner (Boeing 707 – DC8) travelling at 600 mph".[324]

The official story distinguishes between plane impact and subsequent fires, implying that Skilling (who died in 1998), his team and the structural engineering community forgot that a plane might also have fuel on board. *Popular Mechanics* quotes architect Leslie Robertson, Skilling's "chief colleague":

We studied it and designed for the impact (of a Boeing 707). The next step would have been to think about the fuel load and I've been searching my brain, but I don't know what happened there, whether in all our testing we thought about it. Now we know what happens – it explodes. I don't know if we considered the fire damage that would cause.

Rudimentary research would have established that Robertson hardly featured in the original accounts of the buildings. As he told the *New Yorker*: "I only assisted on the team that designed it."[325] The BBC made the same mistake, even describing the World Trade Center as "Robertson's building".[326] Robertson, upset by the events and bullied by the media, may not have been able to remember whether Skilling considered the fuel; but the record is clear. In the wake of the 1993 attack, Skilling stated that he *had* thought about the inevitable fire damage that would result from a collision: "There would be a horrendous fire . . . a lot of people would be killed . . . the building structure would still be there."

"Occam's Razor", a key scientific principle, holds that the theory representing the simplest and most direct explanation is to be preferred. The media's own version of Occam's Razor holds that any major departure from government-supplied expert statements must be wrong. The National Institute for Science and Technology (NIST) skilfully meshed with this fallacy by ignoring the alternatives when it published its final report in 2005. Later it issued a brief response to the controlled-demolition theory and refused any further debate. They could expect little dissent from the scientific community because, outside a small group of handpicked experts, it has been starved of data. Any scientist who pronounces without access to the data rightly faces condemnation.

Responsibility for the decision to limit access to the site and send virtually all the steel for immediate recycling was shared by the New York Police Department under Mayor Giuliani and Bush-appointed FEMA director Joe Allbaugh, described by detractors as a political crony with no disaster-management experience.[327] The destruction of evidence caused an outcry. In January 2002, Bill Manning, editor-in-chief of *Fire Engineering*, demanded a "blue ribbon panel be convened to thoroughly investigate the WTC collapse" and judged the "destruction of evidence" as a breach of fire regulations: "No one's checking the evidence for anything." In a prophetic statement, Manning warned that without the evidence the investigation would "amount to paper- and computer-generated hypotheticals . . . a half-baked farce that may already have been commandeered by political forces whose primary interests, to put it mildly, lie far afield of full disclosure".[328]

Manning highlighted another issue:

> Hoping beyond hope, I have called experts to ask if the towers were the only high-rise buildings in America of lightweight, center-core construction. No such luck. I made other calls asking if these were the only buildings in America with light-density, sprayed-on fire- proofing. Again, no luck – they were two of thousands that fit the description.[329]

Despite its recommendations on everything from police radio quality to US policy on Pakistan, the Commission had nothing to say about hundreds of buildings in America that, according to the spontaneous collapse theory, were vulnerable to attack and inevitable collapse. To skeptics it looked as though they didn't really believe the theory, either.

The first investigation into the collapse of the Towers was led by Gene Corley, nominated by the American Society of Civil Engineers. Corley also led the building performance-assessment team after the Oklahoma bombing, and wrote or co-wrote two reports on the Waco siege.[330] The FEMA report was followed by the supposedly definitive NIST report, based on work started well after the disaster site had been cleared. NIST is a branch of the US Department of Commerce; its chain of command ends not at a professional body or Congress but at the Oval Office. The NIST report was welcomed in the media as a resounding confirmation of the official story.[331]

The only hard information cited in one article was that NIST "filed 10,000 pages of reports examining the Towers' collapse".[332] Others cited the number of participating academics, unaware that most had only been involved in peripheral issues. However, the *Village Voice* in New York noticed a weakness in the report: "NIST's computer simulation stops at the point the collapse begins, and does not document exactly how the rest of the buildings crumbled in ten seconds."[333]

Popular Mechanics agrees with NIST and quotes one expert: "If you look at a modern high-rise building [it's] lighter than balsawood . . . These structures look massive, but they're mostly air . . . Ninety-nine percent of all [modern] high-rises, if hit with a large-scale commercial aircraft . . . would not just collapse, but collapse immediately." In fact, NIST was forced by its examination of the evidence to conclude that the collapses should not have occurred when they did (or perhaps at all) were it not for damage to the fireproofing. This disarray illustrates how little consensus there really is. The real-world complexities of the issue do not allow for definitive proof. Short of building real-life models, structural engineers inevitably deal, as Manning put it, in "paper- and computer-generated hypotheticals".[334]

Kept secret for years, the buildings' blueprints were leaked in 2007. The central core consisted of forty-seven massive, interlinked steel box columns. At ground level, the steel was four inches thick. The columns were 52 x 22 inches. The steel was of high quality, specially prepared in Japan, and the columns were in sections several storeys high and welded together on-site, leaving no connecting bolts to snap. By contrast, here is the Commission version: "These exterior walls bore most of the weight of the building. The interior core of the buildings was a hollow steel shaft, in which elevators and stairwells were grouped."[335]

The results produced by the models are determined by the assumptions fed in. NIST's method was to change the parameters until it got the required result, then announce it had determined what must have happened. But what were the parameters necessary for that result, and do they fit the known evidence? Far from proving the official story, the NIST investigation has come close to disproving it.

NIST reported that it created a computer model of the two near-identical World Trade Center buildings, and when it fed in known data such as the velocity of the aircraft and the temperatures the steel reached, the model showed the start of a building collapse. It argued that a progressive collapse followed because the momentum of the collapsing section overcame the resistance of the relatively undamaged remainder of the building. The speed, the apparently explosive nature and the even, symmetrical pattern of the collapse, as well as the destruction of the central core down to the ground, were all left unexplained.

The speed appears to defy the basic rules of physics. The strength of the construction diminished higher up the Towers because there was less weight to support, so the floors above the impact point on the North Tower made up around 10 per cent of its total mass. Before the event, experts like those cited by the *New Yorker* and Deputy Fire Chief Hayden thought the structural resistance would be so great that the top of the building would not even be able to force its way down at all. Yet the spontaneous-collapse theory says the upper section not only overcame the resistance of the storey below but continued to gain momentum, so that when it reached the next storey it could smash through it as well.[336]

It is conceivable that bolts could have been snapped and welds cracked open in much the same way a karate expert can chop through brick with the undamaged floors below providing little resistance, as the official theory implies. This is the only way the top storeys could

Sections of the collapsing Towers were thrown out with such force that they were embedded in neighboring buildings.

It took immense amounts of energy to break up the buildings, and turn so much of them to dust, yet they still managed to reach the ground at nearly free-fall speed.

© Corbis

reach the ground at anywhere near freefall speed. However, this does not fit the observed data. The collapse generated massive clouds of concrete dust, hurling steel sections horizontally from the building at high velocity, using up energy and according to the basic scientific principle of conservation of energy, slowing the fall. Seismologists quoted by *Popular Mechanics* unwittingly underlined this point: "Only a very small portion of the [gravitational energy] was converted into seismic waves . . . most of the energy went into the deformation of buildings and the formation of rubble and dust."[337] Everyone noticed after the event that the buildings seemed just to have vanished. A lot of rubble could have been absorbed in the six basement levels, but the dust coated a wide area. A fireman was quoted as saying: "You have ten-storey buildings that leave more debris than these two hundred-storey towers . . . Where the fuck is everything? [It's all] turned to dust."[338]

Another drain on the energy of the falling section was the inertia of the sections below. As the falling mass hits each new floor, it must not only expend energy smashing it up, but also share its momentum. The law of conservation of momentum, an immutable law of physics, says that the combined mass must lose velocity during this process. Because the lower part of the buildings had relatively more mass than the upper parts, this represents another massive loss of kinetic energy.

Did NIST at least manage to explain how the collapse started? Mark Loizeaux of Controlled Demolition was a government contractor who happened to be in New York that morning. He was involved in the Oklahoma bombing cleanup and would also be involved in this one. He described the basic scenario to the *New Yorker*:

> First of all, you've got the obvious damage to the exterior frame . . . you've got fires . . . jet fuel fires which the building is not designed for, and you've also got lots of paper in there . . . and you're high in the building up in the wind, plenty of oxygen . . . the airplane is going to skid right through that space to the core, which doesn't have any reinforced concrete in it . . . and the fire is going to spread everywhere immediately, and no fire protection systems are working . . . Floor A is going to fall onto floor B which falls on to floor C; the unsupported columns will buckle and the weight of everything above the crash site falls onto what remains below . . . it has to fall.[339]

However, only 20 per cent of the exterior columns were cut or damaged, while those remaining were designed to take many times their normal load. The building's chief site engineer, Frank A. Demartini, explained in January 2001: "I believe that the building probably could sustain multiple impacts of jetliners", because the structure was "like the mosquito netting on your screen door". According to NIST, the floors must have buckled due to the heat of the fires, pulling the external and internal columns out of line while the core columns were weakened by the heat. To make the theory work it is necessary to assume that the plane impacts knocked the fireproofing off the undersides of the floors but not the upper surface, allowing for a cooking effect.[340]

The temperatures at the periphery were little threat to the integrity of the outer steel columns. The highest temperature NIST identified on an outside column was a mere 250°C. The problem must have been the floors and the core. But NIST had no evidence to show the temperatures were high enough there, either. The assumption was that

Findings – Steel inventory

- NIST has examples of:
  - the many grades of perimeter columns and spandrels,
  - the 2 grades of wide-flange and built-up box core columns (representing 99% of the core columns),
  - the two grades of steel in the floor trusses, and
  - examples of core and perimeter truss seats.
- The collection of steel is considered adequate for the needs of the investigation

NIST

Task 5 - Characterize thermal excursions of steel

June 2004 presentation:

Photographic study

- Recovered panels mapped for pre-collapse exposure to fire

Paint study

- Paint condition used to map upper limits to temperature exposure on 21 perimeter panels
➔ Most perimeter panels (157 of 160 locations mapped) saw no temperature T > 250 °C, *despite pre-collapse exposure to fire on 13 panels*

Today:

- Conventional metallographic study of coarsening of carbide phases
- Correlation with fire model results

NIST

Task 5 - Characterize thermal excursions of steel

Summary of metallographic analysis – Core Columns
- Two core columns in impact area with sufficient paint
- Columns 603 (floors 92-93) and 605 (floors 98-99)
- Paint analyses indicate both columns < 250 °C

Consistent with:
  Impact model results
  - Col 603 (fl 92-93) and 605 (fl 98-99) - Fire proofing intact

  Fire and thermal/structural models
  - Col 603, floors 92 and 93
    - no significant fires near
    - peak temperature of approximately 100 °C
  - Col 605 on floor 98
    - some surrounding fire
    - peak temperature less than 200 °C

NIST

At first NIST said the steel samples were "considered adequate", but they contradicted the official theory of a high temperature fire at the core of each building. NIST changed its line, saying the sample was too small.

the steel had softened, but even at 450C steel retains 75 per cent of its strength. Whistleblower Kevin Ryan was an executive at Under-writers Laboratories, the company that had originally certified the steel. He drew attention to the problem in an email to Frank Gayle, head of the NIST investigation:

> Your comments suggest that the steel was probably exposed to temperatures of only about 500F (250C), which is what one might expect from a thermodynamic analysis of the situation. However the summary of the new NIST report seems to ignore your findings, as it suggests that these low temperatures caused exposed bits of the building's steel core to "soften and buckle" . . . This story just does not add up.

Ryan's e-mail was copied to a recipient who published it without realizing it was confidential. Within days, Ryan lost his job.[341]

The inferno required to precipitate the collapse of the core sections would have left telltale signs on the steel beams, but NIST could not find any example of this on the few beams that had been recovered even though one or two came from the impact area in question. NIST got round this by saying it "did not generalize these results, since the examined columns represented only 1 per cent of the core columns from the fire floors". However, the 2003 report stated the opposite: "The collection is considered adequate for the needs of the investigation."[342] NIST was now confirming what they at first denied and what skeptics and fire experts said all along: by authorizing the destruction of the debris, the evidence, which would have explained how the Towers collapsed, was also destroyed.

By NIST's own admission, the evidence necessary to prove the spontaneous collapse theory does not exist. Did it ever? If the handpicked experts allowed onsite in 2001 were not able to select the right beams for analysis, maybe the right beams were not there. It is agreed most of the fuel burned off in a few minutes. Was there enough paper and other materials and oxygen to keep the ferocious fires raging for forty minutes around the central core? Eyewitness evidence suggests the temperatures were not high enough. In one documentary Brian Clark, a survivor from an upper floor of the South Tower, said there was plaster obstructing the stairwell he used, but he was able to

Some skeptics say relatively weak outer columns should not still be standing when the massive interior core vanished entirely.

CREDIT: FEMA/ Andrea Booher

get through: "You could see through the wall and the cracks and see flames just licking up, not a roaring inferno, just quiet flames licking up and smoke sort of eking through the wall." Firefighters Ronnie Bucca and Chief Orio Palmer of Battalion 7 managed to get up to the seat of the fire in the South Tower. There they saw "two isolated pockets of fire . . . We should be able to knock it down with two lines."[343] Palmer's voice was captured on a tape of Fire Department radio transmissions. The existence of the tapes, owned by the Port Authority, was kept secret for months and released only after a fierce court battle.[344] Bucca, a terrorism expert involved in the 1993 attacks, had studied the building's structures and vulnerabilities.[345]

NIST relied mainly on computer models to estimate the impact damage. Flight 11 hit square on, but the damage was highly asymmetrical, affecting one side of the exterior and presumably mainly one side of the core. Nonetheless, the North Tower went straight down. Video showed the aerial at the centre going down first, and the collapse began symmetrically with the core.

NIST has no explanation for why the core "settled" and precipitated the collapse of the North Tower in such a catastrophic way because its model stopped just as the collapse began. Also, the building had to be simplified – a mere three or four floors with a solid lump above and below – making it easier to explain the hammer effect that initiated the collapse. Since the NIST model was secret, no one tested it independently.

How are we to explain the total destruction of the inner core down to near ground level? It was built on bedrock six storeys down, each thick column welded into one piece of steel and undamaged for most of the height of each building before the collapse began. *Popular Mechanics* simply said the buildings were "mostly air" and collapsed "like a pack of cards". NIST does not address the issue.

THE CONTROLLED-DEMOLITION THEORY

The controlled-demolition theory is not challenged by the issues facing the spontaneous-collapse theory, but has problems of its own. How would the buildings be mined, explosives triggered? How could the collapse be made to start at the impact point of the planes rather than from the base, and how could plotters achieve this without being caught?

In the skeptic scenario massive charges are placed in the basement to knock out the central core along with many smaller charges in the building above. They could all be synchronized by a computer and controlled via radio by operatives within sight of the buildings.

In one of its earlier articles, *Popular Mechanics* ridiculed the controlled-demolition concept (NIST and the 9/11 Commission never considered the possibility), saying that it required miles of cabling that everyone would see. Yet, since a powerful explosive can be detonated from a distance using a device as simple as a modern remote-controlled car key, there is no reason why multiple explosions could not be set off in sequence using similar technology.

By 2006, after dropping this objection, *Popular Mechanics* raised another one. According to Loizeaux, "the explosives configuration manufacturing technology does not exist" to cut through the base columns. Even if it did, claims *Popular Mechanics*, for each tower it could "hypothetically take as long as two months for a team of up to seventy-five men with unfettered access to three floors to strip the fireproofing off the columns and then wire the charges".[346] No evidence is offered to support this unlikely calculation which contradicts the view widely held after the 1993 attack that the terrorists only failed to bring the buildings down because they had not parked their explosives close enough to the cores.

Physics professor Stephen Jones suspects the columns were not blown out with explosives but cut with thermate, a few ounces of which can melt its way through thick steel. He has analysed samples of dust taken from near the site and found chemical traces consistent with his thesis.[347] Other 9/11 skeptics have suggested that if the Pentagon was involved in the plot (or, to follow the reasoning of Cheney and the neocons, if bin Laden had acquired a suitcase nuclear bomb), a small nuclear charge might have been used to knock out the central core.

It would not be difficult to create a computer program to coordinate the collapse sequence with the location of the plane impacts programmed in after the crashes. The collapse could be made to start there, bringing down the section above first and leaving the lower part intact for a few seconds. If charges were set on every fourth floor all round the perimeter and core columns, it might take about 4,000 specially prepared bomblets each weighing a kilo.[348] This is not an impossible task for a trusted team of, say, fifty Special Forces operatives. Though they are trained not to ask questions, they could be given the story that there is an Al-Qaeda attack predicted and that without enough information to stop it the authorities must have the option of bringing down the buildings in a tidy way if necessary.

William Rodriguez, the building manager, has explained that it would be little problem for plotters to position the charges. To place a charge against each column they would simply have had to push up a tile on the drop ceiling. Such tiles are not screwed down. There was little or no security for service staff, particularly at night, and the charges could have been delivered beforehand and distributed to each area as part of a supposed maintenance operation.[349]

Controlled Demolition's Mark Loiseaux says: "If you look at any building that has imploded, the explosives are primarily placed on the ground floor and the basement." Access to the basement areas would be easier for an X-Team, because they are primarily service areas out of bounds to most users of the building. There is powerful evidence from eyewitness reports of massive explosions in the basements at the time of the plane impacts. Engineer Mike Pecoraro was working with a colleague in the lowest basement of the North Tower when the room started to fill with white smoke. Although they had been told to stay put, they decided to ascend the stairs to a small machine shop. "There was nothing there but rubble," Pecoraro told *The Chief Engineer* magazine. "We're talking about a fifty-ton hydraulic press? Gone!" The pair made their way to the parking garage, but found that it, too, was gone: "There were no walls, there was rubble on the floor, and you can't see anything." As they ascended to the B Level, one floor above, they were astonished to see a steel and concrete fire door that weighed about 300 pounds, wrinkled up "like a piece of aluminium foil" and lying on the floor. Having been through the 1993 bombing, Pecoraro recalled seeing

There was no containment of the fireballs to cause an explosion; instead the fireballs expanded outside the building.

© Getty Images/Spencer Platt

similar things happen to the building's structure. He was convinced a bomb had gone off in the building.[350]

Rodriguez narrowly escaped with his life, and has been called the "last man out of the North Tower". He was a national hero and made visits to the White House, but when he testified that bombs had gone off in the basement at about the same time that the building was struck, he was ignored by the Commission and treated as a pariah by the mainstream media in the UK and the US. He has addressed audiences all over the world.

Both Leslie Robertson and the Commission refer to explosions caused by the jet fuel, but the first technical report by FEMA explains:

> Although dramatic, these fireballs did not explode or generate a shockwave. If an explosion or detonation had occurred, the expansion of the burning gases would have taken place in microseconds, not the two seconds observed. Therefore, although there were some overpressures, it is unlikely that the fireballs, being external to the buildings, would have resulted in significant structural damage.[351]

The Commission states: "The fireball exploded onto numerous lower floors", and later: "The explosion had been large enough to send down a fireball that blew out elevators and windows in the lobby."[352] This appears doubly wrong: the express elevators were the only two to run from anywhere near the impact floors to the lobby where everyone agree there was considerable damage or the basement where witnesses thought there were explosions. One of the two was reportedly not affected by the fireballs because the passenger, a man named Griffith, was helped to safety by Rodriguez with only broken ankles and no

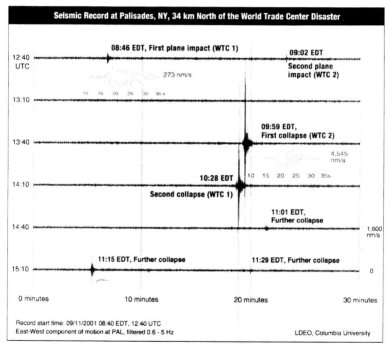

FEMA reports a seismic event at 8.46.20 when Flight 11 hit the North Tower. Later aeronautical evidence shows that Flight 11 impacted at 8.46.40, twenty seconds later. However, in 2007 the same lab supplied data with a different timeline. Both times should have been Universal Standard Time, synchronized to the millisecond. Either FEMA or the seismologists made a crass error, or the new version was doctored to make the official story work.[353]

CREDIT: FEMA

burns. Thus we have one elevator shaft at most to explain burn injuries and extensive further damage in the lobby. It is unlikely too that crashing elevators were the cause of the explosions reported in the basement, their mechanically operated emergency brakes should have operated even without power.[354] The damage and injuries in the lobby are of course easily explained by an explosion in the basement, which had several elevators connecting it to the lobby.

C.2 Sample 1 (From WTC 7)

Several regions in the section of the beam shown in Figures C-1 and C-2 were examined to determine microstructural changes that occurred in the A36 structural steel as a result of the events of September 11, 2001, and the subsequent fires. Although the exact location of this beam in the building was not known, the severe erosion found in several beams warranted further consideration. In this preliminary study, optical and scanning electron metallography techniques were used to examine the most severely eroded regions as exemplified in the metallurgical mount shown in Figure C-3. Evidence of a severe high temperature corrosion attack on the steel, including oxidation and sulfidation with subsequent intergranular melting, was readily visible in the near-surface microstructure. A liquid eutectic mixture containing primarily iron, oxygen, and sulfur formed during this hot corrosion attack on the steel. This sulfur-rich liquid penetrated preferentially down grain boundaries of the steel, severely weakening the

Figure C-1   Eroded A36 wide-flange beam.

C.6 Suggestions for Future Research

The severe corrosion and subsequent erosion of Samples 1 and 2 are a very unusual event. No clear explanation for the source of the sulfur has been identified. The rate of corrosion is also unknown. It is possible that this is the result of long-term heating in the ground following the collapse of the buildings. It is also possible that the phenomenon started prior to collapse and accelerated the weakening of the steel structure. A detailed study into the mechanisms of this phenomenon is needed to determine what risk, if any, is presented to existing steel structures exposed to severe and long-burning fires.

Though FEMA called for further investigation of metal samples that had been eroded by sulphur, no further mention was made of this issue in the NIST report. There was also a sample from WTC 2 with unexplained sulfidation. Sulphur is consistent with the use of thermate and hard to explain otherwise.

CREDIT: FEMA

One can only speculate as to why plotters would detonate explosives at the time of the first plane impacts. Perhaps they calculated that at the beginning of the attacks everyone would be confused, whereas major explosions in the basements just prior to the collapses were unfeasible because the whole world would be paying attention. Perhaps the plotters expected that, as implied by the expert quoted by *Popular Mechanics* who thought the planes impacts should have caused the collapses, the basement blasts would be sufficient to bring the buildings down when the planes impacted.

After the attacks, the mainstream media was full of reports of the fires melting the steel. "The columns would have melted, the floors would have melted and eventually they would have collapsed one on top of each other," an expert told the BBC. Another agreed: "Steel melts, and 24,000 gallons (91,000 litres) of aviation fluid melted the steel. Nothing is designed or will be designed to withstand that fire."[355] This was incorrect, and now media reports explain that the steel was only weakened. *Popular Mechanics* brazenly asserts that the melting steel claim comes from "conspiracy theorists". However, evidence remains that some steel was subjected to far higher temperatures than the fires could have produced, lending weight to the thermate hypothesis.

Dr Jonathan Barnett, a professor of fire protection engineering, told the *New York Times* of unexplained "steel members in the debris pile that appear to have been partly evaporated in extraordinarily high temperatures".[356] This was corroborated by Professor Astaneh Asl of the University of California, Berkeley, who was also involved in the initial investigations. He told Mark Shoofs of the *Wall Street Journal*: "The steel was evaporated", that he had seen "nothing like this". Although he clearly accepted the official story, he testified to Congress that the investigation was hindered by a lack of access to the blueprints.[357]

THE MYSTERIOUS DEMISE OF BUILDING 7

WTC 7 was not hit by plane, although it was damaged by fire and hit by debris from the collapse of the South Tower. At the end of a long day, many videos confirm that the building crumbled into its own footprint, at or very close to free-fall speed. The building gave way from the bottom, collapsing slightly inwards with near perfect symmetry. Dutch controlled-demolition contractor Danny Jowenko has stated that there is no doubt that WTC 7 was a controlled demolition: "I looked at the drawings, at the construction, and it could not have been done by fire. No, absolutely not." He also had an explanation for why colleagues in the US do not say the same: "When FEMA makes a report that says it came down by fire and you have to earn your money in the States as a controlled demolition company, and you say 'No, it was a controlled demolition' . . . you're gone, you know."[358]

Videos of the collapse of WTC 7 are very rarely shown in the mainstream media. Many people even now do not know it happened; fewer know it was the first day in the history of architecture that even one steel frame building collapsed after a fire. The BBC was at the centre of an embarrassing media storm in February 2007 when footage emerged on the Internet of a BBC announcer stating that WTC 7 (which they called "the Salomon Brothers building") had collapsed. In the background, the building was standing, and would do for another twenty minutes. Later, the BBC, which only a week earlier had produced a poorly researched, one-sided documentary on 9/11 issues called *The Conspiracy Files*, issued a statement saying it was "not part of a conspiracy".[359] This may well be right, giving the media advance warning is a standard news-management technique for defusing embarrassment. But how did firefighters predict the collapse of the apparently lightly damaged building so accurately when, six years later, NIST still failed to produce its promised report explaining the collapse?

Lacking NIST's report, the original FEMA report remains the definitive official position. It says the "best hypothesis has only a low probability of occurrence". *Popular Mechanics* explains NIST's "preliminary analysis" five years after the event: Due to the unusual construction of the building, "*if* you take out just one column on one of the lower floors it *could* cause a vertical progression of collapse so that the entire section comes down". (our emphasis) This column is presumed to have been taken out by a combination of structural damage and fire. Though there were tanks of kerosene present, it is agreed that they did not catch fire. *Popular Mechanics* cites the NIST hypothesis that when the building was evacuated electrical pumps were carelessly left running and that these pumped fuel to feed the fires.

In a 2006 interview, New York Police Department officer Craig Bartmer said:

> I was real close to Building 7 when it fell down . . . I walked around it. I saw a hole. I didn't see a hole bad enough to knock a building down, though. Yeah, there was definitely fire in the building, but . . . I didn't hear any indication that it was going to come down. And all of a sudden the radios exploded and everyone started screaming "get away, get away, get away from it!" . . . Somebody grabbed my shoulder and I started running, and the shit's hitting the ground

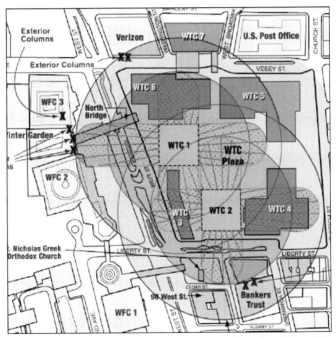

NIST says WTC 7 was more damaged than is generally realized, but this diagram produced by FEMA shows that WTC 7 was barely in the debris field. In spring of 2007 the public was still waiting for their report on how it collapsed so neatly into its own footprint.

CREDIT: FEMA

behind me, and the whole time you're hearing "boom, boom, boom, boom, boom". I think I know an explosion when I hear it . . . That building had a lot of important shit in it and there was enough stuff in that building to bury evidence on other fronts – financial records, government records. There's no way that that just fell down on its own, I don't believe it.[360]

WTC 7 and the Twin Towers were all owned by the same company. Along with Giuliani's high-security Situation Room, WTC 7 housed offices of the Department of Defense and a previously secret CIA station handling espionage at the UN and counterterrorism issues.[361] The Internal Revenue Service and the Securities and Exchange Commission were also there, running criminal investigations into various wealthy individuals close to the Bush White House. All the files for approximately 3,000–4,000 SEC cases were destroyed; many were classified as confidential and had not been backed up elsewhere, reported the *New York Lawyer*.[362] The Secret Service had its largest field office there, with more than 200 employees. One agent was quoted as saying: "All the evidence that we stored at 7 World Trade, in all our cases, went down with the building."[363]

If the building had been badly damaged, it might have made legal and financial sense to bring it down at a time when it would hardly be noticed. A bombshell struck when Larry Silverstein, the New York property developer and long-time owner of WTC 7 who had recently acquired the Twin Towers, made the following comment on the public record:

> [The Fire Department] were not sure that they were gonna be able to contain the fire. I said, you know, we've had such terrible loss of life. Maybe the smartest thing to do is pull it. They made that decision to pull and then we watched the building collapse.

To many people this appeared to be an admission that the building had indeed been brought down by controlled demolition. Some skeptics have accused Silverstein of being a 9/11 plotter, but it hardly seems likely that he would have made this comment if he was. A closer reading of his statement suggests that he may have been strong-armed into agreeing.

What other explanation could there be for Silverstein's apparent gaffe? His office issued a statement saying that he meant that the firefighters should be pulled out of the building, which happened several hours before the building collapsed. Though *Popular Mechanics* quotes Loizeaux and another demolition expert denying that "pull it" has any meaning in their industry, this seems to be contradicted by a phone call with Loizeaux's office that was recorded and posted on the Internet in which the secretary tells an enquirer: "'Pull it' is when they actually pull it in."[364]

Multiple witnesses report that everyone on the ground knew WTC 7 was going to collapse because the Fire Department told them. Google video and Youtube both have clips supporting this. In one, a fireman says: "There's a bomb in the building, start clearing out."[365]

Skeptics argue that an admission of a controlled demolition of WTC 7 will lead to the collapse of the whole 9/11 house of cards. Explosives would have had to be set before the attacks, indicating foreknowledge. Authorities, they say, would not admit the obvious because once an investigation was opened, the whole story would unravel.

10

What Was Going
On at the
Pentagon?

Flight 77 supposedly flew undetected for about thirty-five minutes towards Washington's Reagan International Airport, then made a spectacular descending turn to crash into the side of the Pentagon. Skeptics say it is a highly suspicious coincidence that terrorists struck the only part of the Pentagon updated in the new programme of reinforcements to the wall, largely empty of occupants and due to be reoccupied the following week. Why did Hani Hanjour prolong the risk of being shot down by any Pentagon missiles and introduce an unnecessary new risk, of crashing harmlessly into the lawn as he made an extraordinary high speed ground level approach. Diving into the roof of the five rings or into the large central courtyard would have caused more damage, while hitting the other side of the building might have taken out the top brass or even Rumsfeld himself. *Popular Mechanics* dismisses it all as the one bit of good luck in an otherwise disastrous day.

What would be the motive of a plot to hit the Pentagon? Skeptics have said that Pentagon planners like to kill several birds with one stone. In this case, the attack put war on the top of the response agenda and tested out the newly reinforced wall. Some are suspicious that amongst the relatively few victims many were reportedly financial controllers, while top budget analyst Bryan Jack, head of programming and fiscal economics in the Office of the Secretary of Defense, died on Flight 77. Rumsfeld's admission that "according to some estimates we cannot track $2.3 trillion in transactions" slipped out in a speech the day before the attacks – a Monday, not a Friday, the usual day for bad news.[366]

Official enquiries have little to say about the Pentagon strike. The Commission says "controllers at NEADS located an unknown primary radar track, but 'it kind of faded' over Washington".

> Several of the Dulles controllers observed a primary radar target tracking eastbound at a high rate of speed . . . The aircraft's identity or type was unknown. Reagan National controllers then vectored an unarmed National Guard C130H cargo aircraft [that] identified it as a Boeing 757, attempted to follow its path, and at 9:38, seconds after impact, reported to the control tower: "Looks like that aircraft crashed into the Pentagon, sir."[367]

There is no mention of the oft-cited comments of Dulles controller Danielle O'Brien: "The speed, the maneuverability, the way that he turned, we all thought in the radar room, all of us experienced air traffic controllers, that that was a military plane."[368]

After the cleanup was underway, the American Society of Civil Engineers (ASCE), which ran the first investigation into the World Trade Center collapses, sent only four structural engineers to examine the site for a technical study. "The Pentagon Building Performance Report" never purported to be an investigation into the official story, although the mainstream media often imply that it was. It took as a given that the building was hit by Flight 77. Even so, it identified issues that might have caused a more suspicious investigator to ask questions. In particular, it established that the tail and major parts of the wings could not have entered the building.[369]

If genuine, this must be one of the earliest photos of the attack on the Pentagon. It confirms the approximate point of impact. Note the top line of the facade and the rolls of cables.

The Pentagon Building Performance Report was released in January 2003 by the ASCE, confirming three walls were penetrated and dozens of concrete reinforced steel columns smashed. Some skeptics argue that a 757 could not smash its way through so many obstacles. However, the study established beyond doubt the line of internal damage and hence the angle of approach which will become significant later.

French skeptic Thierry Meyssan claims the small hole, lack of debris and extreme penetration indicate not a passenger jet but a cruise missile. *Popular Mechanics* cites the ASCE report: "When Flight 77 hit the Pentagon it created a hole in the exterior wall of the building approximately 90 feet wide."[370] But this is misleading; the facade was knocked out on one floor across this width, but most of the load-bearing columns, spaced ten feet from centre to centre, were still standing, as seen in the pictures. ASCE makes it clear the hole was at most about forty feet wide.[371]

This photo shows the right-hand side of the impact hole and where the engine might have struck the wall. According to the ASCE report, "no portion of the outer two thirds of the right wing . . . actually entered the building" (p. 35). Skeptics say there should be more remains from the engine and the wing, and more residue from the fireball and wings on the wall.

CREDIT: US Department of Defense/Jason Ingersoll

Popular Mechanics has explained the basic physics needed to make the official scenario work. The entry hole was created as the plane hit the reinforced wall because the plane compacted, explains expert Paul Mlakar, "like taking a Coke can and smashing it against the wall". Midway through this process, the wall gave way and the plane, which had the characteristics of liquid at that point, reached the interior of the building. The mass ploughed on through several reinforced walls and pillars, and eventually the densest part, the undercarriage, punched neatly through the C ring wall. However, the ASCE report says that "the height of the damage to the facade of the building was much less than the height of the aircraft's tail".[372] So what happened to it? Some suggest it might have been rotated and pulled through; others say it must have burnt up in the fireball which, according to the CCTV video (discussed later), lasted only a few seconds.[373]

The hole in the C ring behind the impact aroused the suspicions of skeptics, who said it could not have been caused by the plane's nose. Later, the ASCE investigators said it was caused by the landing gear punching through. Perhaps the hole was enlarged afterwards.[374]

CREDIT: FBI

Mete Sozen, from the ASCE team, told *PM* that the body of an airliner made of thin aluminium is "like a sausage skin", which creates another problem. During the fraction of a second before Flight 77 broke through the wall: why was there no splattering effect, leaving debris stuck to the wall and human remains on the outside of the building?[375]

THE EYEWITNESSES

Eyewitness Allyn Kilsheimer, who was involved in the cleanup operation, angrily asserted: "I held parts of uniforms from crew members in my hands, including body parts, okay?" The Moussaoui trial evidence included pictures of severely charred bodies from the crash site inside the Pentagon. But from these pictures it would appear that Kilsheimer would not have been able to distinguish between uniformed Pentagon personnel inside the building and people onboard the plane.[376] The *Popular Mechanics* report that the remains were "primarily charred heaps of rubble"[377] was confirmed by Fire Chief Ed Plaugher, who told a Pentagon press conference: "There are some small pieces of aircraft visible from the interior during this fire-fighting operation I'm talking about, but not large sections. In other words, there's no fuselage sections and that sort of thing."[378]

According to early reports the Pentagon was hit by a truck bomb. CNN's chief Pentagon correspondent Jamie McIntyre now endorses the official story but at the time he seemed doubtful:

> From my close-up inspection there is no evidence of a plane having crashed anywhere near the Pentagon . . . The only pieces left you can see are small enough that you can pick up in your hand. There are no large tail sections, wing sections, fuselage, nothing like that anywhere around which would indicate that the entire plane crashed into the side of the Pentagon and then caused the side to collapse.[379]

Propaganda documentaries about "conspiracy theories" lay great emphasis on the eyewitnesses to the Pentagon impact (while ignoring the eyewitnesses at the Twin Towers). Many believe they saw Flight 77 fly into the Pentagon but eyewitness testimony is notoriously unreliable – especially in situations where people are taken by surprise. Editor of *Space News* Lon Rains' ambivalent statement makes clear how little eyewitnesses had to go on:

CREDIT: US Department of Defense

Men in uniforms removed debris minutes after the attacks. *Popular Mechanics* said this was normal procedure, but how did the FBI manage to arrive so quickly? Why didn't they record where the pieces were or tag them? Jose Velasquez, at the nearby gas station, thought that his CCTV camera should have captured the event but: "I've never seen what the pictures looked like . . . The FBI was here within minutes and took the film."[380]

At that moment I heard a very loud, quick, whooshing sound that began behind me and stopped suddenly in front of me and to my left. In fractions of a second I heard the impact and an explosion. The next thing I saw was the fireball. I was convinced it was a missile. It came in so fast it sounded nothing like an airplane.[381]

The clearest eyewitness reports came from people who had motives to believe the official story. James S. Robbins, a columnist for the neocon *National Review*, had a spectacular view from his office and declared: "The sight of the 757 diving in at an unrecoverable angle is frozen in my memory." Anyone who denied this was on a par with a Holocaust denier, he continued. But Robbins's account is impossible: the vast majority of eyewitnesses, and indeed the physical evidence from broken streetlights, confirms that the object that hit the building made a flat, ground-level approach, not diving and not unrecoverable.[382]

Captain (now Major) Lincoln Liebner, communications officer for the Secretary of Defense, happened to be on foot "about 100 yards away. You could see through the windows of the aircraft. I saw it hit . . . The plane completely entered the building."[383] William Lagasse, a Pentagon policeman, is quoted as saying: "I could see the windows and the blinds had been pulled down."[384]

Master Sergeant Noel Sepulveda said the plane "flew above a nearby hotel and dropped its landing gear. The plane's right wheel struck a light pole, causing it to fly at a 45-degree angle". The plane tried to recover, but hit a second light pole and continued flying at an angle. "You could hear the engines being revved up even higher," said Sepulveda. The plane dipped its nose and crashed into the southwest side of the Pentagon. "The right engine hit high, the left engine hit low. For a brief moment, you could see the body of the plane sticking out from the side of the building. Then a ball of fire came from behind it."[385] Jim Hoffman has archived multiple reports that broadly agree with these movements, except that the landing gear was *not* down.

Eric Bart collected eyewitness statements from mainstream media sources.[386] Marine Corps officer Mike Dobbs and mortgage broker Jim Sutherland are quoted, indirectly and by the same reporter, as having seen a 737.[387] Former USMC aviator Terry Morin, who was within 100 feet of the plane, said: "It looked like a 737 and I so reported to authorities." Since a 737 is about 30 per cent smaller than a 757, this would go a long way to explain the missing plane tail, lack of debris and so on.

However, the media jumped onto Donald "Tim" Timmerman, described as a pilot, who told CNN he had had a good view and was sure it was a 757: "It didn't appear to crash into the building; most of the energy was dissipated in hitting the ground, but I saw the nose break up, I saw the wings fly forward." Timmerman's statement echoed through the media for several years and was quoted on the US State Department website. But an intensive search of pilots finds only a man of the wrong age by about twenty years. Some suspect this is a plant to shore up the 757 angle essential to the official story.[388]

THE PICTURES

The Internet buzzes with claims that debris was found that positively could not have come from a Boeing 757. However, most of the images are poor quality, impossible to scale, presented without comparison pictures, or all three. Most skeptics have concluded that there is no smoking-gun evidence available.

Taken by US Navy photographer Mark Faram, this is the only known good-quality photo of a large piece of debris with markings from American Airlines, although

there are smaller pieces on poorer quality photos. But how did it escape the crushing effects described by *PM*? If it was blown off in the fireball, why is there no blackening? Some skeptics say that, along with the white flash on the CCTV pictures (below), this is evidence there was an explosion.

CREDIT: US Navy/Mark Faram

This is a normal American Airlines logo taken from the front of a 757. Lines have been added to show where the rivets should be. Some skeptics say the rivets are in the wrong place or the piece on the Pentagon lawn is a different shade of blue.[389]

The Pentagon CCTV video was leaked by Pentagon sources shortly after Meyssan's book appeared, but only the plane's tail is visible. This was apparently due to CCTV retaining fewer images to maximize memory. A video camera monitoring road traffic for the Virginia Department of Transport should have had a perfect view of the aircraft over hundreds of metres, but footage has never surfaced.[390] Also, reports at the time said that a video with a clear image of the rogue jet was seized by the FBI from the nearby Sheraton Hotel.

Despite their poor quality, the CCTV pictures caused a major problem for the official story. The plane appears to be too small, because the nose should be projecting out from behind the pillar. This led skeptics to wonder if the eyewitnesses were right when they thought they saw a 737. In 2006, slightly better versions were issued

This is the best record of what hit the Pentagon. By comparing the two pictures you can see that the tail of the plane is visible behind the white pillar on the left in the first picture.

CREDIT: US Department of Defense

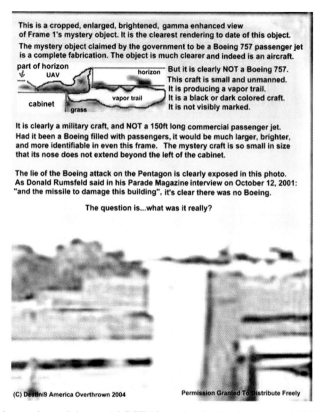

This is a cropped, enlarged, brightened, gamma enhanced view of Frame 1's mystery object. It is the clearest rendering to date of this object.

The mystery object claimed by the government to be a Boeing 757 passenger jet is a complete fabrication. The object is much clearer and indeed is an aircraft.

part of horizon

UAV

horizon

cabinet

vapor trail

grass

But it is clearly NOT a Boeing 757.
This craft is small and unmanned.
It is producing a vapor trail.
It is a black or dark colored craft.
It is not visibly marked.

It is clearly a military craft, and NOT a 150ft long commercial passenger jet. Had it been a Boeing filled with passengers, it would be much larger, brighter, and more identifiable in even this frame. The mystery craft is so small in size that its nose does not extend beyond the left of the cabinet.

The lie of the Boeing attack on the Pentagon is clearly exposed in this photo. As Donald Rumsfeld said in his Parade Magazine interview on October 12, 2001: "and the missile to damage this building", it's clear there was no Boeing.

The question is...what was it really?

(C) Destini9 America Overthrown 2004

Permission Granted To Distribute Freely

Skeptics have enhanced the crucial CCTV frame by altering the colours, highlighting the apparent contrail and the tail. Others say they are falling into a disinformation trap.

Copyright: Destini9 America Overthrown 2004

for the Moussaoui trial, with even less sign of the plane's nose than in the 2002 version. Many dismiss the CCTV photos as disinformation, citing the absence of a shadow thrown by the white flash; the white contrail to the right of the pillar that would not be expected from a passenger jet at low altitude; the incorrect time data; and the suspicious coincidence that the object was not photographed better. However, if the frames submitted to the Moussaoui trial as official evidence in 2006 were faked, a serious offence has been committed.

This car, damaged by a broken lamp pole, is evidence of the plane's low approach.

M-CSP-00001567

In 2006, the FBI's release of a further set of CCTV frames, taken from a slightly different angle but with only the nose of the attack object visible, turned into a public-relations disaster. The media trumpeted it as the final answer to the "conspiracy theorists", but Fox News admitted its disappointment. However, the new frames confirmed that the pilot must have been flying at near ground level for hundreds of meters and would have had a massive ground effect problem to cope with. Said one experienced pilot:

Sep. 12, 2001, 17:37:19

plane

A 757 would have its nose protruding well beyond the pillar. If the CCTV pictures are genuine, they support the eyewitness reports of a 737.
The scaling of the plane was done on autocad for this book by researcher Calum Douglas, based on the known line of approach of the attack plane.

In 2006, after a Freedom of Information action by Judicial Watch, the FBI reluctantly released this picture of the Pentagon attack. The nose of the attack object is just visible on the far right near the horizon.

CREDIT: US Department of Defense

AA77 crossed the highways, knocking down light poles, entered ground effect, didn't touch the lawn . . . Takes a real steady hand to pull that off. I know it would take me a few tries to get it so precise, especially entering ground effect at those speeds. Any slight movement will put you off fifty feet very quickly.[391]

Does this sound like Hanjour, who made instructors nervous in a single-engine plane?

MORE IMPOSSIBLE DATA

A few days after the attacks, AP reported both the data recorder and the cockpit voice recorder from Flight 77

were recovered at about 4 a.m., said Army Lt. Col. George Rhynedance, a Pentagon spokesman. Rhynedance said the recorders were in the possession of the FBI . . . Dick Bridges, deputy manager for Arlington County, Va., said the voice recorder was damaged on the outside and the flight data recorder was charred. But he said the FBI still was confident the data can be recovered from both.[392]

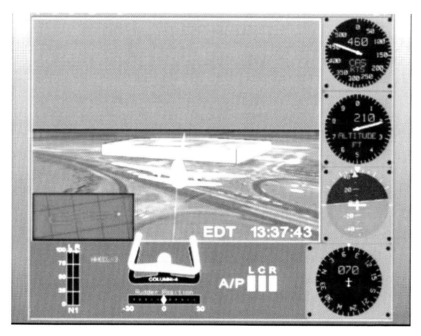

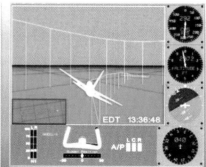

This video was generated by the NTSB from Flight 77's black box, and released under Freedom of Information laws in 2006. If the data has not been tampered with, this plane must have flown over the Pentagon.

CREDIT: NTSB

The voice recorder from Flight 77 reportedly yielded "nothing useful", and this picture was released.[394]

CREDIT: FBI

National Transportation Safety Board
Washington, D.C. 20594

August 11, 2006

The NTSB released the video under a Freedom of Information request.

CREDIT: NTSB

Mr. Calum Douglas
Flat A3E
Cheney Student Village, Cheney Lane
Oxford OX3 0BD
United Kingdom

Re: National Transportation Safety Board (NTSB)
      Freedom of Information Act (FOIA) No. 20060483

Dear Mr. Douglas:

This is in response to your FOIA request dated August 4, 2006, for information regarding the hijacked flights on September 11, 2001. Specifically, you requested NTSB reports of the flight path study for American Airlines Flight 11, United Airlines Flight 175, and American Airlines Flight 77.

The information you requested is enclosed on three CD-ROMs.

In the event that you perceive this response as a denial of some aspect of your request, you may appeal this response by to writing to: Mr. Joseph G. Osterman, Managing Director, NTSB, Washington, DC 20594.

Sincerely,

Melba D. Moye
FOIA Officer

 PILOTS FOR 9/11 TRUTH

Pilots for 9/11 Truth explain that the data in the video implies that Flight 77 did not hit the Pentagon.[395]

CREDIT: Pilots for 9/11 Truth

PRESS RELEASE

FOR IMMEDIATE RELEASE
03/26/07

PILOTS FOR 9/11 TRUTH
www.pilotsfor911truth.org

Contact: Robert Balsamo
e-mail: pilots@pilotsfor911truth.org

OFFICIAL ACCOUNT OF 9/11 FLIGHT CONTRADICTED BY GOVERNMENT'S OWN DATA

Pilots for 9/11 Truth, an international organization of pilots and aviation professionals, petitioned the National Transportation and Safety Board (NTSB) via the Freedom of Information Act to obtain their 2002 report, "Flight Path Study–American Airlines Flight 77," consisting of a Comma Separated Value (CSV) file and Flight Path Animation, allegedly derived from Flight 77's Flight Data Recorder (FDR).

The data provided by the NTSB contradict the 9/11 Commission Report in several significant ways:

1. The NTSB Flight Path Animation approach path and altitude does not support official events.
2. All Altitude data shows the aircraft at least 300 feet too high to have struck the light poles
3. The rate of descent data is in direct conflict with the aircraft being able to impact the light poles and be captured in the Dept of Defense "5 Frames" video of an object traveling nearly parallel with the Pentagon lawn.
4. The record of data stops at least one second prior to official impact time.
5. If data trends are continued, the aircraft altitude would have been at least 100 feet too high to have hit the Pentagon.

In August, 2006, members of Pilots for 9/11 Truth received these documents from the NTSB and began a close analysis of the data they contain. After expert review and a cross check, Pilots for 9/11 Truth has concluded that the information in these NTSB documents does not support, and in some instances factually contradicts, the official government position that American Airlines Flight 77 struck the Pentagon on the morning of September 11, 2001.

Later, officials said the voice data was lost. This is a rare occurrence; "black boxes" (they are in fact normally orange) are designed to resist a crash into a mountainside. The FBI released a picture that seems to bear this out, but it makes nonsense of the original report.[393]

A 2006 Freedom of Information Act request obtained a video reconstruction of Flight 77 from the National Transportation Safety Board (NTSB). The video, which should have been automatically generated from the black box data, ends a few seconds before Flight 77 would have hit the building. At the moment the video stops, the plane's altitude is too high, and it is approaching from the wrong angle. Even if the plane could dive down and hit the Pentagon, it would contradict most eyewitness reports, fail to knock over the lamp poles and leave a different wreckage path. If this video is based on valid data it proves that Flight 77 did *not* hit the Pentagon.

THE PASSENGERS

The details of some of the passengers on Flight 77 are very intriguing. Most high-profile was, of course, CNN's Barbara Olson. In his field, top Navy scientist Bill Caswell was in a similar league. In charge of a team of a hundred scientists at a top-secret facility, even his wife knew little about his work. An obituary in Physics Today praises Caswell's university work: his calculations "are interpreted these days as evidence for both grand unification and low-energy supersymmetry. Thus Bill's work is also crucial to our thinking about physics beyond the Standard Model. As Bill emphasized in his original paper, his calculation indicated the possibility of a qualitatively new behavior in relativistic quantum field theory." One can only speculate over what Caswell, said to be "developing a profoundly new capability for the US Navy", had achieved in twenty years of top-secret work in the Pentagon.396 It was most likely for use in the Pentagon's main advanced technology research: Star Wars. On the unusual passenger list for Flight 77, eleven out of about fifty people were employed by the Pentagon or contractors apparently involved in Star Wars-linked work, related to the tracking of airborne objects. This is a much narrower field than simply working for the government or even the

Pentagon, as many passengers flying out of Dulles would. There is no obvious explanation for this coincidence, such as a conference they were all attending. Curiously, according to the dubious flight manifests (see Chapter 6), neither of the two pairs of colleagues was travelling

Stanley Hall, sixty-eight, of Arlington, Virginia,	Director of Program Management for Raytheon, where he helped to develop and build anti-radar technology. He was described as "our dean of electronic warfare".
John D. Yamnicky Sr, seventy-one,	engaged in top-secret Pentagon work at Veridian Engineering, on air-to-air missile programmes. "He had done a number of black programs – which means top-secret," said his son. "We were given no details."
John Sammartino	an engineer for XonTech Inc, whose website says it specializes in software systems for identifying enemy missiles.
Leonard Taylor	a technical manager for XonTech Inc.
Robert R. Ploger	worked for twenty years at Lockheed Martin, where he was a manager in the Systems and Software Architecture Department.
Chandler Keller	a lead propulsion engineer and a project manager with Boeing Satellite Systems.
Ruben Ornedo	also a propulsion engineer with Boeing, although perhaps in a different division.
Dong Lee	also described as an engineer with Boeing. He is listed in the media but does not appear on the flight manifest.
Robert Penninger of Poway, California	an electrical engineer with BAE Systems, another company with a large presence in the high-tech defence sector.
Wilson Flagg, sixty-three, of Millwood, Virginia	a US Navy admiral and pilot with American Airlines.

together. This list does not include Pentagon financial controller Brian Jack, mentioned earlier or Bill Caswell. Could these people have been involved in the day's hijacking exercise?

CONCLUSIONS

If the data from the CCTV frames and the NTSB video is correct, Flight 77 could not have been the plane that hit the Pentagon. Some skeptics suspect these videos have been cooked up as part of a disinformation operation to distract attention from areas where the plotters are more vulnerable. On the other hand, putting faked data into the public domain would be a risky step. If the official story is true, why go to such lengths to promote conspiracy theories?

Supporters of the official story rightly emphasize the question of what happened to the passengers if Flight 77 did not hit the Pentagon. All but one of the Flight 77 passengers has been identified by DNA technology.[397] The remains were reportedly supervised continuously by FBI agents as they passed to the temporary morgue at the Pentagon, went by truck to a nearby airfield and finally arrived at Dover airbase, where they were analysed.

If the Flight 77 passengers were not in the plane that hit the Pentagon, an X-Team would have to sneak their remains into the transport chain as it carried those of the many more people who were killed inside the building. This is not impossible. But, like the case of the controlled-demolition theory, skeptics need to show a motive and offer possible scenarios, even if they are necessarily speculative at this stage. A possible motive might be to bring the Pentagon into the story, writing war into the script while doing as little damage as possible.

Under any scenario, a 757 might have been seen as too big and too risky. The debris, the eyewitness evidence and the CCTV pictures seem to add up to a 737 in American livery as the best alternative, which is smaller and would explain the vanishing tail.

Who could have been piloting the plane? If it was not the real Hanjour perhaps it could have been another more skilful pilot found by Al-Qaeda to take his place, but highly skilled pilots wishing to commit suicide have proved hard for Al-Qaeda to find (*Note*: Lance op cit provides the most detailed account of how the 911 plan developed and finds little sign of Al-Qaeda recruiting pilots, rather they would try to get their operatives trained, usually unsuccessfully.) Some skeptics conclude that whatever the plane it must have been flying automatically either as a result of computer tampering or because the pilot was sitting in a remote control room.

Since 2001, the use of drone planes in Afghanistan and Iraq has been well publicized, but they were in operation many years even before Operation Northwoods. At the end of World War Two the idea was taken to the advanced planning stage. A recently published history recounts:

> The Americans floated the idea of flying radio-controlled, unmanned "war-weary" bombers loaded with 20,000 pounds of high explosives into industrial targets (that is, cities) in Germany . . . Both the air force and the US Navy had been involved in testing and launching several missions against various sites on the Continent, using worn-out B-17s and B-24s. A pilot and copilot would get the plane airborne, set the remote controls, and bail out. Escort aircraft would then guide the plane by remote control to the target.

By the time of Operation Northwoods, there was no need for pilots at all. In fact, in a programme known as SAGE, NORAD had at its disposal a number of US Air Force General Dynamics F-106 Delta Dart fighter aircraft configured to be remotely flown into combat as early as 1959. These aircraft could be started, taxied, taken off, flown into combat and returned to a landing entirely by remote control, with human intervention needed only to fuel and re-arm them.[398]

By 2001, it was feasible to doctor a plane's computer to be taken over by remote control against the wishes of the cockpit. Clearly this would be an excellent anti-hijacking measure, and the media discussed it after 9/11. This would be "new technology, probably far in the future, allowing air traffic controllers to land distressed planes by remote control", said the *New York Times*. But someone was misleading them. The technology had been tested on a Boeing 727 only a month or two earlier in a joint project between Raytheon and the US Air Force in a programme known as JPALS.[399]

By 2006, Raytheon was describing JPALS as "an all-weather, all-mission, all-user landing system based on local area differential GPS", but even in August 2001 it was possible to modify 727s to land as drones:

> The JPALS system is being developed to . . . be fully interoperable with planned civil systems utilizing the same technology. Raytheon and the U.S. Air Force have been conducting extensive flight testing for JPALS at Holloman over the last three months . . . The FedEx Express 727-200 aircraft at Holloman successfully conducted a total of sixteen Category I approaches. After completing a number of pilot flown approaches for reference the aircraft conducted six full autolands using the JPALS ground station.[400]

Supporters of the official story say normal planes cannot be taken over by remote control in this way, but there are rumours that the Boeing 757 and 767s had a "back door". In any case the planes in the attacks could have had their onboard computers adapted before they took off. If these planes were slated for the hijacking exercises, for instance, this might have been done by operatives working in good faith to test the new system. On the other hand, if real hijackers were under observation the authorities would know which planes and which days they were flying, because many of the tickets were bought in advance. The official plan might be to force the planes safely back to the airports, and the crashes would be blamed on (or perhaps genuinely caused by) rogue operators in the remote-control booths. A simpler system would be to simply rig the computer to ignore instructions once it reaches the right area and head at full speed for a specific location defined by the GPS that autopilots work from. But this would inevitably crash the planes into the buildings, and there could be no cover story.

Can it really be a coincidence that in June 2001 warnings were flooding in of an imminent Al-Qaeda attack; that in August 2001 Bush was being warned of a possible Al-Qaeda hijacking in the US; that in the same month the Air Force was perfecting a GPS-based control system for civilian Boeings; and that on 11 September a secret hijacking exercise coincided with a "real" hijacking. Moreover, GPS is a satellite-based system intimately connected to Star Wars, which involves identifying and shooting down enemy missiles. So it is also odd that Flight 77 had around nine passengers onboard who were probably conducting research in this field. Was this a test of concept trial run that somehow went terribly wrong?

Along with one executive on Flight 77, Raytheon had another three executives aboard Flight 11. Peter Gay, who normally flew on Mondays, was Vice-President of Operations for its Electronic Systems division and had been on special assignment to a company office in El Segundo.[401] This was one of the two facilities developing the remote-controlled Global Hawk plane, but one report said he was supervising Patriot missile development. Kenneth Waldie and David Kovalcin were senior engineers, who also worked for Electronic Systems.

Skeptics say with a proper investigation it should not be difficult to distinguish the very different scenarios to establish what really happened. In the meanwhile we can only speculate. It is time to return to base.

11
Adding Up the
Evidence

This book is not intended to be a complete explanation of what happened in the 9/11 attacks; it is a survey of the evidence and possible explanations. The first phase of the story goes back twenty years to the CIA's Afghanistan war and runs up to the moment the presumed hijackers reportedly boarded the doomed planes.

Bin Laden was a US ally if not a direct asset in the war run by the CIA and Pakistan against the USSR in Afghanistan. Throughout the 1990s the links were maintained between the US and his network, later known as Al-Qaeda. One primary link that has become public is the case of Ali Mohamed, now described as an Al-Qaeda mole in the US but certainly a US mole in Al-Qaeda.

There are many reasons to think that bin Laden, if he is still alive, still maintains contacts with Washington. These include reports of a meeting between bin Laden and the CIA in August 2001; the failure to send US troops to capture bin Laden in November 2001; comments from Rumsfeld and Bush in 2002 that bin Laden was no longer relevant and from such people as the CIA's Buzzy Krongard in 2006 that bin Laden might be of more use to the US if he remained at large; and

2007 reports that the US was once again funding Al-Qaeda-linked groups in attempts to undermine Syria and Iran.

There has been debate over whether Al-Qaeda appeared around 1996, blossomed briefly and has now disintegrated, or whether it was a major player throughout the period. Investigations based on FBI and court materials, primarily by Miller *et al* and Lance, concur with the Able Danger investigation at the Pentagon: Al-Qaeda has been continuously in operation since it was linked to the CIA in the 1980s. It has never been a large organization. It *was* linked to the 1993 New York attack.

After the Oklahoma bombing, wrongly blamed on Arab terrorists, the Clinton White House launched a major review of US policy on terrorism; the still-largely-secret Presidential Directive was issued, and the CIA's covert Alec Station unit was set up, skeptics suspect, to manage the relationship with Al-Qaeda.

Despite later denials by the CIA and Richard Clarke, the Sudanese government offered the US the opportunity to arrest, monitor, contain and effectively disable Al-Qaeda. Instead, the US chose to have bin Laden expelled to Afghanistan, with the unconvincing argument that it did not have enough evidence to indict him. Ali Mohamed, who had trained the cell that carried out the 1993 attack while with the US Special Forces, now helped organize bin Laden's move from Sudan to Afghanistan. There, Al-Qaeda operated as an ally of the Taliban and as an indirect ally of the US and Pakistan.

Al-Qaeda helped the Taliban consolidate its hold on Afghanistan while sending senior aides and fighters to Bosnia and Kosovo again as indirect allies of the US.

Meanwhile, global resistance was growing to the Clinton strategy of peacefully expanding US power through "trade liberalization". There was concern by those who sheltered under the US military umbrella that with the Cold War over, the US might begin pulling back from foreign entanglements.

By 1998, storm clouds were gathering. Hardliners took advantage of the Monica Lewinsky scandal to sabotage Clinton's peace efforts in the Middle East. Al-Qaeda adopted a new policy of striking at US interests, with the African embassy bombs and, in 2000, the USS Cole

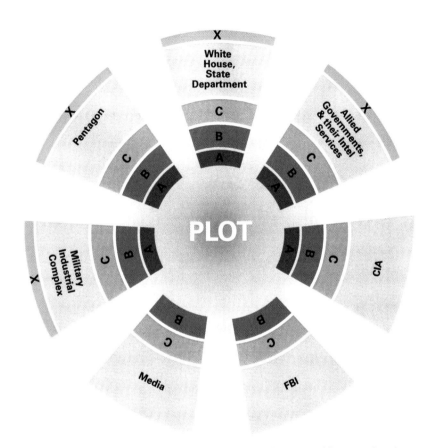

By networking across domestic and foreign agencies plotters could ensure that they all kept quiet afterwards. Nobody would believe any whistleblowers were innocent.

attack. The lack of much public appetite for revenge reaction in the US must have been worrying for Washington and its allies. Meanwhile, the Taliban became less beholden to Pakistan and failed to co-operate over the proposed energy pipeline from Central Asia, a strategic US and Pakistani goal. It was making powerful enemies; Al-Qaeda would become its Achilles heel.[402]

Both the CIA and Clarke devised detailed plans to deal with the new situation, and the paper trail shows these involved placing agents inside Al-Qaeda. Pakistan's ISI set up a joint unit with the CIA focused on Al-Qaeda. Khalid Sheikh Mohammed, under secret indictment in the US but living in Pakistan (reportedly as an ISI agent), approached bin Laden in 1998 and persuaded him to sanction the 9/11 attacks. Intentionally or not, Sheikh Mohammed's role was to manipulate Al-Qaeda into a strategic disaster that would boost support, both in the US and abroad, for Washington's global expansion plans – economic under Clinton, but military under Bush when the plan came to fruition. It would also lead to the takeover of Afghanistan by the Northern Alliance, with whom Sheikh Mohammed was allied when he approached bin Laden.

Some people in Washington already knew of the 9/11 plan, which was discovered on Ramzi Yousef's laptop in 1996. The involvement of the ISI with the ringleaders, the presence in the US of Mossad operators in proximity to the presumed hijackers and on the scene of the attacks (see below) and the more tenuous links with the UK and Saudi Arabia, make it likely that Sheikh Mohammed's attack plan and personnel were monitored by a network drawn from these agencies. Under cover of what may have been a legitimate operation at this stage, unknown plotters may have allowed or facilitated the 9/11 attacks. The involvement of the various parties could have ensured their subsequent participation in the cover-up.

By summer 2001, US policy was set: a ground war was gong to be launched to overthrow the Taliban and destroy Al-Qaeda. The Bush people had another plan, too – to seize Iraq and its oil assets and plant an army at the heart of the Middle East. Neither plan could have been carried out without 9/11, as officials confirmed in testimony to the 9/11 Commission.

In 2002 there seems to have been a major split. The original architects of the 1990s war on terror policy, people like Clarke and more moderate Democrats, wanted to consolidate the successes that 9/11 had brought. The more aggressive wing wanted to press ahead with the occupation of Iraq. The split has led to important information emerging – that, for instance, the White House was committed to an Iraq invasion from its first days in office.

WASHINGTON, SUMMER 2001

Outside the US, the policy was strenuously to disrupt Al-Qaeda cells with a view to aborting any attacks. However, within the US, there was either no strategy (as claimed officially) or a strategy that seemed designed to allow an attack to happen. Different FBI field offices were forbidden from opening criminal cases that might have foiled the attacks. Intelligence cases fell on the other side of the barrier known as the Wall. Inexplicably, officers – mostly from the CIA on the intelligence side of the Wall – effectively sat and watched as 9/11 unfolded, while aggressively blocking FBI field offices from taking any action even though they had identified at least three people as terrorist suspects who were later named as hijackers. Subsequent official investigations into these incidents have been stonewalled by the officers concerned claiming that they could not remember events.

The attempt to explain this by the "Saudi block" theory (i.e. Bush did not want to embarrass his Saudi friends, so he put a block on Al-Qaeda probes) does not make sense. Everyone knew the threat of a mass attack was very real; how could letting an Al-Qaeda attack take place in the US possibly help relations with the Saudis?

According to FBI boss Thomas Pickard, Attorney General John Ashcroft refused to be briefed on the terrorist threat in June 2001. He also refused approaches by trusted conservative political allies to intervene when he was warned that the FBI was being obstructed. In her testimony, Rice stated that the FBI had been tasked to act, and Bush's then-secret 6 August brief, contained the same incorrect information. In his testimony, Tenet told the 9/11 Commission that he did not meet with Bush in August when in fact he had flown to Texas twice – once for a mysterious, day-long meeting.

Nothing so far proves that any of these people were personally aware of a criminal plot to organize or facilitate the 9/11 attacks. There might have been gross incompetence and forgetfulness, a series of misunderstandings and coincidences or some unknown state secret that explains their actions. They might have been duped by plotters operating offstage. However, it can be said that the Commssion failed in its duty to give a full accounting.

There is little evidence that the presumed hijackers had the flying skills, the intent or the organizational capabilities necessary to succeed. People occupying the identites of Atta, Jarrah and al-Shehhi existed in the US, but did not act like suicide operatives. The German police obtained witnesses to substantiate the legend, but only after accusing them of complicity in terrorist offences carrying long prison sentences.

We cannot be sure if the man occupying the identity of Atta in Florida was a drug dealer, an Islamic fanatic, a double agent or a bit of each. Sheikh Mohammed has not been interviewed by anyone outside a tightly knit band of interrogators.

Could it be that, as has been argued in the case of the original Pearl Harbor, the White House simply decided to leave the door open, to look the other way with the feeling – as expressed by Clarke – that "big attacks" would take place sooner or later? For one thing Clarke's view was wrong, Al-Qaeda did not manage anything remotely comparable before 9/11, and has not done since. The FBI block was applied again and again preventing it, legally the lead agency on terrorism under the 1995 Directive, from discovering that al-Hazmi and al-Mihdhar were in the US and from examining Moussaoui's laptop even though he was a known terrorist. And how could officials be so sure that if they turned a blind eye to suspected terrorists Al-Qaeda would not hurl planes into nuclear reactors?

The FBI block can be explained if there was a surveillance operation already running. FBI officers would be putting it at risk, which seems highly likely as agents were told "we know what's going on" and "you might screw something up". Perhaps there was a trusted double agent on the ground reporting everything – Atta, Jarrrah or the mysterious Hanjour. Perhaps the Pentagon or even a top-secret FBI team ran it. More likely, Alec Station didn't trust the FBI's competence and, forbidden itself to take part in domestic surveillance, subcontracted the job to the Mossad, widely respected for its skills in this area. Whatever the nature of this secret team, it failed to stop the attacks.

In 2007, journalist Christopher Ketcham revisited reports that surfaced soon after the attacks: four Israelis, at least two of whom were considered Mossad operatives, were arrested by the FBI on 11 September 2001 after apparently celebrating and taking pictures of the burning Towers. Ketcham quoted ex-CIA counterterrorism chief Vincent Cannistraro: "The FBI investigation operated on the premise that the Israelis had foreknowledge." The *Bergen* [New Jersey] *Record* quoted an FBI source on the investigation as saying the Israelis had "maps of the city . . . with certain places highlighted. It looked like they're hooked in with this . . . It looked like they knew what was going to happen".[403]

Earlier in 2001 the US deported a large number of Israelis suspected of spying – the so-called "art student spy ring" – and a secret US government report was leaked in full on the Internet and gave some addresses for the suspected spies, which in two cases were within a block or two of where some of the alleged hijackers were staying at the time. A spectacular May 2002 report citing unnamed sources in Mossad appeared on the website Globe-Intel, run by Gordon Thomas: Mossad had thoroughly infiltrated the 9/11 hijackers and Israel's Ariel Sharon, angry that Bush was pushing him to accommodate the Palestinians, intended to leak information that the attacks should have been stopped. Whatever the reason, Bush soon changed his position, tilting back to Israel, and no further revelations appeared.[404]

Could 911 have been a Mossad false flag operation? Mossad was more likely to be liaising with its US counterparts for several reasons. Israel would be very unwise to expose itself to being caught in the highly criminal position of monitoring the hijackers and failing to foil the attacks. Deputy Secretary of State Armitage lobbied successfully to have the FBI investigation closed down and the Israelis were quietly expelled even though at least one failed a lie-detector test.[405] The mainstream media gave some support to this report: "According to documents obtained by *Die Zeit*, Mossad agents in the United States were following at least four of the 19 hijackers, including Almihdhar." *Der Spiegel* said the four included Atta. The *Daily Telegraph* said Israel had warned the US and given two names.[406]

The behaviour and comments of the senior FBI officers and the reality of the repeated obstruction of agents on the intelligence side of the Wall appear to make an unacknowledged surveillance operation a near-certainty – but the problem is that it failed. Even the most limited surveillance should have noticed the presumed hijackers' learning to

Ian:

Good afternoon.

I would be happy to assign one of my staff members to determine how we
could respond to your questions. However, we will have to present the
questions to subject matter experts, and that will take a couple of
weeks at least.

Can you wait this long? And may I ask if you are looking for a response
over the telephone, in an interview, or in writing to your
questions?

Ernie Porter

To: "Porter, Ernest J." <Ernest.Porter@ic.fbi.gov>
From: Ian Henshall <crisisnewsletter@pro-net.co.uk>
Subject: RE: Some questions for my forthcoming book
Cc:
Bcc:
Attached:

Hello Ernie,

I am coming up to the book deadline. Here are three questions.

After the Moussaoui trial, why the FBI is still unable to answer
questions and release evidence which would put conspiracy theories
to rest?

Surely you can confirm that Flight 175 was not modified and thus
disprove the "pod theory".

Can you confirm or deny the "plane manifests" as genuine of fake?

The problem is that some people will conclude rightly or wrongly
that there is an intention to create confusion by allowing wild
theories to take root.

I realise that you are bound into a slow moving bureaucracy but you
office did say you can sometimes move fast.

Ian Henshall

Subject: RE: Some questions for my forthcoming book
From: "McKee, Susan T." <Susan.McKee@ic.fbi.gov>
To: <crisisnewsletter@pro-net.co.uk>

Mr. Henshall,

I am sorry to say that the FBI is going to decline your request at
this time. The issues surrounding the events of 9/11/2001 are
documented in the 9/11 Commission Report. We wish you the best of
luck in your endeavor.

Sincerely,

Susan McKee
Office of Public Affairs
Washington, DC

202-324-5348

>From: Ian Henshall [mailto:crisisnewsletter@pro-net.co.uk]
>Sent: Thursday, March 29, 2007 11:29 AM
>To: Porter, Ernest J.
 ...snip...
>Checked by AVG Free Edition.
>Version: 7.5.446 / Virus Database: 268.18.17/732 - Release Date:
24/03/2007 16:36

As these emails show, the FBI is likely under orders not to answer the simplest questions about the 9/11 attacks. Skeptics believe a real enquiry would soon prove their suspicions justified.

fly, buying their plane tickets for the same day and heading to the airports.

A sting operation would explain how the suspects were allowed onto the planes. It might run like this: a double agent, say, Atta, tricks his handlers on the surveillance team into thinking that the planes are going to be flown back to the airports in a spectacular hostage taking, as suggested to Bush in the 6 August memo. The FBI plans a careful ambush, a bloodless wake-up call to Americans to the risks of terrorism. Conservative TV pundit Barbara Olson on Flight 77, described as plucky and adventurous, is to play a hero's role and be a powerful voice in support of the New American Century. Daniel Lewin from Flight 11, ex-Israeli army intelligence[407] from an elite unit specialising in counterterrorism and the freeing of hostages, is to help with the rescue. The hijackers announce a return to the airports to hide their true plans. Then, at the last moment, they wrench the planes into the buildings.

However, a conventional hijacking would not require hijackers to learn to fly. This should have been a red flag to investigators, who should have been aware from Ramzi Yousef's laptop in 1996 – if not from general inference – that Al-Qaeda might be planning a 9/11-type plot. Removing pilots from their seats would not be part of a hostage taking plan so there is no explanation for the silent takeovers – nor for the evidence black hole, the hijackers' lack of flying skills or their unlikely personalities. So the secret surveillance team, even with the adddition of the failed sting operation, provides an extra layer of confusion and a cover story before the event, but hardly exonerates the officials operating it.

THE ATTACKS

There is, to recap, a highly suspicious aura of complicity in Washington. The attacks fit neatly into existing plans on several levels; the FBI has been blocked, and the only justification for that would be a secret surveillance plan that failed, spectacularly and suspiciously. There are other, more general reasons to suspect that the truth is substantially different from an official cockup story, too:

▪ The operational details of the day of the attacks should become clearer with time, but in this case it is the opposite. To take just a couple of examples, the 9/11 Commission changed the Pentagon's timeline so drastically that its official history, already printed, became hopelessly wrong. Five years after the attacks the original visa applications of the three key players are still not available to the FBI, and the NTSB has prepared a video that, if accurate, shows that Flight 77 never hit the Pentagon.

▪ There is a strong smell of planted evidence. Atta's bags, with their still-uncertain but highly incriminating contents; the al-Suqami passport recovered from New York; the elusive pilot who says he clearly saw a 757 at the Pentagon but got the other details wrong; the ten-minute call to a phone supervisor who failed to record it: all are grounds for suspicion that something is amiss.

▪ While dubious evidence leaks to the media, the simple evidence that would remove doubt is missing. Six years after the event, the FBI refuses to answer basic questions, and won't say *why* it won't answer. There are no clear pictures of the presumed hijackers getting on the planes; no pieces of steel that confirm the allegedly furnace-like fires required to bring down the Twin Towers; no explanations offered for the failure of pilots to activate hijack alarms; no pictures corroborating Flight 77's crash into the Pentagon. This is not to say that none of these events happened, but someone does seem to be trying to create a smokescreen.

▪ Several pieces of dubious evidence make sense if plotters were setting up a range of options for possible future use, but then discarded some of them. There is the supposed pilot uniform in Atta's bag, or the story from the planes that hijackers were wielding bombs they could not possibly have smuggled on board. There are the crop-dusting planes Atta made a big fuss over trying to buy,[409] which might have dovetailed into the real anthrax attacks had they not been rumbled as domestic and quickly dropped from the narrative. Even the FBI's John Miller, a devout believer in the official story, expresses bewiderment over Atta's behaviour, remarking that in early 2001 Atta and al-Shehhi "often behaved like men who didn't yet know what their target or method of operation would be".[410]

▦ The highly unlikely coincidence of a hijacking exercise slated for the morning of 11 September surely should at the very least have triggered a search for another Ali Mohamed-type double agent in the Pentagon. Why was it covered up for five years?

▦ There is a stark contrast between the extraordinary paralysis that allowed the attacks to succeed and the lightning speed of the self-serving reaction that followed, with FBI people seizing evidence within minutes at the Pentagon; with CNN briefed that Al-Qaeda was responsible well before the South Tower collapsed; with the CIA global attack matrix approved in principle within twenty-four hours, budgeted and signed off in detail in less than a week.

Finally, what might really have happened on the day of the attacks? In view of the evidence black hole, the record confirming that Operation Northwoods was one signature away from execution and the refusal of the media and the Commission to ask the right questions, wholesale fakery cannot be ruled out. However, none of the jarring evidence that a massive lie might be expected to scatter in its wake has emerged. Moreover, bin Laden is no Fidel Castro. Why *not* use him or his people as patsies, making a plot easier to hide?[411] Here are the circumstances that will have to fit into the explanation, either as core themes or as strange coincidences:

▦ The highly unlikely coincidence of a hijacking exercise on that morning, probably at the very hour the "real" hijackings took place. It is hard to dismiss this as chance because it concerns a central feature of the events, and an obvious *modus operandi* for plotters who would want a smokescreen.

▦ The possibility the planes were involved in the hijacking exercise. The air traffic controller who was assigned to both Flight 175 and Flight 11 believed Flight 11 was not "real traffic". In addition, there is the crossing of the planes in real time, and the fact that Flight 175 waited to report something suspicious until reaching this particular controller.

▪ The filed flight plans for Flights 11 and 93; the actual flight path for Flight 77; the announcements from Flights 11 and 93 and the warning in Bush's 6 August briefing: all suggest the intention was to fly back to the airports.[412]

▪ The silent takeovers of the cockpits without even one hijacking alert issued by eight pilots, at least four of whom were military reservists. It is possible the tapes were scrubbed to cover up evidence of incompetence in responding but tampering with evidence would be a serious step, it has opened up a serious hole in the story, and would have been logistically quite complicated, involving several different locations.

▪ The Pentagon standown with the failed phone connections; the twenty-minute gap at the NMCC; the absences of Rumsfeld and General Winfield; the twenty-six suspected hijackings (NEADS) or thirteen (Clarke/FAA) which acted as a smokescreen and seem to have been based on false information from a hijacking exercise that should have been aborted.

▪ The novice pilots who prebooked their tickets even though they could not have coped with misty or windy weather in New York, and at the Pentagon chose to fly the plane at top speed and at ground level, only to slam into a near-empty section.

▪ The suicide martyrs who had girlfriends, drank alcohol, took cocaine, frequented strip clubs and looked more like drug dealers during the weeks, if not months, prior to the attacks. In Palestine, Sri Lanka and wartime Japan, suicide bombers are and were subjected to prolonged training in supportive environments before being considered reliable.

The bizarre facts must all have some explanation, but they might be very complex and different for each plane. There is a multiplicity of detailed scenarios, that only a major criminal enquiry would be able to penetrate. As the level of involvement mounts, plotters have less scope for cover stories that will stand up after the event. However, the hijacking exercise would help, at least before the event. Here are some broad possibilities:

- The incompetence theory holds that the hijackers were just very lucky, benefitting from a series of cockups and coincidences like the FBI "failures" and the hijack exercise fixed for the same morning. Most of the key circumstances listed above have at best only far fetched explanations.

- A sting operation went wrong. As discussed earlier, this is the most innocent of the other scenarios. It explains the good luck and freedom from interference the hijackers enjoyed, but fails to explain the hijacking issues: the silent takeovers, the flying skills and the unlikely suicide martyrs.

- Any investigation would want to know whether any of the destroyed planes were involved in the hijacking exercise. Several factors suggest they were. Now the possibilities start to multiply. Perhaps the pilots were told to test air traffic controller responses by making a small deviation without signalling a hijacking. At some point the test changes into the real thing. This could partially explain the silent takeovers, the air traffic controller confusion and the Pentagon standown. It would not explain the flying skills issue, the unlikely-martyr issue or the Pentagon attack path.

- Perhaps, given that an Al-Qaeda hijacking was very much on the agenda before 9/11, a remote-control takeover was scripted into the hijacking exercise. The technical feasibility of this was discussed in the last chapter in connection with Flight 77. Again, the exercise somehow turns into the real thing. As the electronics are hijacked, the silent takeovers are now explained. There need be no suicidal intentions, nor flying skills; the ringleaders do not even need to board the planes. They can leave it to the muscle hijackers to order the planes back to the airports. This would explain why several phone calls reported one too few hijackers, and why the authorities are so unwilling to release details like flight manifests, boarding records and so on.[413]

- Alternatively, the computers might have been doctored so that they cut off the transponder signal and flew automatically to the buildings at a certain time or on receiving a signal. Civilian global positioning systems (GPS) may not be quite accurate enough to achieve this but they can be enhanced. Given that the presumed hijackers have bought tickets in advance, this is clearly feasible. The planes might or might not be in the hijack exercise.

One thing is clear: plotters in an X-Team would arouse little suspicion as they went about their falsifications under cover of the exercise, because such exercises are often designed to be highly realistic. As mentioned earlier, Clarke recounted how in one exercise "a special nuclear bomb squad moved in to defuse the weapon, while staff from several agencies pretended to be reporters and peppered officials with tough questions at a simulated press conference". The NEADS operators thought their TV screens might have been tampered with as part of the exercise.

As new evidence emerges, the detailed scenarios and probabilities may change. However, it is noteworthy that, unlike the official story that has continued to flounder, the skeptics' scenarios have narrowed with time. The hijacking exercise and false hijacking reports which

FBI translator Sibel Edmonds stumbled onto a criminal network in Washington with connections to 9/11, and was muzzled by unprecedented court orders when she tried to speak to Congress about it.

CREDIT: Sibel Edmonds

acted as a smokescreen were predicted in detail by Ruppert two years before being confirmed by the NEADS tapes.

It is a logical trap to assume that either "Bush did it" or "bin Laden did it", when probably neither contributed much, and the likelihood is that their people colluded in some way. As veteran Egyptian journalist Mohammed Heikal commented a few weeks after the attacks:

> When I hear Bush talking about al-Qaeda as if it were Nazi Germany or the Communist Party of the Soviet Union, I laugh because I know what is there. Bin Laden has been under surveillance for years: every telephone call was monitored and al-Qaeda has been penetrated by US intelligence, Pakistani intelligence, Saudi intelligence, Egyptian intelligence. They could not have kept secret an operation that required such a degree of organization and sophistication.[414]

An A-Team in a 9/11 plot would probably involve a network of people in places like the CIA, the Pentagon and the ISI, not to mention key private-sector companies. FBI translator Sibel Edmonds was brought in to clear a backlog of untranslated intercepts from Central Asia and muzzled when she started to speak out:

> But I can tell you there are a lot of people involved, a lot of ranking officials, and a lot of illegal activities that include multi-billion-dollar drug-smuggling operations, black-market nuclear sales to terrorists and unsavory regimes, you name it. And of course a lot of people from abroad are involved. It's massive . . . [investigations would] all end up going to the same place, and they revolve around the same nucleus of people. There may be a lot of them, but it is one group. And they are very dangerous for all of us . . . The Department of State is easily the most corrupted of the major government agencies.[415x]

Part 3
What Is To Be Done?

12

The War on Information

THE STRUCTURE OF THE MEDIA

"Why hasn't the media discovered the plot and informed us?" Skeptics must be able to address this question. The media should surely have picked up suspicious murmurs – if not from anyone in a B-Team like the air traffic controller involved in the hijacking exercise, then from peripheral C-Team participants. There must be dozens, if not hundreds, of such people.

The media is good at relaying simple information quickly. It is institutionally very bad at assembling information into a story. The hijacking exercises; the suppression of the FBI investigations; the question of steel in the Towers' fiery collapse; the many warnings received prior to the attacks; Bush's, Cheney's and Rumsfeld's bizarre behaviour on the morning of the attacks: all have crept into the public domain. In this sense the media *has* discovered the truth. But it has been surrounded, in Winston Churchill's phrase, by a "bodyguard of lies" – the official story. There are several closely related reasons for the failure of the mainstream media:

▨ Disgraced President Nixon once observed that it takes two years to listen to two years' worth of tapes. The media needs instead to produce simple summaries of complex events. The "moles and patsies" scenario is more complex than the "bin Laden did it" scenario. As Dutch journalism professor Cees Hamelink explains:

The pressure on journalism is to claim that you know. That's where I think the problem begins . . . There are many different explanations for what happened. One explanation is that it was an external terrorist attack of Al-Qaeda; another explanation is an internal plot by the U.S. Administration . . . It is too early to know which explanation is true and the trouble is that all explanations may all be true at the same time. And that is very shocking for people to realize, but that is what reality is. Reality is chaos.[416]

▨ Newspapers are a declining industry under ruthless pressure from corporate owners. In 2005, prizewinning journalist Laurie Garnett wrote a long goodbye to her colleagues at *Newsday*:

They serve their stockholders first, Wall St. second and somewhere far down the list comes service to newspaper readerships . . . When I started out in journalism the newsrooms were still full of old guys with blue collar backgrounds who got genuinely indignant when the Governor lied or somebody turned off the heat on a poor person's apartment in mid-January . . . It would be easy to descend into despair, not only about the state of journalism, but the future of American democracy. But giving up is not an option. There is too much at stake.[417]

▨ Similarly, CNN founder Ted Turner explained how corporate oligarchies have quietly taken over the media:

In the current climate of consolidation in the media industry, independent broadcasters simply don't survive for long. The U.S. government has changed the rules of the game. Today, media companies are more concentrated than at any time over the past 40 years . . . The Federal Communications Commission defends its actions by saying that we have more media choices than ever before. But only a few corporations decide what we can choose. Disney provoked an uproar when it prevented its subsidiary Miramax from distributing Michael Moore's film *Fahrenheit 9/11*. A senior Disney executive told the *New York Times*: "It's not in the interest of any major corporation to be dragged into a highly charged partisan political battle." There remains only one alternative: bust up the big conglomerates.[418]

Across the English-speaking world, institutions like the Associated Press, Reuters, MSNBC, CNN and BBC dominate the news. The news media hangs together to confront fierce external pressure from government and various lobbies, but this exercises a powerful force for conformity. To question the official 9/11 story is not only to challenge powerful forces in the state, it is to compromise the core product of the cartel: reliable information.

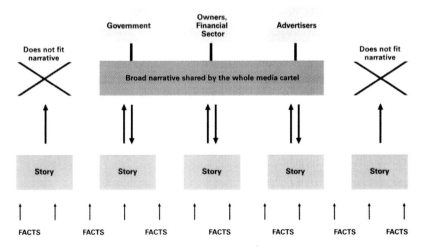

News is not collected in a neutral way and then disseminated. It is filtered and selected to fit a fixed agenda laid down by senior editors and managers who answer to owners, advertisers and regulators.

▨ The government supplies much of the information the media needs for its political coverage, reports on new spending plans, legislation or diplomacy, gossip from the ruling party. The basic product, news, comes from a powerful supplier the media must keep in with. The position of broadcasters is even weaker, because they are directly regulated by the state as well. The shift in public trust from newspapers to broadcasters has returned society to the era when all newspapers were licenced.

MEDIA MANIPULATION

Because the media acts as the eyes and ears of society, the other vested interests have taken advantage of the key structural weaknesses and devised potent stratagems for media manipulation:

▨ Presumed goodwill. The public knows politicians lie, but trusts broadcast news. Therefore, politicians use the newsmedia to launder their lies. The various pressures have combined to bully the media into presuming that on major issues where the national interest is concerned, or where both main parties agree, governments have benign motives and tell the truth. In this sense, the media is as controlled in the US and UK as it was in the USSR. After the WMD affair, current BBC political correspondent Nick Robinson wrote: "It was my job to report what those in power were doing or thinking . . . That is all someone in my sort of job can do. We are not investigative reporters . . ."[419] The anonymous people who write news bulletins often change allegations, little by little over a period, into facts.

▨ False events. Mainstream political reporting depends on long-established personalities and standard left-v.-right debates which evolve only gradually, but a major event can produce overnight change in the political landscape. This strategy is not always successful. Oklahoma bombing and the 2001 anthrax attacks were each blamed on Islamic terrorists at first but fell to bits in the face of starkly contradictory evidence.

911 plotters would probably see a "moles and patsies" scenario as safer.

* Recruit journalists as agents. It emerged during the CIA scandals in the 1970s that hundreds of journalists and editors across the world, including in Washington, were on the CIA payroll. It was famously said that a journalist in Washington was cheaper than a good call girl. I am informed that the situation is similar in London: in every major newsroom there are one or two people reporting to MI5.[420]

* Identify the key outlets. To get the story out quickly, CNN – nowadays the heart and lungs of breaking global news – would be a key target. CNN broke the Al-Qaeda accusation, the Olson phone call and the Timmerman identification of Flight 77. Fairness and Accuracy in Reporting, a centre-left media pressure group in the US, reported in 2000 that army psychological warfare officers had been working on secondment to CNN, which "allowed the Army's covert propagandists to work in its headquarters, where they learned the ins and outs of CNN's operations". An unofficial strategy paper urged military commanders to use the media for, among other things, "executing more effective psychological operations" and "playing a major role in deception of the enemy".[421]

* Feed fake information in a chain. CIA whistleblower Philip Agee explained how baseless information is built up. One recent example: When Bush claimed Iraq was obtaining materials to make WMD, he cited Blair. Blair made the claim citing intelligence reports. The intelligence reports turned out to be fake documents originating in Italy. According to an investigation by the Italian parliament, the originators of the fake documents were Washington neocons.[422]

* The limited hangout. Introduce damaging information a little at a time, like a vaccination, hedged with mitigating factors, suggesting to the reader that the information is not surprising at all. Later it can be described as "nothing new". In the case of 9/11, the prior warnings, intelligence "failures", absence of a significant Al-Qaeda support network in the US, incompetence

in the response, even the hijacking exercise on the morning of the attacks have now all been fed in.

- Shoot the messenger. When under attack, a frequent media protest is, rightly: "Don't shoot the messenger." But the media has its own way of shooting the messengers, calling them "conspiracy theorists" or "conspiracists", an inappropriate term in the 9/11 context, when the official story is *literally* a simplistic conspiracy theory.

  A substantial body of literature from one pro-establishment school of American sociology holds that "conspiracism" is a deviant way of thinking. The lower classes, badly educated and ignorant, are unaware of the essential goodwill of the establishment and the difficulties of administering the complex modern state. Instead, when things go badly, they reach out for false simplistic explanations or may even be deliberately fed them by sinister forces (as in Nazi Germany).

  The conspiracist school correctly cites ways in which false ideas can arise, using terms like "urban legend" and "canard", but fails to understand that the corporate media is particularly vulnerable to the spread of false information. By using its one-sided definition of conspiracy theory as a form of crude name-calling to shut out debate, the corporate media risks putting itself in the same camp as former communist propaganda officials denouncing dissidents as "enemies of the people".

- Gatekeepers. The greatest tactic of political control is divide and rule, famously practised by the British Empire. Now, the global oligarchy uses the same technique by co-opting leftist and conservative journalists as "gatekeepers", building up their credibility as speakers for their respective constituencies so long as they tow the line on the big issues.

THE WAR ON THE PERIPHERY

The mainstream news cartel is powered, like the Wizard of Oz, by a myth of invincibility. It uses the power of mainstream TV news to lay down the narrative, backed up by indignant hysterical gatekeepers to attack dissidents. But as it loses readers and viewers, its power is ebbing away to an anarchic periphery of news websites, independent local newspapers, magazines from *Harpers* to *Hustler*, DVDs, newspaper adverts, Deception Dollars and talk-radio hosts. Long term the most potent force, as marketing experts know, is word of mouth.

Media that is not tied in with the corporate system is skeptical on both sides of the left/right divide. The World Socialist Website (wsws.org) has been a leading investigative resource; the British magazine Red Pepper, the grassroots Democratic website truthout.org and the web-based Indymedia network are all either skeptical or at least even-handed. On the right are antiwar.com with its pro-Constitution conservatism, apfn.org with its vast network of grassroots patriots. The libertarian infowars.org, along with its high-profile campaigner Alex Jones, denounces the official 9/11 story.

Many relatives of 9/11 victims are angry and suspicious, both by the failure to investigate 9/11 honestly and the use of their loved ones to promote the case for war. Bill Doyle, who speaks for one group, told Alex Jones that around half the families in his group are skeptical: "The continuing cover-up is beyond belief . . . It looks like there was a conspiracy behind 9/11 if you really look at all the facts – a lot of families now feel the same way."423

Even in the corporate media chinks are appearing. Commenting on the NEADS tapes, CNN's Lou Dobbs said:

> Incompetence and ineptitude on the part of this government on September 11th and in the weeks and months leading up to it are established. The fact that the government would permit deception after a deception, whether honestly, if you can call it that, honestly intended or not. But the fact that they were [*sic*] continue and perpetuate the lie, suggests that we need a full investigation of what is going on and what is demonstrably an incompetent and at worst deceitful federal government.424

However, many of the people who should be drawing attention to the 9/11 issues are probably the last people who would do. Most mainstream news journalists are probably aware the offical 9/11 story is unsound, but for one reason or another are reluctant to take up the

SECRET//NOFORN

American public, requires that specific boundaries be established for PSYOP. In particular:

> *(U) PSYOP should focus on support to military endeavors (exercises, deployments and operations) in non-permissive or semi-permissive environments (i.e., when adversaries are part of the equation).*

> *(U) DoD should collaborate with other agencies for U.S. Government public diplomacy programs and information objectives. PSYOP forces and capabilities can be employed in support of public diplomacy (e.g., as part of approved theater security cooperation guidelines.)*

> *(U) DoD Public Affairs should be more proactive in support of U.S. Government Public Diplomacy objectives to include a broader set of select foreign media and audiences.*

The Internet is contested territory. The Pentagon's 2003 PSYOPS paper made it clear that foreign websites were fair game for operations "in support of public diplomacy".

issue. Leading 9/11 skeptic David Ray Griffin patiently waited for months, explaining the issues to a journalist with the *Washington Post* who eventually wrote an informed, balanced article.

How has the 9/11 truth movement in the US been able to grow from little more than a handful of dissident Internet sites to the point where, according to a 2006 *New York Times* poll, only 16 per cent of Americans believe the official story in its entirety? The conspiracist school can point to the failure of the war in Iraq, the unpopularity of the Bush administration and disquiet with its flagrant exploitation of 9/11 to undermine human rights at home. If nothing succeeds like success, nothing weakens elites more than losing a war.

Skeptics say their qualified success with public opinion is more the result of a having a strong case. Many cite the power of the Internet to collate information but the battle there has been joined by the Pentagon's psyops agencies, at least outside the US (see illustration). In 2006 the *Guardian* may have been a victim when a thread on their website carried this prominent message:

> If you are going to tell me that the plane that hit the Pentagon 100–150 feet away from me was a missile, you are mistaken . . . I inhaled the jet fumes. Tasted the smoke. It was JP5 jet fuel. I know people who died inside our building. I have seen photos of the American Airlines plane a split second before impact, photos released by the Arlington County Emergency Response Team.[425]

However, Arlington County confirmed that these photos did not exist. Was this persuasive-sounding hoaxer a freelancer, or was she being paid?

Some skeptics think there is an active Internet operation bringing posts like this to high profile sites. Certain standard figures reappear: the hurt "witness" like the one who emailed the *Guardian*; the angry conservative patriot who hates traitors; the exasperated scientist scornfully abusing skeptic scientists while omitting both his own qualifications and any substantive contribution; and the anonymous official claiming from personal experience that governments cannot keep anything secret.

Some skeptics suspect that psyops activities extend to the divide and rule tactic of creating feuds and divisions as happened during the Vietnam era. There should be ample space in the campaign to reopen the 9/11 investigation for both moderates who think plotters allowed an Al-Qaeda plan to succeed and radicals, who think 9/11 was mostly planned in Washington. There is however a difference of outlook between those pressing for political action and those preoccupied with research, which can often mean wild speculation based on inadequate evidence.

There is enough evidence already to convince anyone prepared to be convinced of the case for an enquiry; the problem is that the mainstream media refuses to disseminate it. 9/11 skeptics are confident more will come from muzzled whistleblowers as the legal dam breaks.

13
Conclusion: 9/11 and the Big Picture

Placing 9/11 in the big picture requires a look at where we are today. The landscape consists of a sorry picture of the top third of the planet enjoying relative prosperity based often on technological advances, overwork and consumption of natural resources at an unsustainable level, while the rest live in conditions ranging from traditional poverty to a living hell.

One of the many hidden costs of economic globalization was always going to be a significant increase in state power as governments sought to regulate the increasing mobility of populations. It was very useful to governments everywhere that terrorists from Kandahar should arrive in downtown New York to demonstrate this point in a uniquely dramatic way.

The global elite has emerged as a self-conscious, fully fledged social class. Political and economic power have been sucked away from the citizen as corporations create cartels and politicians spend ever more time in conferences with other politicians.

Washington has led the revolution of the super-rich and set out to dominate it. However, the US has become increasingly resource-poor and heavily indebted. Regional powers such as Europe, Russia, China, India and Brazil are becoming increasingly independent, creating tension within the global elite.

Sociology professor Peter Phillips has identified a Global Dominance Group: "the leadership class in the US . . . now dominated by a neo-conservative group of some 200 people who have the shared goal of asserting US military power worldwide".[426] Similarly, the eminent economist J. K. Galbraith analysed the revolving-door culture of Washington in "The New Industrial State". The constitutional separation of powers has been overridden by the constant rotation of high flying individuals between politics, the executive, business and the media. A similar process has occurred in the UK.

SOME SOLUTIONS

With the war in the Middle East going badly and no end in sight, the Washington oligarchy is confronting a crisis of unpopularity. This could provide the impetus for the fundamental reforms needed in Washington and elsewhere.

- Corporations are already strictly governed by statutes, which can be changed. It can be made clear that human rights apply to humans, not businesses. The Chicago doctrine of investor value can be replaced by stakeholder value. The definition of a cartel can be widened. Media monopolies can be broken up. The ganging together of whole industries to strangle emerging competitors (e.g. the oil industry v. solar power) can be defined for what it is: racketeering.
- The doctrines of executive privilege in America and Crown privilege in the UK have trumped the rule of law and created a zone of impunity for plotters and racketeers by throwing a blanket of secrecy over vast areas of state activity. Statutes

governing secrecy can be revised. A powerful anti-corruption force can be set up, independent of the executive, with the unqualified right to access files and premises anywhere and the power to offer full protection to whistleblowers.

- The power of the lobbies can be broken. Many of the private threats made routinely to elected politicians can be redefined as criminal acts on a par with blackmail and extortion. Funds spent on lobbying can be taxed at very high rates, government contractors could be barred from all involvement in the political process. Journalists can be given the same protection from interference by their employers that other professions enjoy.

- Racketeers are professionally astute at evading the law, but if there *are* laws to evade, real criminal penalties for breaking them and a powerful agency to enforce them, they will at least find life more difficult.

- The UN was not originally designed to be an instrument of Washington. A reformed Security Council could be an honest broker between nations and a neutral investigator of disputes. The World Trade Organization could enforce a new accounting system on corporations worldwide.

Undoubtedly there is a huge problem with these plans. How do we get there from here?

TAKING ACTION

These general issues are unlikely to galvanize the great section of the public that sees no relevance and no hope in political solutions. The left, conservatives and the peace movement have all struggled for over a century against the ever-growing power of Washington's empire. But things seem to be changing. As its power peaks and start to decline, the US faces a familiar choice. Germany in the 1930s took the road of military conquest, while Britain after World War Two chose dignified retreat. Winston Churchill observed that America usually does the right thing, but only after trying out the wrong things first. If so there is still hope that US citizens can find a way to force the right choice on Washington. The 2006 elections showed that Americans have woken up to the danger, but so far it's business as usual as Democrats vote for funds to expand the war and the leading Presidential candidates prostitute themselves to the usual lobbies.

With the oligarchy in control of the two major parties in Washington, the traditional left will have to form a new movement with conservatives who believe in constitutional rights, business people who think war is bad business and religious people who put human rights before the greed for oil. The process of divide-and-rule can be overcome:

- The movement should reward its friends and punish its enemies, ignoring appeals by leaders to party loyalty. The first question for any aspiring politician must be: how many times have you defied your party leadership in the interests of peace, truth or justice?
- Tactical voting. Let no party wield a big majority. In the UK, Blair's power began to wane when his majority was slashed. In the US, voters may soon have the luxury of weeding out Washington's fake Democrats without the risk of bringing pro-Bush Republicans to power.
- Ignore the media's judgement about who is electable. Consider "dark horse" candidates. Bush won a second term because the media pushed Democrats into supporting John Kerry against their better judgement. Howard Dean was no hero, but his positions were clear and he opposed the war.
- Recognize the law as a key weapon. The racketeers of the power elite are not invulnerable, particularly in government where there are paper trails. Torture, for instance, is a crime under international law. Dozens of CIA officers are already the subject of arrest warrants, pursued by European magistrates on charges that could ensnare a swathe of senior politicians.

THE BIG ONE

This is where the 9/11 truth movement comes in. Carol Broulliet, an early activist and member of the US Green party, thinks 9/11 was an act of desperation. Skeptics argue that the sheer audacity of the scam, the ensuing wars, the number of senior people covering it up (through an inability to question authority, wilful ignorance or criminal complicity), together lay bare the reality of the Washingon power elite.

As investigations gather momentum into crimes like torture or the faked documents used to justify the attack on Iraq, skeptics say it is a no-brainer to add 9/11 to the list. As time goes on US goals in Iraq and Afghanistan, and hence the motive for a Washington plot, become ever more transparent. 9/11 cannot be brushed under the carpet; as the wars become more unpopular it is one of the few justifications that still have any credibility. Its beneficiaries need to keep the memory alive.

In the words of California Senator Barbara Boxer, the evidence should be followed "wherever it leads". We now know it leads to flagrantly misleading statements about lack of forewarning, incompetence at both the operational and policymaking levels, and the deceitful use of the tragedy to launch a war that was already planned. Even if the Al-Qaeda side of the official story is broadly correct, the evidence still points to collusion by plotters somewhere in Washington.

As public anger mounts at this or the other unfolding scandals, a permanent and effective independent commission against high level racketeering could be set up for what it would cost to run a medium-sized department at the Pentagon. Teams of prosecutors, with overlapping jurisdictions, could be backed up by a few hundred investigators and given special powers to override secrecy obstacles. They might seek advice from investigators abroad with experience in rooting out high-level corruption. Precedents include post-war Germany's denazification programme or South Africa's Truth Commission.

9/11 skeptics and believers can agree on one thing: another 9/11 Commission is not an option, starved of resources, packed with politicians and blind to the possibility of official wrongdoing. The corporate media and Congress have also failed to provide adequate answers or to ask the right questions. As more information slips through the FBI's embargo, the occupation of Iraq grinds on, and the revulsion increases in the US and abroad, the demand for a powerful independent criminal commission into the 9/11 attacks can only grow.

WEBSITES

There is a multiplicity of websites on aspects of 9/11, most should be found through the sites listed here.

911dossier.co.uk
The author's website for this book, updates, extra research notes, key sources mirrored

911Truth.org
Original campaigning site

911blogger.com
All the latest news

911Research.WTC7.net
Physicist focuses on Twin Towers and building 7 collapses

911review.org
Compendium of research, including more radical theories

cooperativeresearch.org/project.jsp?project=911_project
911 researchers bible, timeline of mainstream press reports from 1990 on

journalof911studies.com
Scientific papers on various issues

globalresearch.ca
The big political picture

patriotsquestion911.com
Ever growing compendium of high profile 9/11 doubters who have spoken out, often from senior positions

pilotsfor911truth.org
Research into the piloting issues

thememoryhole.org/
Archives vital documents which it fears may be scrubbed from the Web. This book is indebted to this site

Daily updated news websites that distrust the official story on the 9/11 attacks:

prisonplanet.com, clg.org

informationclearinghouse.info

whatreallyhappened.com

List of Frequently used Acronyms

AA	American Airlines
AFB	Air Force Base
ATC	Air traffic control, controller or control centre
BBC	British Broadcasting Corporation
BND	German Intelligence
CAPPS	Passenger screening system
CIA	Central Intelligence Agency
CNN	Cable News Network
DOJ	Department of Justice, in charge of FBI
EST	Eastern standard time
FAA	Federal Aviation Administration, in charge of air traffic controllers
FEMA	Federal Emergency Management Agency, in charge of crash sites, initial WTC investigation
FISA	Foreign Intelligence Surveillance Act, used to limit FBI investigations
ISI	Directorate of Inter-Services Intelligence, Pakistani Intelligence
MOSSAD	Israeli intelligence
NATO	North Atlantic Treaty Organization, military structure set up as a defensive US/Europe alliance, now claims worldwide scope

NEADS	North East Air Defense Sector, the US military directly involved in scrambling aircraft to intercept the hijacked planes
NIST	National Institute for Science and Technology, scientists responsible for investigating collapse of Twin Towers and WTC7, answerable to White House
NMCC	National Military Command Centre
NORAD	Sector of US military charged with defending continental US from attack, in charge of NEADS
NSA	National Security Agency, handles electronic and other surveillance
NSC	National Security Council, Presidential agency for dealing with foreign affairs issues
NTSB	National Transportation Safety Board
NYPD	New York Police Department
PBS	Public Broadcasting Service
PNAC	Project for a New American Century
USAF	United States Air Force
WMD	Weapons of mass destruction
WTC	World Trade Centre
WTC7	(or Building 7) collapsed at the end of the day

Bibliography

Ahmed, Nafeez Mosaddeq, *The London Bombings*, London: Duckworth, 2006.

Brzezinski, Zbigniew, *CFR: The Grand Chessboard: American Primacy and Its Geo-Static Imperatives*, New York: Basic Books, 1997.

Burke, Jason, *Al Qaeda*, London: I. B. Tauris, 2003.

Clarke, Richard A., *Against All Enemies*, New York: Free Press, 2004.

Coll, Steve, *Ghost Wars*, New York: Penguin Press, 2004.

Dunbar, David and Reagan, Brad (eds), *Debunking 9/11 Myths*, New York: Hearst Books, 2006. The case made by *Popular Mechanics* contributors in favour of the official 9/11 story.

Fouda, Yosri and Fielding, Nick, *Masterminds of Terror*, Edinburgh and London: Mainstream Publishing, 2003.

Ganser, Daniele, *Nato's Secret Armies*, London: Frank Cass, 2005.

Griffin, David Ray, *Debunking 9/11 Debunking*, Northampton. MA: Olive Branch Press, 2007.

Kean, Thomas and Hamilton, Lee, *Without Precedent*, New York: Knopf, 2006.

Lance, Peter, *Triple Cross*, New York: Regan Books, 2006.

Miller, John, Stone, Michael and Mitchell, Chris, *The Cell*, New York: Hyperion, 2002.

Morgan, Rowland, *Flight 93 Revealed*, London: Constable, 2006.

Musharraf, Pervez, *In the Line of Fire*, London and New York: Free Press 2006.

National Commission on Terrorist Acts Upon the United States, *The 9/11 Commission Report*, 2004.

Posner, Gerald, *Why America Slept*, New York: Ballantine, 2003.

Ruppert, M. C., *Crossing the Rubicon: The Decline of the American Empire at the End of the Age of Oil*, Gabriola. BC: New Society Publishers, 2004.

Scheuer, Michael, *Imperial Hubris*, Virginia: Potomac Books, 2004.

Suskind, Ron, *The Price of Loyalty*, New York: Simon and Schuster, 2004.

Suskind, Ron, *The One Percent Doctrine*, New York: Simon and Shuster, 2006.

Tarpley, Webster, *9/11 Synthetic Terror – Made in USA*, Joshua Tree, CA: Progressive Press, 2006.

Tenet, George, *At the Centre of the Storm – My Years at the CIA*, New York: Harper Collins, 2007

Thompson, Paul, *The Terror Timeline*, New York: Regan Books, 2004.

Notes

CHAPTER 1
THE FIRST DRAFT OF HISTORY

1   See http://www.defenselink.mil/transcripts/2001/t09162001_t0915wbz.html.
2   Richard A. Clarke, *Against All Enemies*, 2004, p. 22.
3   Clarke, p. 30.
4   Clarke, p. 32.
5   See http://www.thememoryhole.org/9/11/managing-wmd.htm last picture.
6   James Bennet, "A Day of Terror", *New York Times*, 12 September 2001.
7   Ron Suskind, *The One Per cent Doctrine*, 2006, pp. 14–15.
8   Ibid, p. 17.
9   Ibid, p. 20.
10 Dana Priest, "CIA covert action program biggest since Cold War", *Washington Post* 30 December 2005; see http://www.sfgate.com/cgi-bin/article.cgi?file=/c/a/2005/12/30/MNGVDGF5S91.DTL.
11 See http://www.whitehouse.gov/news/releases/2001/09/20010920-8.html.
12 Ibid.
13 Ibid.
14 See http://www.muckrakerreport.com/id267.html#_ftn1.
15 See http://www.september11news.com/PresidentBushUN.htm.
16 See http://www.whatreallyhappened.com/framingarabs.html.
17 M. C. Ruppert, *Crossing the Rubicon: The Decline of the American Empire at the End of the Age of Oil*, p. 270.
19 See www.whatreallyhappened.com/anthraxsuspect.html.
20 Suskind, *One Per cent Doctrine*, p. 337.
21 See http://www.angus-reid.com/polls/index.cfm/fuseaction/viewItem/itemID/13469.

CHAPTER 2
THE SKEPTICAL VIEW DEVELOPS

22   See http://www.bbc.co.uk/blogs/theeditors/2006/12/too_much_conspiracy. html.

23   For a sympathetic view of Strauss, see "The Demonization of Leo Strauss" at http://www.nysun.com/article/32841; for a critical view see Webster Griffin Tarpley, *9/11 Synthetic Terror: Made in the USA*, pp. 364–72.

24   See http://talknationradio.com/?p=67.

25   See http://www.informationclearinghouse.info/article4068.htm.

26   When they did, 9/11 had "changed everything". The media announced that this was no time for petty bickering, stating unconvincingly that Bush really had won. Investigative journalist Robert Parry argued cogently that Bush had lost; the BBC's Greg Palast discovered that thousands of mostly Democratic black voters had been denied the right to vote at all after being wrongly listed as convicted felons by Republican officials.

27   Many historians downplay such events, preferring what could be called the "inevitability theory", that wars have deeper causes, i.e. "trigger" incidents are irrelevant. But is this always true? The US entry into World War One, after a German attack on the arms-laden American "passenger ship" *Lusitania*, came about amidst huge opposition and served to wreck a German peace proposal.

28   How they intended to produce bogus relatives is unknown. A massive sector of US society is under the control of the military, with its culture of following orders unconditionally. Perhaps people living on army bases (beyond the reach of stray reporters) could have been paid to claim non-existent relatives; perhaps there was an unwritten plan to murder real people.

29   This section is based on *NATO's Secret Armies*, 2005, by Daniele Ganser of the Centre for Security Studies at the Federal Institute of Technology, Zurich. His sources include parliamentary enquiries, investigations by Italian magistrates and confessions made on record to journalists by former terrorists.

30   Ganser, p. 82.

31   Ganser, p. 136; the US State Department claims the *Manual* was a Soviet-era forgery, but does not address its inclusion as evidence in the Italian enquiry: see http://usinfo.state.gov/media/Archive/2006/Jan/20-127177.html.

32   Neil Mackay and Louise Branson, "British double-agent was in Real IRA's Omagh bomb team", *Sunday Herald*, 19 August 2001; see http://web. archive.org/web/20011230123418/http:/www.sundayherald.com/17827.

33   See http://sinnfein.ie/pdf/stevens_inquiry.pdf.

34   See http://www.serve.com/pfc/pf/StevensWestminster.html.

35   Fulton, cited in Nafeez Mosaddeq Ahmed, *The London Bombings*, 2006, p. 115.

36   Ganser, for instance, relates that several right-wing terrorists who began confessing their involvement with the military were found hanged in their prison cells.

37   The moles and patsies theory achieved prominence with Webster Tarpley's book (see Bibliography).

CHAPTER 3
THE INVESTIGATIONS

38   The FBI refused to divulge the results of its massive trawl pending Moussaoui's trial (five years away). Even then, vital documents were missing, including the original passenger manifests for the apparently hijacked planes and the visa applications for the alleged ringleaders.

39   Ruppert, pp. 271–9. McKinney returned to Congress in the next election, but the Democratic leadership refused to give her back her seniority. She succumbed to a similar electoral tactic in 2006.

40   Tarpley, pp. 33–5. A similar fate befell Representative Curt Weldon when he exposed the Able Danger scandal, discussed later.

41   See http://web.archive.org/web/20050307213256/www.cbsnews.com/stories/2003/09/09/national/main572343.shtml. One intriguing exception: they could still sue a "knowing participant in any conspiracy to hijack any aircraft or commit any terrorist act". This was probably aimed at making trouble for the Saudi government, but could conceivably open the door to future civil action against 9/11 plotters at home.

42   Tarpley, p. 51.

43   See http://www.consortiumnews.com/2000/110500b.html; http://www.btinternet.com/~nlpwessex/Documents/hamiltoniran-contra.htm; and the chapter on Kean/Hamilton, David Ray Griffin, *Debunking 9/11 Debunking*, 2007.

44   Peter Lance, *Triple Cross*, 2006, p. 389.

45   See http://dir.salon.com/story/news/feature/2003/11/21/cleland/print.html.

46   See http://www.cbsnews.com/stories/2003/12/17/eveningnews/main589137.shtml.

47   "Wanted: a commission to investigate the 9/11 commission", *Irish Times*, 15 August 2005; cited at http://www.indymedia.ie/article/71226.

48   Ian Henshall and Rowland Morgan, *9/11 Revealed*, 2005, p. 108.

49   See http://georgewashington.blogspot.com/2006/07/interview-with-april-gallop.html; http://screwloosechange.blogspot.com/2006/07/april-gallop-speaks-on-this-blog.html.

50   For Keller, Grapentine and Frederickson, see http://www.madcowprod.com/10042006.html.

51   See http://www.dailykos.com/storyonly/2006/1/22/11595/1945; and Ellsberg's book *Secrets: A Memoir of Vietnam and the Pentagon Papers*, Viking, 2002.

CHAPTER 4
THE CIA AND AL-QAEDA

52   For a collection of bin Laden's statements see http://www.robert-fisk.com/ understanding_enemy.htm; for the confession tape see www.whatreallyhappened. com/osamatape.html; for official transcript www.defenselink.mil/news/Dec2001/ d20011213ubl.pdf.

53   Audiotapes of bin Laden claiming responsibility for the attacks, intended for Islamic audiences, were previously released by Al Jazeera.

54   For more on voice cloning technology, see chapter 7.

55   See http://transcripts.cnn.com/TRANSCRIPTS/0410/29/lkl.01.html.

56   See Fisk's website at http://www.robert-fisk.com/*Washington Post* 14 May 2002.

57   Yosri Fouda and Nick Fielding, *Masterminds of Terror*, 2003, p. 103.

58   Steve Coll, *Ghost Wars: The Secret History of the CIA, Afghanistan and Bin Laden, from the Soviet Invasion to September 10, 2001*, 2004, p. 163.

59   See http://sunday.ninemsn.com.au/sunday/cover_stories/transcript_923.asp.

60   Coll, pp. 165, 167, 202.

61   See http://www.nybooks.com/articles/16823.

62   Musharraf, p. 218.

63   Robin Cook, "The struggle against terrorism cannot be won by military means", *Guardian*, 8 July 2005; see www.guardian.co.uk/terrorism/story/0,12780, 1523838,00.html.

64   Bunel quoted by Wayne Masden at http://www.globalresearch.ca/index.php? context=viewArticle&code=BUN20051120&articleId=1291.

65   Musharraf, p. 219.

66   Coll, p. 204.

67   Miller *et al*, p. 54. The implied source is the FBI, with which Miller has close links, despite being a journalist when the book was written; in 2007 he was reported as working in its public affairs division.

68   Robert Friedman, "The CIA's Jihad", 17 March 1995; cited in Lance, p. 19.

69   Miller *et al*, p. 54.

70   Ibid, p. 45.

71   Lance, p. 34.

72   Lance, p. 29.The *Boston Globe* was told much later that Mohamed was secretly a CIA asset, while the *New York Times* was told federal officials deny so, but "could not rule out" some other agency.

73   Lance, pp. 34, 47.

74   Miller *et al*, p. 46.

75   Ibid, p. 75.

76   See http://www.lectlaw.com/files/cur46.htm; see also http://www.time. com/time/magazine/article/0,9171,979171–2,00.html; http://pdr.autono.net/ Kunstler_wtc.html.

77   Lance, p. 182.

78   David Rose, "The Osama Files", *Vanity Fair*, 8 December 2001, cited in http://archives.cnn.com/2001/US/12/02/ret.terror.sudan/index.html; see also "Resentful west spurned Sudan's key terror files", *Observer*, 30 September 2001 (see http://observer.guardian.co.uk/waronterrorism/story/0,1373,560675,00.html). Journalist Greg Palast has a similar tale concerning a prohibition by senior FBI officials against receiving documents from a Saudi defector; see http://www. gregpalast.com/did-bush-turn-a-blind-eye-to-terrorism-bbc/.

79   Coll, p. 323; Tenet's *At the Center of the Storm*, p. 103.

80   Clarke, p. 142.

81   Miller *et al*, pp. 151–2.

82   Lance, p. 223. Lance quotes Jack Cloonan and "terrorism expert" Steve Emerson. Cloonan presumably bases his assertions on Mohamed's statements after his arrest in 1998. Mohamed's ties to the CIA, FBI and Special Forces lead Lance to call him a "triple" agent.

83   National Commission on Terrorist Acts Upon the United States, *The 9/11 Commission Report*, 2004, chapter 4, note 2, p. 479; Miller *et al*, p. 150.

84   Coll, p. 318.

85   *The 9/11 Commission Report*, chapter 3.6, p. 101; Clarke, p. 92. For an unclassified synopsis see http://www.ojp.usdoj.gov/odp/docs/pdd39.htm.

86   The *Daily Telegraph* reported in 1993 that Bosnia's 6,000-strong fanatical Handzar division was "trained and led by veterans from Afghanistan and Pakistan, say UN sources". See Robert Fox, "Albanians and Afghans fight for the heirs to Bosnia's SS past", *Daily Telegraph*, 29 December 1993; see also Richard J. Aldrich, "America used Islamists to arm the Bosnian Muslims", *Guardian*, 22 April 2002 (http://www.guardian.co.uk/print/0,3858,4398721-103677,00.html).

87   See http://www.prisonplanet.com/us_supported_al_qaeda_cells_during_ balkan_wars.html.

88   For various mainstream newspaper quotes and links see http://www. btinternet.com/~nlpWESSEX/Documents/shaylergatehtm.htm; for the capture of al-Liby see http://www.usatoday.com/news/world/2003-03-02-alqaeda-list_x.htm; note that this is a different man to Abu-Faraj al-Liby later described as overall Al-Qaeda operations chief.

89   Lance, pp. 269, 298.

90   Caroline Lees, "Oil barons court Taliban in Texas", *Daily Telegraph*, 14 December 1997; see http://www.telegraph.co.uk/htmlContent.jhtml?html=%2 Farchive%2F1997%2F12%2F14%2Fwtal14.html; see also http://news.bbc.co.uk/2/ hi/world/west_asia/37021.stm.

91   For Pakistani pressure on the Taliban, see Burke, pp. 187–8 and Musharraf, p. 203.

92   Gerald Posner, *Why America Slept*, 2003, p. 149.

93   Miller *et al*, p. 194.

94   Zbigniew Brzezinski, *CFR: The Grand Chessboard: American Primacy and Its Geo-Static Imperatives*, 1997, p. 211; cited in http://www.fromthewilderness.com/free/ww3/zbig.html 211.

95   Clarke, pp. 185, 196.

96   Coll, p. 389; *The 9/11 Commission Report*, chapter 4.5, p. 142; see also chapters 4.2, 4.5, 6.3.

97   Senate briefing, cited in Coll, p. 413.

98   Coll, p. 455. Black is described by most sources as a gung-ho type who would not be worried by bureaucratic constraints.

99   Miller *et al*, p. 330. The context is that nothing happened until 2001.

100   Lance, p. 7.

101   Coll, p. 484.

102   James Bamford, *A Pretext for War*, 2005, New York: Anchor Books, cited in Lance, p. 337. It is suspicious that Clarke, presumably the White House official concerned, makes no mention of the incident in his otherwise voluble book. For original NSA reports, see *The 9/11 Commission Report*, chapter 8.2, section on June 2001.

103   Lance, p. 334, citing Bamford, Cloonan and *Stern* Magazine.

104   Clarke, p. 224.

105   Ibid, p. 225. In an off-the-record 2002 briefing, later leaked, Clark denied there was any plan in place when Bush came to power. This is an example of how an off-the-record briefing can be used to mislead journalists while giving them the impression they are "in the know". It was aired by Fox News, seeking to discredit Clarke in 2004; see http://www.foxnews.com/story/0,2933,115085,00.html.

106   Ron Suskind, *The Price of Loyalty*, 2004, p. 70; the source is O'Neill, who was present. See also Suskind, *One Per Cent Doctrine*, p. 22 and Clarke, p. 30.

107   Clarke, p. 245.

108   Suskind, *One Per Cent Doctrine*, p. 97.

109   *The 9/11 Commission Report*, chapter 6.4, p. 202.

110   Ibid, chapter 6.5, Staff Statement No. 6.

111   Jean-Charles Brisard and Guillaume Dasquie, *Forbidden Truth: US-Taliban Secret Oil Diplomacy and the Failed Hunt for Bin Laden*, quoted at http://www.wsws.org/articles/2001/nov2001/afgh-n20.shtml. The authors are respected French experts on oil and intelligence respectively. Additionally, the BBC reported: "Niaz Naik, a former Pakistani Foreign Secretary, was told by senior American officials in mid-July that military action against Afghanistan would go ahead by the middle of October." (George Armey, "US 'planned attack on Taleban'", BBC News, 18 September 2001; see http://news.bbc.co.uk/2/hi/

south_asia/1550366.stm.) See also Jonathan Steele, Ewen MacAskill, Richard Norton-Taylor and Ed Harriman, "Threat of US strikes passed to Taliban weeks before NY attack", *Guardian*, 22 September 2001 or http://www.monitor.net/monitor/0209a/pc2001.html.

112   *The 9/11 Commission Report*, chapter 5.1, chapter 5 note 14. Based on the generally unreliable Sheikh Mohammed confession transcripts, there is nevertheless no motive for the story to have been imposed by his interrogators. Perhaps there was corroboration from the Northern Alliance, now allies.

113   Significantly, both men are secular and Westernized; their first cabinet meeting was held in English. Musharraf, p. 146; Burke, pp. 187–8.

114   *The 9/11 Commission Report*, chapter 6.2 plus footnotes; Coll, p. 509.

115   Ibid, *The 9/11 Commission Report*.

116   SAPRA (New Delhi), 22 May 2001, quoted at http://www.cooperativeresearch.org/context.jsp?item=a0501armitage#a0501armitage; Clarke, p. 232; Coll, p. 552.

117   See http://www.globalresearch.ca/articles/CHO308C.html, citing Agence France-Presse, 28 August 2001. A sting operation plot would be a closely guarded secret, so one can only speculate on the details of the diplomacy: the problem must have been to square the Pakistani elite's new dislike of the Taliban with their long investment in it, and the inevitable loss of influence if it were removed. In 2006 Musharraf blamed Armitage for a threatening message, relayed by Ahmad, that Pakistan would be bombed back to the Stone Age if he did not cooperate. See www.cbsnews.com/stories/2006/09/21/60minutes/main2030165.shtml.

118   See http://www.karachipage.com/news/Sep_01/091001.html.

119   See http://globalresearch.ca/articles/CHO206A.html. Only the Federal News Service carried the unedited version. There is a link from this website so listeners can check the soundtrack for themselves.

120   Kathy Gannon, "Musharraf Set to Cut Ties between Spy Agency and Islamic Militants", AP, 21 February 2002, mirrored at http://s3.amazonaws.com/911timeline/2002/ap022102.html. Ahmad was said to have been sent to Kabul to persuade Mullah Omar to extradite Al-Qaeda, and instead encouraged them not to. But with US policy after 9/11 set firmly on invading Afghanistan and destroying Al-Qaeda, this is the last thing it would have wanted. More likely, having sprung the sting operation on Al-Qaeda and the Taliban, Ahmad wanted to make sure they did not wriggle out of the trap they were in.

121   Manoj Joshi, "India helped FBI trace ISI-terrorist links", *Times of India*, 9 October 2001; see http://timesofindia.indiatimes.com/cms.dll/articleshow?xml=0&catkey=-2128936835&art_id=1454238160&sType=1; mirrored at http://www.ratical.org/ratville/CAH/linkscopy/ToI100901.html.

122   Agence France-Presse,10 October 2001, quoted at http://globalresearch.ca/articles/CHO206A.html.

123   B. L. Kak, "FBI, CIA benefit from RAW's input", *Daily Excelsior*, 18 October 2001; see http://www.*dailyexcelsior*.com/01oct18/news.htm.

124   See http://www.globalresearch.ca/articles/KUP310A.html for a fascinating article analysing press reports and intelligence "leaks" over nearly ten years in support of the author's thesis that Al-Qaeda is an entirely bogus construct.

125   *The Times* and the *Daily Mail* cited in Ahmed, p. 171. For Musharraf on Sheikh as MI6/CIA, see *The Times* 25 September 2006; see http://www. timesonline.co.uk/tol/sport/rugby/article649692.ece. See also *Pittsburgh Tribune-Review*, 3 March 2002 (http://www.pittsburghlive.com/x/pittsburghtrib/s_20141.html), for allegations that Sheikh was working with the ISI on 9/11. Syed Sheikh has another curious element in his CV, too. He was released from an Indian prison after an Al-Qaeda plane hijacking/hostage-taking, so his presence in the 9/11 legend makes this possibility more credible as a cover story for 9/11 too (whether concocted by plotters in Washington or by Al-Qaeda).

126   Posner, p. 215; Coll, pp. 77–9. See also Arnaud de Borchgrave, "Arabian Medicis", UPI, 27 December 2006 (http://www.upi.com/InternationalIntelligence/view.php?StoryID=20061227-082153-2822r).

127   Democratic candidate John Kerry publicly put his defeat down to the video. According to Suskind, CIA analysts concluded: ". . . bin Laden's message was clearly designed to assist the President's re-election." Suskind, *One Per Cent Doctrine*, p. 337.

128   Musharraf, pp. 220–1. I was told a German company delivered dialysis equipment to bin Laden. CNN quoted Musharraf as saying Pakistan "knew" bin Laden had taken such a delivery "specifically for his own personal use". Coll says the CIA heard about bin Laden's apparent health problems on more than one occasion, and was unsure whether to believe them. Bin Laden's last fully authenticated videos show him looking extremely gaunt. See http://edition.cnn.com/2002/WORLD/asiapcf/south/01/18/gen.musharraf.binladen/.

129   "*La CIA aurait rencontré Ben Laden en juillet*", *Le Figaro,* 31 October 2001; translated at http://www.scoop.co.nz/mason/stories/HL0111/S00018.htm.

130   Anthony Sampson, "CIA agent alleged to have met Bin Laden in July", *Guardian*, 1 November 2001; see http://www.guardian.co.uk/waronterror/story/0,1361,584444,00.html.

131   Perhaps realizing the very serious implications, anchorman Dan Rather credited the report to sources in the ISI and "one of the best foreign correspondents in the business, CBS's Barry Petersen". See http://www.cbsnews.com/stories/2002/01/28/eveningnews/main325887.shtml.

132   Suskind, *One Per Cent Doctrine*, p. 59.

133   See http://www.msnbc.msn.com/id/8853000/site/newsweek/.

134   Suskind, *One Per Cent Doctrine*, chapters 3, 4, 5 have many details on the hunt for Al-Qaeda after 9/11, for capture of KSM see chapter 5.

135   Tony Allen-Mills, "Let Bin Laden stay free, says CIA man", the *Sunday Times*, 9 January 2005; see http://www.timesonline.co.uk/tol/news/world/article410125.ece.

136   See http://www.fromthewilderness.com/free/ww3/izvestia_story_pic.html.

137   David Wastell and Philip Jacobson, "Israeli security issued urgent warning to CIA of large-scale terror attacks", *Daily Telegraph*, 16 September 2001; see http://www.telegraph.co.uk/news/main.jhtml?xml=/news/2001/09/16/wcia16.xml and http://www.fromthewilderness.com/free/ww3/izvestia_story_pic.html.

138   Sarah Goodyear, "I Spy", *Village Voice*, 25 September–1 October 2002; see http://www.villagevoice.com/news/0239,goodyear,38630,1.html.

139   See http://www.whitehouse.gov/news/releases/2002/05/20020516-4.html.

140   Michael O'Hanlon, quoted at http://www.wsws.org/articles/2002/may2002/bush-m18.shtml. I am unable to trace the original, but the point clearly stands.

141   Bruce Johnston, "Bush to live on aircraft carrier at G8 summit"; *Daily Telegraph*, 27 June 2001; see http://www.telegraph.co.uk/news/main.jhtml;jsessionid=GDSBP3WFEASTTQFIQMGCFGGAVCBQUIV0?xml=/news/2001/06/22/wsum22.xml.

142   "Italy Tells of Threat at Genoa Summit", *Los Angeles Times*, 27 September 2001; see http://prisonplanet.com/Italy_Tells_of_Threat_at_Genoa_Summit.htm.

143   Bryan Bender, "Pentagon crash 'too unrealistic'", *Boston Globe*, 14 April 2004; see http://www.boston.com/news/nation/washington/articles/2004/04/14/pentagon_crash_too_unrealistic/.

144   Steven Komarow and Tom Squitieri, "NORAD had drills of jets as weapons", *USA Today*, 18 April 2004; see http://www.usatoday.com/news/washington/2004-04-18-norad_x.htm.

145   *The 9/11 Commission Report*, chapter 8, p. 257.

146   Barton Gellman, "Before Sept. 11, Unshared Clues and Unshaped Policy", *Washington Post*, 17 May 2002; see http://www.washingtonpost.com/ac2/wp-dyn/A30176-2002May16?language=printer.

147   Clarke, p. 237.

148   Reuters, 12 July 2001; cited at Cooperative Research, see http://www.cooperativeresearch.org/context.jsp?item=a071201watsonwarns&scale=0#a071201watsonwarns.

149   "Ashcroft Flying High", 26 July 2001; see http://www.cbsnews.com/stories/2001/07/26/national/main303601.shtml.

150   Posner, p. 73.

151   *The 9/11 Commission Report*, chapter 8.1, p. 262.

152   9/11 Commission hearings, ninth public hearing with testimony from Condoleezza Rice, 8 April 2004, transcript p. 9; see http://www.9-11commission.gov/archive/hearing9/9-11Commission_Hearing_2004-04-08.htm.

153   See http://www.newsday.com/news/nationworld/nation/ny-rice0410,0,3695500.story?coll=ny-nation-big-pix.

154 *The 9/11 Commission Report*, chapter 8, note 37, p. 535.

155 Ibid, chapter 8.1, p. 260.

156 9/11 Commission hearings, ninth public hearing with testimony from Condoleezza Rice, 8 April 2004, transcript p. 9; see http://www.9-11commission. gov/archive/hearing9/9-11Commission_Hearing_2004-04-08.pdf.

157 Ibid, p. 68.

158 Clarke, p. 237.

159 Charles Hurt and Stephen Dinan, "Memos show Gorelick involvement in 'wall'", *Washington Times*, 29 April 2004; see http://www.washtimes.com/ national/20040429-122228-6538r.htm.

160 *The 9/11 Commission Report*, chapter 8.1, p. 257.

161 Ibid, p. 263.

162 For Black's testimony, see http://www.fas.org/irp/congress/2002_hr/092 602black.html.

163 *The 9/11 Commission Report*, chapter 6.1, note 44, p. 502.

164 Ibid, chapter 8.2, p. 269.

165 Miller *et al*, p. 304.

166 Lance, p. 339.

167 *The 9/11 Commission Report*, chapter 8.2, section on Aug 2001, p. 270. For Choicepoint, see http://www.breakfornews.com/articles/QuestionsAboutFBI.htm.

168 Lance, pp. 377–8.

169 Rowley's memo was widely published. I use the *Time* website's version, which includes the vital footnotes; see http://www.time.com/time/covers/ 1101020603/memo.html. For Moussaoui transcripts, see: http://www.rcfp.org/ moussaoui/.

170 *The 9/11 Commission Report*, chapter 8.2, note 94, p. 540.

171 Rowley memo, see http://www.time.com/time/covers/1101020603/memo. html. The Commission accepted FBI HQ's argument: they could not prove Moussaoui was in Al-Qaeda, thus there was not enough evidence against him to apply for a warrant. But a warrant should have been easy to obtain; Moussaoui had overstayed his visa and was no longer in any sense a "United States Person"; see William C. Banks and M. E. Bowman, "Executive Authority for National Security Surveillance", *American University Law Review*, vol. 50, no. 1, October 2000 (http://www.wcl.american.edu/journal/lawrev/50/banks.pdf?rd=1).

172 Rowley memo, see http://www.time.com/time/covers/1101020603/memo.html.

173 Lance, p. 377.

174 *The 9/11 Commission Report*, chapter 8.2, p. 275.

175 French Interior Minister Daniel Vaillant met with the FBI on 5 September 2001. The French cooperated thoroughly. Vaillant confirmed: "There was nothing held back." See ABC News, 5 September 2002, mirrored at http://www.btinternet. com/~nlpWESSEX/Documents/WATWhatWAT.htm.

176 Rowley memo, see http://www.time.com/time/covers/1101020603/memo.html.

177 See http://www.youtube.com/watch?v=M27ZbfL-Iwg.

178 US Department of Justice, Office of the Inspector General, "A Review of the FBI's Handling of Intelligence Information Related to the September 11 Attacks: Special Report (November 2004), released publicly June 2006, chapter 4, section 13; see http://www.usdoj.gov/oig/special/s0606/chapter4.htm.

179 Rowley memo, see http://www.time.com/time/covers/1101020603/memo.html.

180 See http://www.judicialwatch.org/printer_2469.shtml.

181 Brian Ross and Vic Walter, "FBI Called off Terror Investigations", ABC News, 19 December 2002; see http://abcnews.go.com/Primetime/story?id=131907 &page=1.

182 "Report Says FAA Got 52 Warnings Before 9/11", *Washington Post*, 11 February 2005; see http://www.washingtonpost.com/wp-dyn/articles/A13203-2005Feb10.html.

183 John Dougherty, "Armed pilots banned 2 months before 9/11", Worldnetdaily.com, 16 May 2002; see http://www.wnd.com/news/article.asp?ARTICLE_ID=27647.

184 Michael Isikoff and Evan Thomas, "Storm Warnings", 29 March 2004; see http://www.msnbc.msn.com/id/4571338/.

185 See http://en.wikipedia.org/wiki/Michael_Chertoff. I am grateful to Lila Rajiva for researching the details of the Elamir case; see Allan P. Duncan, "New Jersey and Terrorism . . . Perfect Together", OpEdNews.com, 2 September 2004 (http://www.opednews.com/duncan_0090304_NJ_terrorism1.htm) and Wayne Guglielmo, *Medical Economics*, 25 October 1999 (http://www.memag.com/memag/article/articleDetail.jsp?id=124049).

186 See http://www.wnd.com/news/article.asp?ARTICLE_ID=25008.

187 *The 9/11 Commission Report*, chapter 8.1, p. 265.

188 9/11 Commission hearings, tenth public hearing on "Law Enforcement and the Intelligence Community", 13–14 April 2004; see http://www.9-11-commission.gov/archive/hearing10/9-11Commission_Hearing_2004-04-14.htm.

189 AP, "Tenet misspoke about not meeting Bush in August 2001", 14 April 2004; see http://www.scoop.co.nz/mason/stories/WO0406/S00098.htm.

190 Dana Priest, "Forgotten Briefings of August 2001", *Washington Post*, 14 August 2004; see http://www.washingtonpost.com/wp-dyn/articles/A12951-2004Apr14.html.

191 Source: The White House; see http://www.whitehouse.gov/news/releases/2001/08/20010825-2.html.

192 Suskind, *One Per Cent Doctrine*, pp. 20, 21, 52.

193 John B. Roberts II, "Potential Bush-CIA crisis", *Washington Times*, 31 August 2005; see http://www.washingtontimes.com/op-ed/20050831-091719-1217r.htm.

194 Ibid.

CHAPTER 6
THE HIJACKERS: TERRORISTS OR PATSIES?

195   Seymour Hersh, "What Went Wrong", *New Yorker*, 1 October 2001; see http://web.archive.org/web/20020614095512/http://www.newyorker.com/fact/content/?011008fa_FACT. Hersh broadly accepted the official story.

196   Ibid.

197   Ibid.

198   "Brown backs tougher terror laws", BBC News, 13 February 2006; see http://news.bbc.co.uk/2/hi/uk_news/politics/4708444.stm. Brown's figure seems quite out of line with other reports, but the claim was made in a set-piece speech and, presumably, carefully checked.

199   "Hijack 'suspects' alive and well", BBC News, 23 September 2001; see http://news.bbc.co.uk/1/hi/world/middle_east/1559151.stm.

200   Timothy W. Maier, "FBI Denies Mix-Up of 9/11 Terrorists", 11 June 2003; mirrored at http://www.prisonplanet.com/fbi_denies_mix_up_of_911_terrorists.htm. See also David Harrison, "Revealed: the men with the stolen identities", *Daily Telegraph*, 23 September 2001 (http://www.portal.telegraph.co.uk/news/main.jhtml?xml=/news/2001/09/23/widen23.xml).

201   Joel Mowbray, "Visas that should have been denied", *National Review*, 6 October 2004; see http://www.nationalreview.com/mowbray/mowbray100902.asp.

202   Michael Springman, Alex Jones Radio Show, www.infowars.com, 1 May 2002; see http://www.infowars.com/transcripts/springman.htm. Springman also gave an interview on BBC's *Newsnight*; see http://news.bbc.co.uk/1/hi/events/newsnight/1645527.stm.

203   *The 9/11 Commission Report*, chapter 1.1, note 5, p. 451.

204   9/11 Commission hearings, seventh public hearing, on "Borders, Transportation, and Managing Risk, 26 January 2004, transcript pp. 3–4; see http://www.9-11commission.gov/archive/hearing7/9-11Commission_Hearing_2004-01-26.pdf.

205   Michael Dorman, "An untold story of 9/11", *Newsday*, 17 April 2006; mirrored at http://www.amny.com/news/nationworld/nation/ny-uslugg0417,0,1751421.story?coll=am-topheadlines.

206   Yosri Fouda and Nick Fielding, *Masterminds of Terror*, 2003, pp. 110–11.

207   Fisk wondered if the CIA's translators had misrepresented it. He recently told me he never saw the Arabic version. See Robert Fisk, "What Muslim Would Write: 'The Time of Fun and Waste is Gone'?, *Independent*, 29 September 2001; see http://www.commondreams.org/views01/0929-07.htm.

208   Burke, pp. 238–9.

209   Fouda, pp. 80–1.

210   Burke, pp. 238–9; Miller *et al*, p. 243.

211 "Atta's father praises London bombs", CNN, 20 July 2005; see http://edition.cnn.com/2005/WORLD/meast/07/19/atta.father.terror/index.html.

212 See Hopsicker's website, www.madcowprod.com/02212006.html; the witness is on film in Hopsicker's video, *Welcome to Terrorland*.

213 "When our World Changed Forever: Terrorism in the US", special report, *Observer*, 16 September 2001; see http://observer.guardian.co.uk/international/story/0,,552749,00.html. The staff later said Atta did not drink alcohol, but they were very aware of the session at the time; they considered the men problem customers, and Shuckums does not look from photographs like a busy location on a Friday afternoon – perhaps the change in story is due to FBI pressure.

214 Jackelyn Barnard, "Exclusive: 9/11 Hijacker Stayed at Jacksonville Hotel", First Coast News, 24 August 2004; see http://www.firstcoastnews.com/news/local/news-article.aspx?storyid=23296.

215 Don Van Natta Jr and Kate Zernike, "Hijackers used brains, muscle and practice", *New York Times*, 4 November 2001; mirrored at http://www.sptimes.com/News/110401/Worldandnation/Hijackers_used_brains.shtml.

216 Elizabeth Neuffer, "Hijack suspect lived a life, or a lie", 25 September 2001; see http://web.archive.org/web/20010925123748/boston.com/dailyglobe2/268/nation/Hijack_suspect_lived_a_life_or_a_lie+.shtml. See also articles cited in Rowland Morgan, *Flight 93*, pp.103–19.

217 For Jarrah's family's views, my source is a reliable intimate of the family, with whom I have communicated personally.

218 Carol J. Williams, "Friends of terror suspect say allegations make no sense", *Los Angeles Times*, 23 October 2001; mirrored at *Orlando Sun-Sentinel* site: http://web.archive.org/web/20020203214236/http://www.sun-sentinel.com/news/local/southflorida/sns-worldtrade-jarrah-lat.story. Jarrah may also have disliked fundamentalists and/or been a double agent. The Commission reports that Jarrah took an interest in the Hamburg mosque only after returning from a visit to Lebanon. His interest in aviation also preceded his apparent conversion. While away from Hamburg he still failed to attend prayers, according to the *Los Angeles Times*.

219 Morgan, p. 114, citing Jere Longman *Among the Heroes*, 2002, pp. 101–2.

220 *The 9/11 Commission Report*, chapter 5, note 97, p. 496; Sheila MacVicar and Caroline Faraj, "September 11 hijacker questioned in January 2001", CNN, 1 August 2002; see www.cnn.com/2002/US/08/01/cia.hijacker/index.html.

221 See, for example, Dennis B. Roddy *et al*, "Flight 93: Forty lives, one destiny", *Pittsburgh Post-Gazette*, 28 October 2001 (http://www.post-gazette.com/headlines/20011028flt93mainstoryp7.asp).

222 The infowars site linked the company that appeared to be the ultimate owner of the tape to a military intelligence reservist on Rumsfeld's staff, and quoted mainstream US sources as saying the military had possessed the tape since 2001. See http://infowars.net/articles/October2006/051006Rumsfeld.htm.

223 Daniel Hopsicker has masses more research on his website; see http://www.madcowprod.com.

224   Amy Goldstein, Lena H. Sun and George Lardner Jr, "Hanjour a Study in Paradox", *Washington Post*,15 October 2001; see http://www.washingtonpost.com/ac2/wp-dyn?pagename=article&node=&contentId=A59451-2001Oct14&notFound=true.

225   Ross Coulthart, "Terrorists Target America", msn.com; see http://sunday.ninemsn.com.au/sunday/cover_stories/transcript_923.asp.

226   "When our World Changed Forever: Terrorism in the US", special report, *Observer*, 16 September 2001; see http://observer.guardian.co.uk/international/story/ 0,,552749,00.html.

227   Mark Oliver, "Suspected hijacker sought loan for crop duster", *Guardian*, 25 September 2001; see http://www.guardian.co.uk/wtccrash/story/0,,557948,00.html.

228   See http://web.archive.org/web/20041226035609/http://www.ou.edu/cas/psc/atlargedeptnews.htm.

229   Michael Wright, an Oklahoma-based researcher, has uncovered most of the information in this section for his thesis, which includes the suggestion that some of the hijackers' airline tickets were purchased by an unknown, non-Middle Eastern person at the University of Oklahoma; see http://journals.aol.com/mpwright9/michael.

230   Tami Watson, "CIA Officer: Terrorism Is Still a Threat," *Norman Transcript*, 12 February 2002; see http://members.aol.com/mpwright9/sting.html.

231   See http://en.wikipedia.org/wiki/Mounir_El_Motassadeq. This story has been extensively covered in the mainstream German media, e.g. Frankfurter Rundschau 12, 13 August 2004.

232   Fouda, p. 116. The details appear convincing, but the account stumbles on the role of Moussaoui. At this stage the official story was still casting Moussaoui as one of the plotters, and Fouda is told his arrest sped up the plan. However, the 9/11 Commission heard bin al-Shibh's testimony that he was unaware of the arrest and would have aborted the operation had he known. A third version was introduced later at the trial: Moussaoui was regarded as too unreliable, and was never part of the operation.

233   Suskind, pp. 156–7.

234   Suskind gives several examples of such sting operations; see for instance p. 181.

235   Paul Thompson, "Is There More to the Capture of Khalid Shaikh Mohammed Than Meets the Eye?"; see http://www.cooperativeresearch.org/essay.jsp?article=essayksmcapture, for secret January 1996 indictment of KSM see Lance pp. 192, 271, 283.

236   Philip Shenon, "Second Officer Says 9/11 Leader Was Named Before Attacks", *New York Times*, 23 August 2005; see http://select.nytimes.com/gst/abstract.html?res=FB061EFA3A5A0C708EDDA10894DD404482.

237   John Diamond, "Four hijackers ID'd as al-Qaeda before 9/11, officer says", *USA Today*, 17 August 2005; see http://www.usatoday.com/news/washington/2005-08-17-911-hijackers-identified_x.htm.

238 Lance, p. 392.

239 Donna De La Cruz, "Weldon: Atta Papers Destroyed on Orders", AP, 15 September 2005.

240 Lance, pp. 392–3.

241 See http://cryptome.org/able-danger2.htm.

CHAPTER 7
THE HIJACKINGS

242 Greg Gordon, "Prosecutors play Flight 93 cockpit recording", McClatchy Newspapers, Scripps Howard News Service, 12 April 2006; see http://www.knoxstudio.com/shns/story.cfm?pk=MOUSSAOUI-04-12-06&cat=WW. See also http://www.physics911.net/projectachilles and www.physics911.net/cellphoneairliners.htm.

243 William Arkin, "When Seeing and Hearing Isn't Believing", *Washington Post*, 1 February 1999; see http://www.washingtonpost.com/wp-srv/national/dotmil/arkin020199.htm.

244 Clarke, p. 175.

245 Morgan, pp. 50–1, 70, 132–3. Griffin, chapter on NORAD tapes; see also http://www.tomburnettfoundation.org/tomburnett_transcript.html.

246 See http://www.nylawyer.com/news/01/09/091701i.html; http://www.fed-soc.org/BKOlsonMemorialLecture/bkolsonlecture-111601.htm. *Daily Telegraph*, 5 March 2002, see http://s3.amazonaws.com/911timeline/2002/telegraph030502.html.

247 The Commission writes in Chapter 1, note 57: "The records available for the phonecalls from American 77 do not allow for a determination of which of four 'connected calls to unknown numbers' represent the two between Barbara and Ted Olson, although the FBI and DOJ believe that all four represent communications between Barbara Olson and her husband's office (all family members of the Flight 77 passengers and crew were canvassed to see if they had received any phonecalls from the hijacked flight, and only Renee May's parents and Ted Olson indicated that they had received such calls)."

248 *New York Observer*, 17 June 2004; see http://web.archive.org/web/20040712043148/http://inn.globalfreepress.com/modules/news/article.php?storyid=470; see also http://news.bbc.co.uk/2/hi/americas/1556096.stm.

249 Morgan, p. 97.

250 op. cit., p. 53.

251 See http://www.post-gazette.com/headlines/20010912crashnat2p2.asp.

252 The detour appeared in early reports, then vanished from media accounts. Was this sloppy research by the Commission or an anomaly it was unable to airbrush out?

253 See http://web.archive.org/web/20030307124832/www.september11-tribute.org/NewsArticles/AAL77Transcript.htm.

254   See http://www.csmonitor.com/2001/0913/p1s2-usju.html.

255   *New York Observer*, 17 June 2004; see http://web.archive.org/web/20040712043148/http://inn.globalfreepress.com/modules/news/article.php?storyid=470 http://csindy.com/csindy/2004-07-08/cover.html.

256   See http://www.guardian.co.uk/wtccrash/story/0,1300,575518,00.html; *The 9/11 Commission Report*, chapter 1.2. Associated Press, 12 August 2002, reporting a press conference by Boston ATC, confirmed the 8:37 exchange with Boston controllers.

257   *The 9/11 Commission Report*, chapter 1.2, p. 21.

258   See http://s3.amazonaws.com/911timeline/2001/nyt101601b.html.

259   Ibid.

260   *The 9/11 Commission Report*, chapter 1.1, p. 7.

261   See http://www.cooperativeresearch.net/context.jsp?item=a852hansoncall.

262   *Boston Globe* articles cached at: http://911research.wtc7.net/cache/planes/attack/globe_planes_reconstruction.htm.

263   See http://pilotsfor911truth.org/pentagon.html.

264   See http://www.arlingtoncemetery.net/cfburling3.htm.

265   *The 9/11 Commission Report*, chapter 1 and chapter 1, note 66.

266   See http://www.911review.org/Wiki/Flight77TowerConversations.shtml; also a semi-official version from ATC union can be found at http://web.archive.org/web/20030307124832/www.september11-tribute.org/NewsArticles/AAL77Transcript.htm.

267   *The 9/11 Commission Report*, chapter 1.1, p. 9.

268A   See http//www.presidency.gov.eg/html/25-Oct2001_press.html.

268B   See http://www.prisonplanet.com/articles/february2006/210206impossibility.htm.

269   See http://www.foxnews.com/story/0,2933,52408,00.html.

270   *Debunking 9/11 Myths* op cit pp. 5, 6.

271A   See http://www.baltimoresun.com/news/custom/attack/bal-te.md.terrorist09sep09,0,5567459.story?coll=bal-attack-storyutil.

271B   See http://www.amics21.com/911/shadows.html.

CHAPTER 8
THE NORAD EXERCISES: EMPTY DESKS IN THE CHAIN OF COMMAND

272A   *The 9/11 Commission Report*, chapter 1.2.

272B   See http://www.fromthewilderness.com/timeline/2001/bostonglobe091501.html.

273   See http://emperors-clothes.com/9-11backups/mycon.htm. For an amusingly sarcastic account of Myers's apparent incompetence and America's love affair with "dumb blondes", see http://www.Public-Action.com.

274   See Commission testimony from Larry Arnold, multiple press reports. Pentagon's history of 9/11, *Air War Over America*, author Leslie Filson, published Air Force ISBN 0-615-12416-X. See Ruppert, ibid p. 443.

275   9/11 Commission hearings, X public hearing with testimony from General Larry Arnold, 2004. The Commission was hardly blameless: they said that the NEADS tapes were corroborated by "taped conversations at FAA centers; contemporaneous logs compiled at NEADS, Continental Region headquarters, and NORAD; and other records." So why did they not pick up the story themselves from one of these sources? (*The 9/11 Commission Report*, chapter 1.2, p. 34.)

276   *The 9/11 Commission Report*, chapter 1.2, p. 26. Even so, the two planes from Langley should have been nearby, but instead flew out over the Atlantic Ocean. The Commission explains this was because the lead pilot and local FAA controller incorrectly assumed that standing orders superseded the original scramble order.

277   Kean and Hamilton. For incorrect statements, see www.vanityfair.com/politics/features/2006/08/norad200608.

278   *Minneapolis Star Tribune*, 31 July 2004.

279   Griffin discusses the phantom Flight 77 in chapter 2.

280   See www.vanityfair.com/politics/features/2006/08/norad200608.

281   When United 93 team was in production, a researcher approached me for information. I spent some time briefing her and advised that the only way they would get any information at all from the US government would be to promise to uphold the official story. I had no idea they would follow this advice quite so literally. Perhaps I am overstating my role, though. Morgan, in his book, details the funding stream for the film, suggesting it was little more than a feature-length commercial paid for by the military-industrial complex.

282   Bronner; see www.vanityfair.com/politics/features/2006/08/norad200608. headlines04/1019-01.htm.

283   Arnold may be referring to a different part of the exercise; see Ruppert, p. 444. For other reports see http://www.cooperativeresearch.org/entity.jsp?entity=vigilant_guardian.

284   *The 9/11 Commission Report*, chapter 1.2, plus footnote 116. An ambiguous comment from General Arnold appeared in the Commission's transcripts, but never made it into the report: "... Frankly, we do hijacking exercises as we go through these exercises from time to time ... we had reviewed the procedures of what it is we do for a hijacking, because we were in the middle of an exercise." Noting that the Commission ignored this in its final report, I concluded in *9/11 Revealed* that while the Commission was probably misleading its readers,

it remained uncertain whether the exercise that day contained a significant hijacking element. We now know this to be the case. See http://www.9-11 commission.gov/archive/hearing2/9-11Commission_Hearing_2003-05-23 .htm.

285 See http://www.cnn.com/2004/US/04/19/norad.exercise/.

286 Ibid.

287 Ruppert, many references, e.g. p. 442.

288 NORAD public affairs officer Don Arias emailed Ruppert that the "Guardian" designation indicates that this was not a live exercise. "Warrior", according to Arias, is the designation for live exercises. See Ruppert, pp. 368, 445. There was a diversion of an unspecified number of NORAD fighters to an exercise in Canada called "Northern Vigilance"; see Ruppert, p. 340. There was also an exercise called "Northern Guardian" that drew planes away to Iceland. See http://www. cooperativeresearch.org/entity.jsp?entity=vigilant_guardian.

289 *USA Today*, 18 April 2004.

290 See http://emperors-clothes.com/indict/update630.htm.

291 *The 9/11 Commission Report*, chapter 1.3, p. 44.

292 9/11 Commission hearings, twelfth public hearing, oral evidence.

293 Ibid.

294 This memo was circulated on 11 May 2003 to clarify the testimony to the Commission earlier that day. It was sent to interested parties, including Washington-based investigative journalists Tom Flocco and Kyle Hence of the website www.911truth.org. The mainstream media appears to have ignored it.

295 Commission chap 1.3.

296 See www.vanityfair.com/politics/features/2006/08/norad200608.

297 *The 9/11 Commission Report*, chapter 1.3, p. 37, including extracts from notes.

298 *The 9/11 Commission Report*, notes to chapter 1.3.

299 Ibid., p. 37.

300 See note 284.

301 See Chairmen of the Joint Chiefs of Staff instructions, June 2001, ref 3610.01A, which refers to a 1993 document, ref 3025.1. The document from 1997, ref 3025.15, is a much broader discussion of military assistance to civil authorities. It is not clear which document the new one replaces. It may not have been changed, but the reissuing is of interest.

302 See http://www.nps.edu/News/ReadNews.aspx?id=634&role=pao&area=news.

303 *The 9/11 Commission Report*, chapter 1.3, p. 44.

304 "Cheney is not the man I used to know"; see http://msnbc.msn.com/ id/11436302/site/newsweek/page/6/.

305 Clarke, p. 18.

306 One minute seems rather fast for Cheney's move to the basement. It seems the Commission prefers the testimony of Cheney's wife, cited in the final report, to that of Mineta, who was not cited. See http://transcripts.cnn.com/TRANSCRIPTS/ 0109/11/bn.06.html.

307 9/11 Commission hearings, X public hearing with testimony from Norman Mineta, 23 May 2003; see http://www.9-11commission.gov/archive/hearing2/9-11 Commission_Hearing_2003-05-23.htm#panel_one.

308 *The 9/11 Commission Report*, chapter 1.3, p. 45. This timeline, implicit throughout Mineta's testimony, includes the evacuation corroborated by CNN. Mineta could hardly have been referring in error to Flight 93 half an hour later: he was explicit that it was the plane that hit the Pentagon, and Flight 93 was much further than fifty miles out.

309 *The 9/11 Commission Report*, chapter 1.2. This timeline suggests an X-Team would have detected Flight 77 earlier. The NEADS tapes show otherwise.

310 CNN reported an unexplained white jet circling over the White House at around 9.40; see also http://transcripts.cnn.com/TRANSCRIPTS/0109/11/bn. 06.html; see also http://z9.invisionfree.com/Pilots_For_Truth/index.php?act=ST&f= 5&t=483 and http://rense.com/general76/missing.htm. When Reynolds Dixon, an English professor, contributed an article to the *Journal of 9/11 Studies* on the subject, he received death threats. See also http://www.ts9/11t.org/ ThirdJetEvidence.html; http://www.williambowles.info/9/11/scholars_9/11_ under_attack.html.

311 Tarpley, pp. 279–91. All references here are to this passage. Tarpley quotes articles over several days from reporters citing a range of sources.

312 Suskind, p. 174. Several reports say such exercises were normally in October. Their rescheduling is suspicious. By October the new wing of the Pentagon would have been filled with people. However, this refers to "Global Guardian". I have been unable to penetrate the bewildering range of codenames to ascertain whether "Vigilant Guardian" was the same exercise.

313 See http://archive.salon.com/politics/feature/2001/09/12/bush/index.html. There appears to be an announcement on the general counterterrorism brief that I have been unable to source. See http://www.whitehouse.gov/news/ releases/2001/05/20010508.html. The link given by the Commission for this press release is incorrect. The relevant passage runs: "Today, numerous Federal departments and agencies have programs to deal with the consequences of a potential use of a chemical, biological, radiological, or nuclear weapon in the United States ... To maximize their effectiveness, these efforts need to be seamlessly integrated, harmonious, and comprehensive. Therefore, I have asked Vice President Cheney to oversee the development of a coordinated national effort ... I will periodically chair a meeting of the National Security Council to review these efforts."

314 Ruppert, p. 367.

315 9/11 Commission hearings, public hearing with testimony from Mayor Giuliani, 19 May 2004. Giuliani was explaining how this good luck helped on 11 September, providing a ready-made command centre, enabling his team to abandon its specially built Office of Emergency Management (OEM) command centre in World Trade Center 7 soon after the attacks. Ruppert dug out a press

release (OEM, 22 May 2002) confirming the involvement of "The Office of Justice Programs, through its Office for Domestic Preparedness", but this may refer to the New York ODP rather than Cheney's task force.

316   AP, 21 August 2002 cited in Ruppert, p. 340. AP mentions that the crash scenario was not supposed to be terrorist-related.

317   See http://www.9/11truth.org/article.php?story=20060718232126585. Everett wonders if another exercise was planned for the day of the attacks, citing a series of reported coincidences. From the same clinic another medic reports: "I was just on the phone with the FBI, and we were talking. 'So who has command should this happen, who has the medical jurisdiction, who does this, who does that?' and we talked about it and talked about it, and he helped me out a lot. And then the next day, during the incident, I actually found him. He was out there on the incident that day."

318   See http://public.cq.com/public/20060911_topten_2368204.html.

CHAPTER 9
WHY DID THE TOWERS COLLAPSE?

319   See http://www.usc.edu/dept/engineering/illumin/vol3issue3/wtc/page5.html.

320   See http://www.firehouse.com/terrorist/911/magazine/gz/hayden.html.

321   *The 9/11 Commission Hearings*, chapter 9.4, p. 320.

322   *Albuquerque Journal*, 21 September 2001; mirrored at http://www.maebrussell.com/Articles%20and%20Notes/WTC%20Explosives.html.

323   See http://transcripts.cnn.com/TRANSCRIPTS/0109/11/bn.05.html.

324   See http://wtc.nist.gov/NISTNCSTAR1-2.pdf P421.

325   See http://www.newyorker.com/fact/content/articles/011119fa_FACT.

326   See http://www.pbs.org/wgbh/nova/transcripts/2907_wtc.html.

327   See http://www.washingtonmonthly.com/archives/individual/2005_09/007023.phpa.

328   *Fire Engineering*, January 2002; see http://fe.pennnet.com/Articles/Article_Display.cfm?Section=OnlineArticles&SubSe%20ction=Display&PUBLICATION_ID=25&ARTICLE_ID=131225.

329   Ibid.

330   See http://www.fas.org/irp/congress/1998_hr/h980604-corley.htm; http://www.apologeticsindex.org/pdf/wetherington.pdf page 4.

331   See http://wtc.nist.gov/. The relevant chapter of the NIST report can be found at http://wtc.nist.gov/NISTNCSTAR1-6D.pdf.

332   See http//education.guardian.co.uk/higher/worldwide/story/0,,1864657,00.html.

333   Skeptic Jim Hoffman believes, based on videos, the collapses may have taken longer than the Commission cites, perhaps fifteen seconds; see http://911research.wtc7.net/essays/demolition/seismic.html#evidence_of.

334   *Debunking 9/11 Myths*, p. 30.

335   *The 9/11 Commission Report*, chapter 9, note 1, p. 541. For core and blueprints see http://9/11research.wtc7.net/wtc/arch/core.html.

336   See http://www.newyorker.com/fact/content/articles/011119fa_FACT. NIST believes it proved the momentum would increase with the first impact, but its model assumed that the upper floors were a solid lump that did not allow for dissipation effects.

337   *Debunking 9/11 Myths* quoted this in another context without realizing the implications for the energy equation, which it fails to address. It is conceivable that the buildings collapsed because they were substandard, and the concrete and metal had deteriorated before the events of the day. However, NIST tested the steel and found it was of the right quality.

338   Christopher Ketcham, *Salon.com*, 19 September 2001, mirrored at http://911research.wtc7.net/wtc/evidence/contents.html.

339   See http://www.newyorker.com/fact/content/articles/011119fa_FACT.

340   See http://www.jonesreport.com/articles/210207_wtc_designers.html.

341   See http://www.911truth.org/article.php?story=20041112144051451; http://wtc.nist.gov/media/P3MechanicalandMetAnalysisofSteel.pdf.

342   For 2003 report see figure; for 2005 quotes, see wtc.nist.gov/pubs/NCSTAR1-3ExecutiveSummary.pdf.

343   See http://www.pbs.org/wgbh/nova/transcripts/2907_wtc.html.

344   See www.thememoryhole.org/911/firefighter-tape.html.

345   Lance, pp. 324–5, 380–1.

346   *Debunking 9/11 Myths*, p. 46.

347   See http://www.journalof911studies.com/volume/200609/WhyIndeedDidtheWorldTradeCenterBuildingsCompletelyCollapse.pdf. For spheroids of molten iron see http://ae911truth.org/twintowers.php.

348   I understand that state-of-the-art explosives would require far less than this, but the plotters would not want to leave their signature behind if something went wrong.

349   Source: personal correspondence with Rodriguez.

350   *The Chief Engineer*; see http://www.chiefengineer.org/article.cfm?seqnum1=1029.

351   The FEMA report "World Trade Center Building Performance Study" is not available online but can be ordered from FEMA; however, the relevant section and some interesting comments can be found at http://911research.wtc7.net/mirrors/guardian2/wtc/WTC_ch2.htm.

352   *The 9/11 Commission Report*, chapter 9.2, p. 285.

353   See http://news.bbc.co.uk/2/hi/americas/1540044.stm.

354   Source: personal correspondence.

355   See FEMA report, pp. 1–11; *The 9/11 Commission Report*, chapter 1.1.

356   *New York Times*, 29 November 2001; see http://select.nytimes.com/gst/abstract.html?res=F10812FF3F590C7A8EDDA80994D9404482.

357   Shoofs recently confirmed the interview by email; see Mark Shoofs, *Wall Street Journal*, Friday 5 October 2001.

358   Source: phone call transcript, early 2007; see also http://www.911blogger.com/node/2807 and http://www.youtube.com/watch?v=t_z8VMKL1ww.

359   See http://www.youtube.com/watch?v=C7SwOT29gbc; www.prisonplanet.com/articles/february2007/280207timestamp.htm.

360   See http://www.prisonplanet.com/articles/february2007/100207heardbombs.htm.

361   See http://archives.cnn.com/2001/US/11/04/inv.newyork.cia.office/.

362   See http://www.wanttoknow.info/010917natllawjournal.WTC7SECfiles.

363   See http://www.g4tv.com/techtvvault/features/27904/Ground_Zero_for_the_Secret_Service.html?detectflash=false&.

364   See http://www.pumpitout.com/phone_calls/controlled_demolitions.mp3.

365   See http://video.google.com/videoplay?docid=-4574366633014832928.

CHAPTER 10
WHAT WAS GOING ON AT THE PENTAGON?

366   See www.defenselink.mil/speeches/2001/s20010910-secdef.html.

367   *The 9/11 Commission Report*, chapter 1.2, p. 26.

368   See http://web.archive.org/web/20011024150915/http://abcnews.go.com/sections/2020/2020/2020_011024_atc_feature.html.

369   See http://www.fire.nist.gov/bfrlpubs/build03/PDF/b03017.pdf.

370   *Debunking 9/11 Myths*, p. 66.

371   ASCE, "The Pentagon Building Performance Report", pp. 20, 24.

372   Ibid., p. 36.

373   See http://web.archive.org/web/20030802142312/http://perso.wanadoo.fr/ericbart/witness.

374   Ibid.

375   *PM*, p. 69.

376   We have not published the pictures from inside the Pentagon out of respect for the victims. They can be found at http://www.vaed.uscourts.gov/notablecases/moussaoui/exhibits/prosecution.html.

377   *Debunking 9/11 Myths*, pp. 64–5.

378   See http://www.defenselink.mil/transcripts/transcript.aspx?transcriptid=1617.

379   See http://thewebfairy.com/9/11/pentagon/27_1-mcintyre.swf.

380   See Bill McKelway, *Richmond Times-Dispatch*, 11 December 2001; http://news.nationalgeographic.com/news/2001/12/1211_wirepentagon.html.

381   See http://www.space.com/news/rains_september11-1.html.

382   See http://www.nationalreview.com/robbins/robbins040902.asp.

383   See www.usmedicine.com/article.cfm?articleID=384&issueID=38.

384   *Debunking 9/11 Myths*, p. 63, quoting ABC's *Nightline*.

385   See http://web.archive.org/web/20020925205057/http://www.af.mil/news/Apr2002/n20020415_0585.shtml; http://9/11research.wtc7.net/pentagon/evidence/witnesses/details.html.

386   See http://web.archive.org/web/20030802142312/http://perso.wanadoo.fr/ericbart/witness.html.

387   See http://web.archive.org/web/20030803161516/www.abqtrib.com/archives/news01/091201_news_dcscene.shtml.

388   See http://www.cnn.com/TRANSCRIPTS/0109/11/bn.32.html. For a skeptical angle on Timmerman's credibility see http://9/11exposed.org/Witnesses.htm. For a skeptical list of eyewitnesses and their links with the Washington establishment, see http://911review.org/Wiki/PentagonAttackWitnessesBlast.shtml.

389   For more pictures of the debris and detailed scaling see http://77debris.batcave.net/AA.html.

390   This French site has details of the traffic cameras: http://perso.wanadoo.fr/jpdesm/pentagon/pages-en/fct-videos.html.

391   See http://pilotsfor9/11truth.org/pentagon.html.

392   See http://www.firehouse.com/terrorist/14%5FAPboxes.html.

393   See http://www.cooperativeresearch.org/timeline.jsp?timeline=complete_9/11_timeline&the_post-9/11_world go to September 13-14.

394   See http://www.firehouse.com/terrorist/14%5FAPboxes.html.

395   For this and more information on professional pilots endorsing Pilots for 9/11 Truth see www.pilotsfor911truth.org.

396   See http://www.physicstoday.org/pt/vol-54/iss-12/p74.html.

397   See http://www.washingtonpost.com/ac2/wp-dyn?pagename=article&node=&contentId=A61202-2001Nov20&notFound=true.

398   See http://www.facsnet.org/issues/specials/terrorism/aviation.php3.

399   See http://topics.nytimes.com/top/reference/timestopics/subjects/a/air_traffic_control/index.html?query=BUSH,%20GEORGE%20W&field=per&match=exact.

400   See http://www.raytheon.com/products/amhs/navigation/; http://www.prnewswire.com/cgi-bin/micro_stories.pl?ACCT=742575&TICK=RTNB&STORY=/www/story/10-01-2001/0001582324&EDATE=Oct+1,+2001.

401   See http://www.usatoday.com/news/nation/2001/09/12/victim-capsule-flight11.htm; http://911review.org/Sept11Wiki/Raytheon.shtml.

CHAPTER 11
ADDING UP THE EVIDENCE

402   Some skeptics speculate that the Africa bombings and the Cole attack were also manipulated events, part of the process of setting up Al-Qaeda as an enemy and entrapping the Taliban. Miller *et al* make it clear that these events could easily have been foiled, and Lance that Ali Mohamed was quite closely involved in the embassy bombings.

403   Christopher Ketcham, "What Did Israel Know in Advance of the 9/11 Attacks?", *Counterpunch*, 7 March 2007; see http://www.counterpunch.org/ketcham03072007.html. Ketcham quotes the *Bergen Record* and spoke to Cannistraro directly. Article now available by subscription only. Ketcham appears unaware of the FBI block, and assumes the Israelis were acting independently. The high-level warnings from Mossad to the White House could have been an insurance policy against what happened: a chance arrest by the FBI that made it look as though Mossad had prior knowledge and failed to act.

404   See http://www.gordonthomas.ie/104.html. I have confirmed from a one-time colleague of Thomas's that he does indeed have contacts in Mossad.

405   For translations of the German reports see http://summeroftruth.org/atta.html. See also Rob Broomby, "Report details S 'intelligence failures'", BBC News, 2 October 2002; see http://news.bbc.co.uk/2/hi/world/europe/2294487.stm.

406   In his report (see note no. 2 in this section), Ketcham quotes the Israeli newspaper *Ha'aretz* on the Armitage decision.

407   See http://www.cooperativeresearch.org/context.jsp?item=a820lewinattack #a820lewinattack.

409   Mark Oliver, "Suspected hijacker sought loan for crop duster", *Guardian*, 25 September 2001; see http://www.guardian.co.uk/wtccrash/story/0,,557948,00.html. See Miller et al, p. 278.

410   Miller *et al*, p. 278.

411   Many skeptics would say there is plenty of evidence. However, extraordinary claims require strong and corroborating facts with no alternative explanations. I have spent a lot of time trying to check out some of these claims, and have got nowhere.

412   For pilot announcements see 9/11 Commission, For Flight 11 flight path to Kennedy airport see http://web.archive.org/web/200109/11202702/http://www.csmonitor.com/earlyed/earlyUSA5.html , for Flight 93 to fly to an unidentified East Coast destination see Morgan op cit P101 citing ABC news Peter Dizikes, 13 September 2001.

413   It would also explain the report from Flight 11 that the pilot was still at the controls, the pressure on the air traffic controllers not to talk, the reported statement by Barbara Olson that no one seemed to be in charge and the report from Atta's father that his son was still alive after 9/11.

414   See http://www.guardian.co.uk/g2/story/0,3604,566516,00.html.

415   See http://antiwar.com/news/interview.html http://www.justacitizen.com/.

CHAPTER 12
THE WAR ON INFORMATION

416   See http://www.deepjournal.com/p/7/a/en/457.html.

417   See http://www.editorandpublisher.com/eandp/news/article_display.jsp?
vnu_content_id=1000819198.

418   See Washington Monthly (July/August 2004); www.washingtonmonthly.com.

419   *The Times*, 16 July 2004.

420   See http://www.whatreallyhappened.com/RANCHO/POLITICS/MOCK/
mockingbird.html.

421   See http://www.fair.org/index.php?page=1748.

422   Philip Agee, *CIA Diary: Inside the Company*, 1975, Penguin Books.

423   See http://www.prisonplanet.com/articles/july2006/080706government
complicit.htm.

424   See http://transcripts.cnn.com/TRANSCRIPTS/0608/09/ldt.01.html.

425   See http://media.guardian.co.uk/site/story/0,,1764955,00.html; http://news.
bbc.co.uk/2/hi/americas/4655196.stm. Personal email exchange with four
Arlington officials.

CHAPTER 13
CONCLUSION: 9/11 AND THE BIG PICTURE

426   See http://www.projectcensored.org/downloads/Global_Dominance_Group.
pdf.